DESIGNING THE INDUSTRIAL STATE

DESIGNING THE INDUSTRIAL STATE

The Intellectual Pursuit of Collectivism in America, 1880–1940

by JAMES GILBERT

QUADRANGLE BOOKS, Chicago, 1972

DESIGNING THE INDUSTRIAL STATE. Copyright © 1972 by
James Gilbert. All rights reserved, including the right
to reproduce this book or portions thereof in any form.
For information, address: Quadrangle Books, Inc., 12 East
Delaware Place, Chicago 60611. Manufactured in the
United States of America. Published simultaneously in
Canada by Burns and MacEachern Ltd., Toronto.

Library of Congress Catalog Card Number: 73–152091

ISBN 0–8129–0219–X

For my parents, Marjorie and Philo Gilbert

Preface

THIS BOOK was written to satisfy two impulses. The first is my dissatisfaction with the quality of political analysis that appears in contemporary magazines of liberal persuasion. These journals have been a source of extracurricular political education in America for several decades; their weaknesses are now the heritage, I think, of two generations of intellectuals. In reading these magazines it gradually occurred to me that I no longer trusted the meanings of commonly used terms, and that I was encountering a language of politics which often evaded reality in order to defend clichés. I wondered whether there were some American intellectuals, principally before World War I, who looked at the enormous concentration of economic power in America at the turn of the century and speculated about its social effects without using the crude designations "liberal" and "conservative." Obviously there were, and I wished to explore the nature of their arguments and the validity of their predictions.

The second impulse for this book came from my reading of much of the history now being written about the United States at the turn of the century. As a new literature this work is exciting yet incomplete in a way which is enormously interesting. If one accepts, as I largely do, the works of historians who have stressed the obvious about capitalist industrialism at the beginning of the century—that new economic forms in turn created new social forms, often in the guise of reformism—one cannot help but be troubled by unresolved historical questions. Clearly business interests inspired and shaped much reform legislation, though some businessmen must have winced at the raw exposés of industrial practice that filled the popular press of the day. But then, what of the reformers? How could men and women who were so clearly admirable in other respects become the shock troops for conservative reform, settling for those areas of human concern, such as poverty and education, left over after the larger questions of social organization had been disposed of? Was Jane Addams no more than a corporate liberal?

One is tempted to answer "Perhaps," though ultimately such an interpretation makes no historical sense. The perspective of the present must not prevent us from judging the meaning of political writings and intellectual statements in their own contexts. What, indeed, did reformers of the time think was happening to society? How did they understand contemporary social processes? What were their aims? To what extent did they agree with the prevailing economic and social institutions of their day? I cannot hope to answer all of these questions, nor speak for all intellectuals, but I have attempted to reconstruct one crucial category of political thought which suggests a fresh interpretation of the theory behind modern reform.

In writing this book I have been greatly helped by my friends and colleagues, who have both encouraged and challenged some of my ideas. I am indebted to Fred Ciporen, William R. Taylor, Harvey Levenstein, James Weinstein, my wife, Susan Olivia Gilbert, Francis Haber, Herman Belz, Ken Lee, Paul Buhle, James O'Brien, Alan Horlick, and Donald Miller. I am also grateful to Ivan Dee of Quadrangle Books for his critical reading and helpful suggestions.

One of the great pleasures in writing and research is the discovery of new sources. The story of Edmond Kelly's life, in particular, was fascinating to me, and ultimately became accessible because of the enormous help and interest shown by Mrs. Shaun Kelly of Boston, who lent me her personal manuscript collection. Other members of the Kelly family, especially Sean Kelly of Washington, D.C., were also generous in helping me to assemble the details of Kelly's life. I am indebted to the Union College Library of Schenectady, New York, for allowing me to use the Steinmetz collection there. I also had the good fortune to find other Steinmetz papers buried under mannequins, rockers, and old papers—and near a dead squirrel—in the attic of the Schenectady County Historical Society. Finally, I wish to thank Max Shachtman of the Socialist party and George Novack of the Socialist Workers party for discussing the career of James Burnham with me.

The University of Maryland provided a summer grant in the initial stages of my work, and the National Endowment for the Humanities granted me a Junior Fellowship to complete a major portion of the book. I wish, finally, to acknowledge three excellent libraries: the Wisconsin Historical Society, the Butler Library at Columbia University, and the Library of Congress. So much historical work depends at the outset upon accident. The filing of books in close proximity, the general caliber of holdings, the completeness of purchases in certain fields—all conspire to give a special impression about a period or an event. These three libraries offer outstanding collections and are themselves a fascinating part of our historical consciousness.

Contents

DESIGNING THE INDUSTRIAL STATE

Introduction

SOMETIME in the early 1960's the popular language of American politics became useless. It no longer made sense to describe the American political or economic system as a decentralized democracy of competing pluralistic groups, or a small-town democracy writ large. It became more difficult to claim that a man could make his way to success or fulfillment without first bargaining away his liberty to some institution. The awareness that political language itself might be the foundation of a myth often provoked the accusation that the history of American thought since 1890 had been one of intentional obfuscation. Moreover, if the rote language of popular politics described nothing real, then perhaps political reality held the secrets of unfinished revolutions or discarded possibilities for truly radical change. Going a step further, it was tempting for historians to think that intellectuals had somehow become the willing instruments of an increasingly bureaucratized and static political system. That clandestine government organizations were found to be financing important and respectable magazines and conferences seemed to confirm the suspicion that prestige and money could, with little difficulty, turn intellectuals into ideological agents.

Perhaps the greatest impetus for the decline of faith in older political concepts was the Cold War. By turning almost all political description into propaganda—"free world," "captive nations," "iron curtain," and so forth—those bleak years after World War II created a kind of critical amnesia about the period before the war, as well as a sense of frustration about the time since. The creation of a greatly Americanized world seemed to diminish the need for a thoughtful discussion of American institutions. American ideas and assumptions, which were often exported as the packaging for American technology, influenced the rest of the world until it seemed as if the American experience would become universalized as the inevitable and only road to industrial or social development. In a sense, power and technology replaced ideas, and Americans came, at least temporarily, to feel no need for a justifying ideology.

Those critics in the 1950's who called the American political system into question were often dismissed as right-wing cranks or left-wing camp-followers of the Soviet Union. To many liberals, the arguments that American society was becoming too centralized or that individualism was a crucial problem sounded like anti–New Deal madness. To many conservatives, suggestions for serious political and economic reform were evidence of the secret inroads of bolshevism. With these absurd—but real—limits of political discussion in the 1950's, it is no wonder that so many political scientists and historians turned to analyzing power relationships or interest groups, thereby shrinking the size and implications of their work.

At the beginning of the twentieth century, the terminology of politics had already taken on a double meaning which was the source, I think, of much political confusion. On one level, political rhetoric was still constricted by the demands of traditional institutions and processes; on another level, political discussion cut deeper to take account of the new mass society. Histories of this era have almost always emphasized the traditional language of American politics, lauding its practical aspects and vote-getting compromises while neglecting the new political ideas that explored deeper problems of the new industrial world. It was the latter ideas, however, that showed a well-developed utopianism and a desire to test new social arrangements within the institutions of the new society. Thus there were men and women concerned to express the newness of their situation, who had thought deeply about the course of American development. It is in the work of these intellectuals that one has the best opportunity to get behind the language of traditional politics and establish some sense of the kind of society that social reformers wished to achieve. These intellectuals predicted many of the social patterns of the present and foresaw the institutions that would come to dominate America in the middle of the twentieth century. They took seriously the indications that America was becoming a mass society—a collectivity and not a chaos of competing egos and regions. In fact, one can identify among these thinkers an idea that appears at the turn of the century and persists until the late 1930's: the idea of a collective society.

Few periods in American history have been subject to better-documented or more interesting historical scholarship than the Progressive era, stretching from around 1900 to 1920. But historians, in the course of tracing the reform impulses of progressivism, have produced an enormously contradictory literature. One can find, as various historians have, intellectuals, politicians, and movements characterized by pessimism or optimism; men and women searching for goals as different as social order or compensations for their own lost status; business as well as labor in chief roles in reform movements and in urban political machines. The reforms that inundated American politics after the turn of the century were variously proposed by Anglo-Saxon Americans, immigrant social workers, Southerners, Westerners, women, the urban middle classes, and businessmen.[1] All of a hundred movements were part of "progressivism," and each sentiment—of optimism, of pessimism, of doubt, and even of self-deception—was part of the complex attitudes held by men toward the society they sought to change.

The ease with which the events and ideas of the period can be divided among contradictory interpretations demonstrates nothing so clearly as the partial correctness of each view. Progressivism could mean a great variety of things to a great variety of people because historians fashioned the word to describe one or another set of ideas which they then isolated from one central fact: they were dealing with a whole society entering modernity. Beyond the central movement which called itself Progressive, one discovers great differences of opinion among divergent forces and movements, each seeking to convert its own special experience into the reform consciousness of the nation. Each of these forces was in its own way progressive.

Because of its vagueness, the term progressive now seems to be of little help to historians. But more than semantics are in question. For example, does it make much sense to limit the discussion of reform impulses—or, more broadly, the development of political attitudes—to one period in time? Is it wise to use the arbitrary boundaries of decades to delimit ideas or events? Certainly some elements of our present attitudes toward American political institutions are echoes of earlier decades. The dominant ideas of the Progressive era were neither invented in 1900 nor discarded in 1920. Nor does it make much sense to compare two artificial structures of time, such as the Progressive era from 1900 to 1920 and the depression decade from 1929 to 1939, in a search for continuity and change. Such historical constructs generally tell us more about our own intellectual acrobatics than about the matters we study.

In writing a descriptive book about the development of political ideas, one cannot take intellectuals and their ideas to represent a specific movement, unless it be primarily an intellectual movement. Thus the frame of reference for many of the intellectuals I shall discuss in these pages is as much their own careers and their relationships with other intellectuals— their interests, what they read, even their language—as it is their connection with established reform movements. Often the reform role of the intellectual was quite distinct and self-consciously different from the interests of the rank-and-file of reform movements. The intellectual's assumptions and the implications of his actions were sometimes special for the very reason that they expressed the interests of a developing intellectual elite as well as allegiance to a set of reform ideas.

The intellectuals I have chosen to examine in this book— admittedly a selective group—were all convinced that American society was experiencing a revolution in its economic relationships. They saw these new economic relationships as the forewarning of a wholly new social orientation. Their task, as they conceived it, was to close the cultural lag between economic fact and social understanding, and to make comprehensible, if only to themselves, the new society that had come into being with the creation of corporations and functional groups. At the same time, these intellectuals sought to carve out for themselves an indispensable role in the increasingly organized intellectual life of the twentieth century.

I call these intellectuals "collectivists" because I think this word (which, incidentally, some of them used to describe themselves) expresses the general shape of their thoughts about the new mass society. I believe it more effectively describes the content and connotations of their political thought and carries a good deal less confusion than such labels as "liberal" or "conservative," because it relates to social organization, not political abstractions. More important, the idea of collectivism signifies the general area of agreement among those intellectuals who committed their careers and hopes to such different movements as socialism, progressivism, and managerialism. Finally, the term collectivism distinguishes the elements that linked many of the most critical social thinkers to the object of their criticism, the mass society.

Because collectivism is a relatively new term to describe political ideas that were only sometimes associated with socialism, I have felt it necessary to define the term broadly and to take up my first few chapters in discussing its implications. This necessarily means also examining what intellectuals thought was happening to economic and social institutions as well as how they wished to change them. The collectivist vision of a reformed society was, as we shall see, explosive with potential for social change. If these ideas were not always politically practicable, they were nonetheless immensely useful as interpretive tools, and by the 1920's and 1930's a whole body of literature produced by intellectuals (primarily for other intellectuals) embraced the precepts of collectivist thought.

Collectivism, then, emerged as a general theory of society in which economic institutions were the key element. Possibilities for social interaction and political reform derived from the mass nature of these economic institutions. Although many collectivists wished to preserve such older values as individualism, they were nonetheless forced by their understanding of the scale of social problems to consider as a solution pitting social organization against injustice, or translating such older economic ideas as laissez-faire competition into theories of competing groups. Pluralism, a variant of collectivist thought, is an example of one direction which these assumptions often took. But other concrete theories also expressed the same central assumptions about social organization; only the details varied.

In examining the collectivist response to the inrush of modernity, I have been guided by several questions. First, I have asked how intellectuals viewed their own contributions, real or potential, toward adjusting society to modern technology and organization. I have done so because from the very first I found that the role of intellectuals in organizations, and the great value they placed on the tools of the mind, provided one leg of contemporary political theory. In other words, intellectuals often universalized their own experiences and transformed their own roles into theoretically necessary functions.

I have also inquired about the conception of the good society as it appears among those writers who saw the collectivist nature of modern institutions. Particularly important was the source of their model of a good society. In most cases I found this model to be a chunk of America itself, with some small revisions. It was often a characteristic of reformers of the time to argue that some special development that had recently come into being, such as the corporation, would dominate the future. Reform often meant little more than extending the present system, or, sometimes, spreading the fruits and opportunities of middle-class life to those who were less fortunate. Often the patterns of the future as projected by intellectuals represented merely the bare structures of their own society without the shadows of poverty, ignorance, and vice.

I have been most interested in those intellectuals who viewed the emergent corporation as the prototype for the perfect society. Elaborate organizational patterns and corporate power frightened such intellectuals not in the least. The social relationships within the corporation, once abstracted from self-interest and profit-making, looked a great deal more promising than the traditional social divisions and organizations that then divided and dominated the United States. For one thing, the corporation was organized for use, not waste. This being so, problems of regionalism and special interest appeared to have no hold. Science, not personality, political pressure, or ideology, was the backbone of this new organization. True, the corporation also divided men, and sometimes sharply; but the functional categories of worker, owner, manager, and—on the outside looking in—consumer, seemed to produce strong, self-interested commitments to the good of the whole. This discovered commonality of interests was far more attractive to many intellectuals than a theory of class struggle or perpetual economic warfare.

One question I discovered I could not answer was why the various descriptions of a collectivist society did not become useful in political debate, for they were far more realistic than such slogans as Woodrow Wilson's "New Freedom." There are, of course, many easy explanations for this failure, such as the persistence of traditional political mythology. But such answers simply force one to ask, Why does the traditional persist? In any event, I have tried to show that collectivist assumptions are, whether acknowledged or not, at the heart of much of twentieth-century reform thought.

Two distinct divisions in this book are designed to deal with two sides of the question of collective theory, for any interesting set of ideas is better understood both in general theoretical terms and in the specialized isolation of biography. The first portion of the book tears ideas from their context, assembling arguments as if they were building blocks, in order to describe the ideological edifice of collectivism. Since very few intellectuals were totally absorbed by the collectivist ideal, and none can really be considered the perfect collectivist thinker, I have had to fashion the wholeness of the collectivist argument myself. I do this not from a desire to invent agreement but in order to place ideas within the context of their implications and broader meanings.

The second portion of the book uses biography to reveal collectivist expressions in their full diversity. I have examined the lives and writings of six men who developed the central notions of collectivism in six different directions, yet each of whom contributed to explaining the meaning of the general collectivist orientation toward society and social problems.

The collectivist intellectual displayed five broad concerns. Of the five, modern economic institutions received the most attention. For many intellectuals these institutions represented the possible foundations of a new social order. In a sense, the problem of reform became the need to untangle contemporary confusions about specialized roles in these institutions. What was, for example, the role of a manager, an owner, a worker, and a consumer in relation to the corporation? A second area of concern, the terrible dilemma of a divided society, preoccupied those collectivist thinkers who were anxious to find a substitute for Marx's perpetually imbalanced and revolutionary diagram of proletarian versus capitalist. The nature of the modern state was a third vital concern, though what was assumed, and thus only briefly noted, was often as important as rare substantive discussions of the nature of government. The formulation and practical application of political knowledge was a fourth great concern. Thus the origins of sociological concepts were often closely examined, and the uses which intellectuals and reformers might make of such tools were carefully considered. Finally, intellectuals wanted to find a way to describe society that would express its general form and mechanics. This fifth concern was an attempt to answer two questions: Was society an organism or a mechanism? How did its parts interrelate? In sum, collectivists were deeply interested in what they felt was the enormous social and political revolution implied in the relationships of modern economic organizations, and their utopias were by and large distended models of those relationships.

To assemble the various parts of the collectivists' argument and consider the implications of the ideas involved was, I found, by itself not enough. Distinctly different programs of reform seemed to flow from the same general assumptions. This intriguing diversity illustrated the extremely personal nature of political thought at the turn of the century as well as the connections between apparently conflicting programs.

The reasons for this diversity can be found in the second part of this book. For one thing, collectivist ideas always seemed to be a part of other arguments or preoccupations. They encompassed not just one program but many related ones. These fascinating twists and turns, together with the political and social encounters that men made in developing their ideas, are an important story, which is revealed in the intellectual biographies of six men who contributed to the enormous variety of modern collective theory.

My criterion for choosing these six men has been neither their political importance (though several were important political writers), nor the ease with which one might place them in categories of collectivist thought. They were selected instead because of their uniqueness and the fascinating way in which each illustrates the snarled relationships between general ideas and specific intellectual conduct. Each of these men was a collectivist but also, inevitably, himself and, as such, deeply concerned with personal questions of career, occupation, and family.

The first biography is of Edmond Kelly, a founder of the New York City Club and an international lawyer. Kelly's career led from the elegant surroundings of the urban gentleman's club and his own magnificent chateau in northern France to the rough and tumble politics of New York City and, finally, into the Socialist party. Kelly exemplified the extraordinary means that some men would adopt in order to preserve (and grant to everyone) an old-fashioned world of stern morality, culture, and propriety. To save this world, Kelly embraced socialism and envisioned a state with a social system that would eliminate economic individualism.

William English Walling held a very different view of collectivist thought. One of the most original American socialist thinkers, Walling was worried by the popularity of collectivism, especially by the variety of forms in which it was taken up among other socialists, and he warned of its ensnaring difficulties. Refusing to pretend that nineteenth-century individualism was all bad, Walling ingeniously used the works of Herbert Spencer and the anarchist Max Stirner to rebut the argument that the modern state ought to emulate corporate organization. Although Walling ultimately changed his mind, his writings still stand as an important indictment of collectivist assumptions.

A third biography, that of King Camp Gillette, the inventor of the safety razor, offers a picture of a businessman who explicitly and crudely transformed the corporation into the basis of a good society. Gillette's proposals, which called upon the nation to reconstruct itself into a vast business organization, were politically unfeasible. Probably few people read his books. But Gillette rightly sensed the future importance of the corporation. Although his grandiose schemes were impossible, his assumptions intrigued a diverse group of reformers.

Charles Steinmetz's book *America and the New Epoch,* published in 1916, offers another dimension of collectivist thought. Steinmetz wrote of a future society modeled on the modern aspects of the business world, a surprising book for a socialist to write. There were other surprises in Steinmetz's career as well, particularly his proposals for public and corporate education, and his activities in their behalf. He was a man whose life was defined by the General Electric Company and who from his experience argued that the good society of the future ought to be guided by the best relationships then to be found in the business world.

Reinhold Niebuhr's sense of the collective society was far different from that of earlier thinkers, for he was a commentator on what had become by the 1930's a tradition of collectivist theory. Deeply imbedded in Niebuhr's revised version of collectivism was his theological rejection of modern optimism and rationalism which until then had been the dominant tone of collectivist thought. At first frightened by class struggle and wishing to eliminate it, he transformed this fear into the belief that the clash within the corporation and between the functional units of economic power in society provoked the creative forces of progress. Justice, if ever it were to appear again, would emerge from the violence men threatened but did not do to each other, and the compromises they subsequently reached. Thus while Niebuhr held true to the central tenets of collectivism, he strained these ideas through the filter of his own pessimistic theology.

Finally, the works of James Burnham illustrate another variety of collectivist thought and, as a fitting conclusion, a dead end. In the early 1930's, Burnham was acutely critical of the massive, bureaucratized society that he felt was emerging in America under the guise of reform—one variant, in other words, of the collectivist prediction. During the depression years, however, his socialist commitments and his preoccupation with centralization began to be replaced by a great distaste for the Soviet Union. Ultimately, Burnham rejected both the New Deal and communism on the same grounds, and sought refuge in the pristine past of laissez-faire individualism. Yet his rejection of collectivism, like Walling's, was clear evidence of the importance these ideas had acquired as descriptions of the modern state. Burnham's "managerial society" was really intended as a picture of American corporate society, minus politics. His deeply ambiguous attitude toward that society revealed both the possibilities and pitfalls of his theory.

1

The Collectivist Tendency

THE UNITED STATES must have seemed like a strange and grandiose spectacle in 1906. In the midst of urbanization and an industrial revolution accomplished with a good measure of violence, American political thinkers nonetheless seemed to halt at the borders of the city, preferring older rural virtues. It was an unusual society that could proclaim the physical frontier closed, yet cling to the political and social virtues of the moral frontier. Perhaps these cherished virtues were a natural outgrowth of the New World environment; still, it was clear they had no place in the emerging society. Everything was changing in America save the understanding of change itself. So it seemed to H. G. Wells, a frequent visitor and lecturer in the United States. The American mind, Wells complained, "still seems lacking in any of that living sense of the state out of which constructive effort must arise. . . ." The pace of reform was breakneck, but the reforms themselves appeared haphazard and directionless. Partly from his own well-developed elitism, Wells argued that reformers must take hold of society at the national level or they would see change deflected and misappropriated. They must understand the meaning and utility of the modern political state. Yet Americans seemed little concerned about the national state, at least not enough to write about it seriously. When they did mention it, their remarks tended to be like Clarence Darrow's conception of the perfect political entity: "the sheltering home of all."[1] Who could take such words seriously?

Wells was neither the first nor the last observer to notice the gap between ideas and action in American political life. Others before him wondered how Americans could institute reforms apparently without considering their metaphysical implications. At a time when the people more and more relied upon the federal government as the instrument of national policy and social salvation, only a scanty literature dealt specifically with the state, and most of this writing was imported. Nor was there any widely accepted set of political ideas that could be invoked to judge social schemes.

Yet among an immense number of proposals for municipal, state, and national regeneration, one might discern a common thread and a comprehensive, though vague, set of answers to immensely complicated questions about the new social order, the possibilities of industrial progress, and the nature of the modern state. Wells was wrong to assume an absence of "abstraction or generalization" in American political thinking. He was looking in the wrong place. While Americans rarely studied the state in isolation during this period of amazing change, they were very much concerned with the gigantic economic institutions that had suddenly appeared in the guise of the trusts. In schemes for the future and reforms for the present, the state appeared most often as an instrumentality, a means to an end, a neutral body already withering away, soon to be an administrative organ for the dictates of the community. Among a great many efforts to understand the nature of the new industrial society, few were built upon European theories of the state.

Van Wyck Brooks agreed with Wells: Americans had so far failed to think of the state in organic terms. They had not yet systematized the emerging national consciousness into a political scheme. Thus, Brooks wrote, Americans "are unconsciously engaged in works of an almost appalling significance for the future of society. A trust is a work of this kind, and whether it is to be a gigantic good or a gigantic evil depends wholly upon whether its controlling minds are more conscious of their individual or their social function."[2] Here was the key question and an implied answer. Americans had created a new industrial civilization in which the giant business organization was the dominant force and the prevailing idiom in the thinking of a great many reformers. Whether an antiquated individualism or a new collectivism would emerge to mold this new industrial society was the most pressing consideration of the day. Had Wells looked to American writings about industrial society, he would have found an enormous literature which was often deeply speculative, theoretical, and profoundly utopian.

A new attitude toward American society was most apparent among those intellectuals who were becoming social entrepreneurs, those men and women who saw new social relationships emerging in the movement toward a centralized, modern economy. The kinds of occupations they held and the attitudes they shared are key to an understanding of the nature of their thought and the meaning of their proposals.

Most characteristically, these new social entrepreneurs were bound together first by a self-consciousness, not necessarily as like-minded intellectuals but as to their own special role in an industrialized society. They were, by and large, oriented toward national issues, for only on such a grand scale could they find the means for the general social reorganization they proposed. Many thought the past a useless record of disproved systems, or, more optimistically, an illustration of the possibilities for rapid evolution. Still, these same intellectuals were not reluctant to find models for their thought in the great writings and discoveries of the nineteenth century—in Darwinism, in the newer social sciences, and in the utopian speculations of such writers as Edward Bellamy. All of their efforts and experiences confirmed two general hypotheses: first, that economics and economic relationships were the dominant causes of social maladjustment or progress; second, that their own interests as intellectuals and reformers could be linked to the most progressive forces of modern social change. These assumptions led them to propose a collective society to control the forces of economic change, and to propose themselves as the interpreters and scientific observers who would work out the generalized schemes for regulating that new society.

If many of these reformers and intellectuals agreed on the nature of the problems facing American society, what is to explain the lack of a cohesive political ideology which they could share? Why have these people as a force remained obscure?

One reason is that the premises they agreed upon could be used toward such different theoretical ends. Municipal reformers, prohibitionists, single-taxers, and many socialists championed their divergences, not the views they shared with others about the direction and future shape of American society. A hundred irrelevant, simpleminded, and single-cause reform movements testify to the lack of cohesion and direction at one level of American reform thought before World War I. No wonder, then, that historians have courted the contradictions between such movements and tried to make them speak for very different interpretations of a "Progressive era." Consequently, the beginnings of modern reform have been variously pictured as an attempt to adjust modern America to a new political and economic reality; as a manifestation of status insecurity, or conversely, of a new optimism; or as an attempt by corporations to use intellectuals to absorb and blunt radicalism. If generally true, such theories nonetheless make the reform intellectual seem uncomfortable and ill-placed. Now he seems to be working for a liberal cause, now for a conservative one. One must ask if this intellectual ever understood what he was doing, or whether he was perhaps acting cynically all the while. Inevitably, in searching for subconscious motivations, historians have often fallen back on interpreting the intellectual's role in terms of self-deception.

The general insights of intellectuals, or their agreements about the basic outlines of a reformed society, were either compromised or hidden behind the drive for specific legislation. The new society admired the cash value of ideas, and the theories underlying social reform often seemed remote from practical measures. For example, did the question of the organic nature of society have anything to do with the direct election of Senators? These two levels of reform theory, one speculative and one immediate, were separated and complicated by the personalities of reformers, by practical politics, by geography, by class, and by the amazing variety of reform organizations, all clamoring for similar changes. The main effect of this separation of speculation and practice was to prevent deeper ideas from becoming politically noticeable. Even socialism, to many radical intellectuals, was merely a set of demands completely divorced from a specific system of empiricism. The ideological distinction between a Progressive and a socialist intellectual could often be eliminated by juggling their demands.

While even the most distant of intellectual utopias could often be translated into some form of political activism, truly partisan utopian thinking was rare. A man such as Herbert Croly, who temporarily attached his weighty sociological system to the political cause of Theodore Roosevelt, was almost unique. He addressed Roosevelt's political movement as if it proposed to create a new social system, and thus set an important precedent for making Presidents the commander-in-chiefs of reform. In most cases the separation between assumptions and political strategy persisted. Ideas which now appear to be apt descriptions of the direction of society did not then become politically usable ideas. They remained detached insights, mere glimpses of reality. When intellectuals enlisted in a particular reform plan, such as the initiative and referendum, scientific management, or industrial democracy, their insights were exiled to the realm of metaphysics. The irony of this distinction between practicality and impracticality was the heavy burden it placed upon success. Given their values and their own purchases of political futures, intellectuals failed at first in their attempt to convince society to accept their reform schemes, and, worse, failed to unite themselves. Yet what is most important about them—and most often ignored by historians—is not, as they believed, their many pragmatic and transitory suggestions for reform, but their agreement in theory.

Beyond the most obvious progressive thinkers (the autobiographers and journalists), a great many intellectuals wrote about society in a serious and sustained manner. Together with more practical or politically involved intellectuals, they provided a surprising range of literature about their society and its future. To a special few, that future would be dominated by some form of collectivism which drew its inspiration from organizational and functional changes in modern industry. Some writers felt they had discovered the structures of a new form of society, a step beyond laissez faire in the evolution of civilization from barbarism and slavery to feudalism and capitalism. The most important group of collectivist intellectuals believed that the good society could be realized by harnessing the most aggressive and dangerous elements of change in the social and economic structure. Reform, they argued, was man's way to complete the natural growth of society. The twentieth century would be a collective epoch in terms of social organization. And community—if ever that illusive feeling should reappear—would necessarily arise out of the organic relations created by the new industrial state. Just as the tensions and clashes of older forms of political economy had been smoothed over by elaborate social custom and political practice, so too the tensions of modern industrial society might be sublimated. As socialist Laurence Gronlund wrote: " . . . This Commonwealth will be a Society all of whose units have a sense of belonging together, and of being responsible for one another; a Society pervaded by a feeling of what we, using a foreign word, call SOLIDARITY, but what we not ineptly may in English term CORPORATE RESPONSIBILITY."[3] The surprising fact is not that so many intellectuals agreed with this general formulation, or even with a much more specific vision of the future, but that such basic agreement could be molded into such a wide variety of immediate panaceas, and then lost.

What has been called collectivist thought refers precisely to this wide agreement among intellectuals that modern social organization ought to emulate the contours of industrial organization. Most reform intellectuals saw their position in society as a happily ambiguous one between the massive power units which grew up around the work roles of employers and employees in the new giant corporations. Perceptive as these general insights were, they did not emerge as a popular ideology. America was far too involved with traditional political myths to rely upon ideas that sounded strikingly new; assumptions about the mass nature of society remained assumptions. Yet these intellectuals before World War I helped to create a tradition that for fifty years provided a core of ideas which were used and reused by America's leading social thinkers. Collectivism became a loose set of ideas which explained American society to other intellectuals, if not to the nation. They were ideas born in between the public and private realms of ideology.

For those intellectuals and practical reformers who spoke of the new collective society, two descriptive metaphors illustrated the dangerous and exciting possibilities of the present. One defined the modern period as a revolutionary one, with its roots perhaps in the Civil War. New economic and social forms had suddenly coagulated into a different kind of civilization, splendid in its potential but still aggravated by class hostilities and outmoded social conventions. The revolutionary idiom was a way of expressing the newness of the society that seemed imminent. A second metaphor came from the language of modern science. Many writers worked hard to incorporate Darwinism in orderly sociological and political laws which would explain rapid social change. This attempt to be scientific was most often conservative in the sense of preserving order, and yet progressive because it sought to continue the momentum of change. Together these two metaphors of revolution and orderly progress strained the imagination of many social thinkers, forcing them to grasp at utopias, or in some cases to believe in present perfection. Such writings had little to do with the practical politics of reform, yet they often provided the assumptions for Christian socialism, prohibition, single-taxism, nationalism, municipal reform, Industrial Democracy, and a hundred other causes.

Who were these collectivist intellectuals and reformers? They came largely from a new group of social scientists, "experts," and academics—what might be designated a "national reform bureaucracy." Socialist William James Ghent called them the "social service class." Sociologist Franklin Giddings named them the "protocracy," which "comes into existence and begins its career as a little band of alert and capable persons who see the situation, grasp the opportunity, and in the expressive slang of our modern competitive life, 'go to it' with no unnecessary delay." To William Tolman, director of the American Museum of Safety, they were social engineers, a new professional class with special skills to solve socio-industrial problems with a "world experience in life and labor."[4]

Coming from different parts of the country, they were based in universities, settlement houses, reform clubs, popular reform journals, in the Socialist party and countless reform organizations and leagues, and at the periphery of labor unions and corporations. Many knew each other or at least often read their names side by side on the letterheads of national reform groups. In major urban areas such as Boston, New York, and Chicago, they tended to belong to the same social clubs, for example, the City Club of New York and the Sunset Club of Chicago. Divided as they always were on the specifics of immediate reform, they nonetheless created an interlocking literature which described the new social order. If anything, they were both students of and professors to the modern industrial organization and to the growing class of business executives just descended from the Robber Barons.

Their writings were explicitly based upon new economic theories. The momentous rediscovery of economic motivations by history and the social sciences was at the base of their thought. Like most intellectuals of the day, they recognized that the corporation (which they sometimes confused with industrialism in general) symbolized all that was new and dynamic in American society. Because of their economic emphasis, they defined society in terms of its functional and productive elements. The leading sectors of social progress which they chose to discuss were innovative in the form and organization of economic activity. Society was defined as an economic organism; the intellectuals were the social entrepreneurs. When they spoke of a new nationalism or a new organic society, theirs was no abstract patriotism. They often had in mind the kind of model society they imagined the new corporations to represent, one in which the conflicting roles of owner, worker, and manager would be united in a commitment to production and efficiency. When these intellectuals thought about the future, they often perceived a new social order emerging naturally out of the old, propelled into existence by the velocity of the industrial process. Some even proclaimed their faith in socialism as the inevitable future, though quite frequently they vehemently attacked the Socialist party.

While collectivist intellectuals were expansive about the possibilities of the future, they were certain that the past had been dim and narrow. They denounced Social Darwinism and economic individualism, declaring their rebellion against these old tyrants of the social mind and their supporters in the business world. Yet they never made much of an effort to see if such social theories were really widespread, or if they were really responsible for the social evils of the day. They simply labeled laissez-faire individualism the enemy of progress, and held that competition threatened America with a violent and dramatic end. They denounced social theories that defined some persons in society as inherently creative, intelligent, and deservedly rich, and the majority as no more than a springboard for a few lucky individuals. They were often quite explicit in their collectivism, but only because they recognized that a mass society had already arrived as a collective entity of competing groups under the new economic system. They placed the values of the community above those of individuals, if only as a way to save individualism.[5]

In their hesitating and incomplete way, these "social service" intellectuals helped to sketch in the characteristics of a society whose problems could be solved, they thought, only through constructive action. Their ideas did not become political slogans except in the guise of specific reforms. Still, they helped to explain one vital direction of thought which lay behind the enormous activity directed toward transforming American society. They suggested that one of the major themes of American political thought in the twentieth century —albeit a subversive theme—would be the collective nature of industrial society.[6]

Collectivist thought had two distinct roots in the nineteenth century. The first grew out of European, and especially German, economic and philosophic literature, and was incorporated into the rebuttal of Social Darwinism advanced by American economists and sociologists in the 1880's and 1890's.

The other root was the curious and widely read statement of the collective utopia in Edward Bellamy's *Looking Backward.* Both of these sources contained assumptions which collectivists thought they had shed in their disgust for Spencer and economic individualism.

It is difficult to demonstrate a direct link between Bellamy's Nationalist movement and the varieties of collectivist thought that followed some years later. There is evidence for such a connection in the careers of individual reformers and in the history of such magazines as the *Twentieth Century,* which changed in the mid-1890's from explicit support of Bellamy's Nationalism to a more industrial version of socialism. But, most important, Bellamy's famous book appears again and again as a kind of unconscious archetype in writings about the solution to industrial problems. It echoes through new social schemes because it was based upon many of the same assumptions as the writings of collectivist intellectuals. Like Bellamy, these later writers often appeared to have a clear vision of the future, though they were perhaps more optimistic than he about the present. They wrote of the future as if it existed at the edge of contemporary society. They found the outlines of utopia in the predicted success of the reform movements they entered. The most extreme statements of this sort were found in the Social Gospel movement. As Christian Socialist Walter Rauschenbusch wrote, the kingdom of heaven on earth was imminent: "Its consummation, of course, was in the future, but its fundamental realities were already present."[7]

If anything, Bellamy was more radical and explicit about his collectivism than his utopianism. The society he foresaw in 1887 anticipated the new corporations in a total sense that few later intellectuals could have imagined. Looking backward to preserve cultured Boston society and its social manners, he drew plans for an extraordinary community which was to be determined by the absolute expansion of corporate organization until it encompassed almost all social activity. The individual was to be dissolved into the life of the economic and administrative community. But instead of destroying autonomy, as one might expect, this new society would liberate the individual. All those social problems caused by partial industrialization and centralization would be eliminated by merging government and industry. Individualism would reappear with the fulfillment of collectivism. Thus Jonah could command the whale which swallowed him.

The greatest promise of the year 2000, however, was a new sense of social solidarity. Bellamy contrasted the worrisome class-consciousness of his own day to the devotion to all of society which was to be characteristic of his utopian residents. The unpleasant, rigid meritocracy which he proposed would be the cost for creating an absolute equality of consumption. Thus, as he implied, economic and political questions were to be treated as questions of social arrangements. Neither Bellamy nor many of the later collectivists were greatly concerned with the precise functioning of the economy or with problems of economic growth. They were more interested in harvesting the implications of economic change, and were immensely excited by the possibility that new forms of economic organization would revolutionize social loyalties and destroy class, religious, and ethnic allegiances.

Bellamy's amateurish economics were really no more naive than the speculations of some important collectivists who followed him. His belief in distributive equality was extreme, so much so that he even rejected socialism. Yet he shared with later writers a belief that waste was responsible for most poverty. To his own world, a world in which one could begin to talk about ending poverty, equality seemed to be a matter of distributing goods, and wastefulness a most criminal misuse of human production. A utopia based upon mechanical speed and social manipulation was within the grasp of humanity, if only efficiency could be made a pattern of social behavior. The potential for ending poverty would have enormous impact, as John Dewey wrote in *Democracy and Education:* "To subjugate devastating disease is no longer a dream; the hope of abolishing poverty is not utopian." This promise of a democracy of consumption was repeated again and again. Intellectuals equated class-consciousness and social chaos—and, in fact, most major social problems—with the existence of residual poverty.[8]

Traces of Darwinian evolutionary metaphors are apparent

in *Looking Backward* as they are in the works of later collectivists. In their eagerness to find the few small keys that could unlock the enormous doors of social control and progress, collectivists looked first to the perfectability of existing institutions. Bad as the corporations were, and selfish as were the men who commanded them, both could be redeemed. Thus the object of reform, the corporation, was also the instrument that could drive social progress forward. Darwinism seemed to justify this notion, for it was a theory that made chaos and contention the raw materials of the laws of evolution.[9] Collectivists thus repeated Bellamy's double-vision by which they saw the instruments of destruction and the engines of reform as very much the same thing. They wrote of change as if it amounted to a turning of the social focus to sharpen some images and make others disappear. If vulgarized, John Dewey's insistence that ends and means were continuous would bolster such an argument.

This interest in evolution linked Bellamy's utopian model to the other root of collectivism—the revolution in economic thought which originated in Europe in the latter part of the nineteenth century and profoundly affected American thought for many years after. "Forty years ago," sociologist Albion Small wrote in 1912, "the most influential body of social scientists ever found in the world 'deliberately repudiated the fundamental capitalist conception [laissez faire] on which English and American policy still rests.' "[10] Just as Bellamy had suggested that human guidance could be substituted for the rule of self-interest in social evolution, the new European economists, influenced by reform Darwinism, attacked the unplanned economy. Positive state action, they asserted, was necessary to manage an industrialized economy. This new economic thought inspired the founders of the American Economic Association and appeared in the early sociological works of such men as Lester Frank Ward, who tried to synthesize a model for modern social behavior. In rejecting the strict laissez-faire economic and social model, intellectuals proposed instead that institutions alleviate man's problems in adjusting to modern industrial life. One strong impulse behind the organization of the American Economic Association was a feeling on the part of younger economists such as Richard Ely that conservative economics must be challenged. These young economists never isolated themselves from the larger implications of their ideas, nor from other reformers. Men with callings other than economics were also interested in the new economics; thus Lyman Abbott and Washington Gladden, two ministers, were among the founders of the AEA.[11] More than mere economics and sociology, the new theories were also a moral and a political science.

The essential problem for the new economics was a dilemma already confronted by socialist thought and by traditional laissez-faire economics—the problem of division and unity in modern society. As municipal reformer Frank Parsons put it, all political persuasions wished to eliminate social strife. "This agreement upon the desirability of eliminating competition and attaining a more perfect organization of industry is the common truth at the heart of capitalism and socialism. These sworn antagonists are in accord upon this one momentous proposition. Organized labor also and the great mass of our science and philosophy face the same way."[12] So too the goal of collectivist thought was to eliminate the effects of competition in society and to translate chaos into law. Whether intellectuals called themselves socialists, capitalists, Progressives, or conservatives, many were united on this essential point, and this unity influenced their receptiveness to different social theories which promised cohesion, community, and an end to strife. Modern economic theory, especially as it appeared in the political and sociological writings of the first decades of the twentieth century, helped to shake a number of important intellectuals loose from their traditional laissez-faire heritage. Thus economic and sociological theories found their way into the most important American forms of collectivist thought because they promised an institutional answer to what had previously been considered an individual —and possibly an insoluble—problem. Society, the new theories claimed, might indeed be reorganized to run smoothly without division.

One result of this new communion of utopia and social theory was that intellectuals often felt a special relationship to socialism and to socialist movements in the United States. Often this assumed relationship betrayed a confusion about socialism, as, for example, when Nicholas Paine Gilman wrote in 1893, "The phenomena of scientific socialism in this country were set forth in 1886 by Professor R. T. Ely in 'The Labor Movement in America.' . . ."[13] As Gilman implied, much of what American intellectuals learned about socialism they acquired from the writings of American reformers who could hardly be called socialists. Such leaders of modern American socialist movements as Daniel DeLeon and Eugene Debs had themselves been involved in movements such as Bellamy's Nationalism early in their careers, and later moved to high positions in the socialist movement. Reform thought often seemed to parallel socialism because both criticized prevailing economic theories and stressed the need for community action. Above all, both wished to control the chaotic system of unbridled individualism which they identified as America's prevailing economic ideology. Both saw the common enemy as capitalistic exploitation. Because of this close ideological relationship, reformers and socialists were enriched by their mutual encounter.

The growth of collectivist thought was an important element in the rise of a national reform consciousness. From their own experiences, many intellectuals had concluded by the turn of the century that social change could be initiated only by the centralized administration of national laws. Indeed, from the 1890's until the First World War, one of the most striking changes in American intellectual life was the close association of intellectuals with national institutions, and, at the same time, the transformation of provincial reform organizations, centered in large cities, into national groups. Based in such organizations, intellectuals were preparing themselves to help government inquire into social problems, or to aid in arbitrating labor disputes. Many intellectuals were becoming, in fact, a kind of professional public interest. In this way they acquired a power and influence which did not depend primarily upon their political allegiances and positions. As American political society became bureaucratized, intellectuals achieved a security that party politics could never offer.

Many activities at the turn of the century, but particularly the academic, scientific, and publishing fields, offered joint educational and reform possibilities. One exemplary organization which incorporated both was the settlement house—the university in the slums. By 1901 there were more than one hundred settlement houses in American cities, as well as a national organization and magazine. Local figures such as Jane Addams and Robert Hunter became national reform celebrities and expanded their activities and influence into associated fields. Just as the settlement house reached out to young students, the university also extended itself to deal with social problems. Teaching became the base of operations for a number of important reformers, and the university a safe haven (from small storms) for dissenting opinions. In a sense, academic freedom could be defined as the right to practice expertise. As sociologist E. A. Ross argued, one way to settle class conflict would be to allow freedom of academic expression by teachers and researchers untouched by "molestation on account of their utterances." The most important universities became national institutions. Prominent and controversial professors such as John Dewey, John R. Commons, and Richard Ely each taught in several different sections of the country. The formation of national professional organizations such as the American Economic Association and the American Historical Association reinforced the national orientation of teaching and research. Universities such as Wisconsin and Columbia often lent their names and energies to reform projects. Professors in the new, expanding social sciences made poverty, economic change, and modern social structure their primary fields of study.[14] The appearance of mass-circulation magazines at the turn of the century provided another outlet for the enormous amount of research and writing undertaken in the name of reform. Journals such as the *Outlook,* the *Independent,* and, later, the *New Republic,* and a host of more popular magazines provided intellectuals with an audience for their work. It encouraged them to join research with journalism and abstract truths with practical problem-solving.

The Socialist party offered intellectuals many of the same possibilities of status, position, security (occasionally in the form of paying jobs), and stimulation as did the settlement houses and universities. A generation of important thinkers were full-time Socialists, and many of their friends or acquaintances belonged to associated groups such as the Inter-Collegiate Socialist Society. This traffic in revolutionary ideas helped to shape the questions and answers about society posed during the period before World War I. It also stimulated the collectivist perception of the times. Profoundly different men, such as Edmond Kelly, the founder of the City Club of New York, scientist Charles Steinmetz, urban reformer William James Ghent, and sociologist Albion Small, believed in their own way that America's future was socialist.

In keeping with collectivist thought, the corporation, which we now know as the textbook enemy of the Progressive movement and the target of much muckraking journalism, was at the same time often pictured by some of the intellectuals who worked in business as the model of reform and a microcosmic blueprint for the good society. And working in a corporation was credentials enough for some writers to pass judgment upon the future. Lyman Abbott, who published the *Outlook,* wrote that his unique position made him a sort of Everyman of the industrial world. "I have a little stock in The Outlook Publishing Company; to that extent I am a capitalist. I am one of the directors of The Outlook Publishing Company; to that extent I am an employer of labor. I am a wage-earner in The Outlook Company; so I belong with the laboring classes."[15] Experience in the corporation could also be the source for such practical experiments as scientific management or more generalized arrangements such as Industrial Democracy.

Despite the tempo of activity in the universities, publishing, and socialist politics, reform organizations were the chief stamping grounds for intellectuals searching for a new national cohesiveness. Each of these organizations expressed in its own way the notion that progress and development were synonymous with reform. These uncounted organizations provided a kind of itinerary in the reformer's educational grand tour. The Fabian Society of the 1890's, the Nationalist movement, the Civic Reform Leagues, organizations of Christian Socialists, Consumers' Leagues, national research foundations such as the Russell Sage Foundation, the NAACP, the National Civic Federation, the Women's Trade Union, prohibition movements, single-tax groups—from all these sources intellectuals could gain broad experience with reform projects and an acquaintance with the various theories designed to speed social progress. This experience was recorded in a common literature which exposed society's shortcomings, proposed plans to end them, and estimated the price. This literature often became raw material for the work of intellectuals who nominally had a very different political orientation. Thus a book such as Robert Hunter's *Poverty* was cited to support the contentions of socialists as well as Progressives because it was one of the first studies of its kind in the United States. Inevitably, Hunter's methods and findings affected the writings of those who relied upon them.[16]

Institutions designed to promote social reforms and a self-conscious reform spirit helped to shape the content of specific proposals. Just as activity and change were often identified with social progress, so also the reform organization sometimes appeared in the minds of its members as the prototype for the ideal society. This urge projected the settlement house, the university, the Socialist party, a world corporation, an industrial efficiency system, or even a particular factory arrangement as the ideal social system to be copied and universalized. In this fashion, and despite the interest in national reforms, intellectuals sometimes practiced a parochial empiricism, based upon no more than their own experience. "During the last twenty years," Van Wyck Brooks remarked in 1915, "modern thought has been dominated to an extraordinary degree by men who have been educated solely through the movements in which they have taken part: seldom has there been so universal and so hectic an empiricism." In the theoretical projection of their own activities, collectivist intellectuals often imagined they had found the elusive national community which they sought.[17]

These private visions, whatever their narrowness, had to be transformed into some sort of public statement. The rapid growth of state and federal reform activity meant that every question of social transformation had a political connotation.

Jane Addams commented on this phenomenon: "The question, whether one looks at it from the viewpoint of philanthropy or from the viewpoint of science or from the viewpoint of humanitarianism, it seems to me is again the same question. The line is wavering between the philanthropic action and government action. There is perhaps no one thing in American life at present which is changing so rapidly as the dividing line between private beneficent effort and public governmental effort. . . ." Whatever their pretensions, reformers were forced to think in terms of the government's role in directing social regeneration. After all, their own futures were at stake.

A key element in the formation of collectivist thought was therefore the position which the intellectual carved out for himself in the contemporary social structure. This position generally reflected not only his need to participate in the new bureaucracy but often his awareness of a particular status and social position. In broad terms, intellectuals often emphasized their own neutral position above the conflicts of competing interest groups—they could not be influenced by the bias of capitalists, nor constrained by the narrow views of the working class. Occupying a position above the dialectic of social struggle, they felt able to judge the aspirations of the other classes. To support this position they invoked social science and the assumed objectivity of scientific observation. This became a common ideal which ran through much reform and socialist thought, and which developed as a guiding assumption of the academic world, of much modern legal theory, of research organizations and foundations, and of civil service and government bureaucracies. In effect, this emphasis upon expertise was a reverberation from similar theories which claimed that the state could be impartial toward competing social classes; or that technology had a neutral, guiding function in the development of industry; or even that behind the process of evolution was a benign, directing nature. Neutrality and scientific impersonality were decisive weapons in the struggle to achieve social justice in a world of bias and corruption. As Lester Frank Ward argued, in such circumstances science meant ethical behavior. Inevitably, efficiency and the application of scientific methods to wasteful economic prac tices became one test for progress. William Graham Sumner's "Forgotten Man," who was once trapped along the jagged edges of two contending classes, could rise above the struggle to occupy a special position as an expert in society. No longer a pawn in the fight over the spoils of progress, he could now judge their proper distribution.[18]

The loose groupings of collectivist intellectuals whose works created a new view of America were sometimes identified by contemporaries as having special qualities. To John Martin, writing in the *Atlantic,* these intellectuals represented a militant upper class: "The men and women who aim at a social betterment in both the getting and spending of fortunes are the advance-guard of the soldiers of the coming change," he wrote in 1908. Brooks Adams had much the same thought in mind when he proposed that a new class of men replace the narrow-minded intellectuals who supported ruthless capitalism. A new class could organize "conflicting social energies in a single organism, so adroitly that they shall operate as a unity." Or perhaps these new intellectuals and technicians would become the political baronry of the benevolent feudalism that William James Ghent had predicted for the United States.[19] If nothing else, such descriptions suggest the potential for self-indulgent prediction by some writers.

Reform work by the end of the nineteenth century had become a profession to some and an avocation to many others who before might have entered the ministry, law, teaching, or politics. Intellectuals trained for other work chose to devote their full energies to reform or to academic or research work that armed the reformers. Economist Henry C. Adams, for example, was originally a minister. Richard Ely was trained as a philosopher but became a social scientist. Charles Edward Russell began his career as a newspaper compositor, then became a reporter and finally an important socialist intellectual. Lyman Abbott succeeded Henry Ward Beecher at Brooklyn's Plymouth Church, then became a magazine editor.[20] A good deal of mobility among professions was natural in a period of proliferating academic disciplines and reform organizations. Such mobility also indicates that intellectuals were developing a base of operations outside the ministry, academics, politics, or private patronage.

Perhaps because of the prevailing social unrest—or the potential for reform—many reformers belonged simultaneously to organizations which in retrospect appear to have had conflicting purposes. Moreover, the rapid turnover in the membership of reform organizations suggests that single causes often had a faddish attraction for intellectuals. Many of the same persons alternately joined the Nationalist Club, the Fabian Society, the National League for Promoting the Public Ownership of Monopolies, communitarian experiments such as Upton Sinclair's Helicon Home Colony in New Jersey, the Society of Christian Socialism, the Collectivist Society, the various settlement house organizations, the Mediator Society (which strove to eliminate labor disputes), civic reform clubs such as the City Club of New York, a wide variety of offshoots from the Socialist party, the scientific management movement in all of its variations, Industrial Democracy, guild socialism, or discussion clubs such as the X Club of New York. Some intellectuals had no difficulty in alternately calling themselves collectivists, Nationalists, Fabians, socialists, or, simply, reformers.

Science, especially, seemed to lend itself to reformist sentiments. Thus philosopher Robert Sellars wrote of the socialist movement in 1916: "There are signs . . . both in America and abroad that socialism is allying itself with the modern social sciences, content to learn from the results of economics and sociology and psychology while holding before these sciences the stimulating ideal which is its dearest possession."[21] Here, as Sellars suggested, was a generation of reform scientists and radicals—social scientists in the most meaningful contemporary definition of that term. Given this commitment to experimentation in pursuit of utopia, many collectivist intellectuals were open to an amazing range of responses to America's speedy industrialization. Almost any proposal to end industrial disarray seemed relevant, if not always practical.

One of the most striking characteristics which set these intellectuals apart from the political movement known as progressivism was their disdain for politics. Pedagogy, not politics, was thought to be the means for spreading a new message of social cohesion. New forces could be harnessed to bring about social change. In their experience as administrators, journalists, arbitrators, and experts, these intellectuals felt they had been stymied by politics at every crucial turn-ing.[22] Certainly the party system was an obstacle to reform, they concluded, and so was the old and primitive style of eco-nomic regulation imbedded in the Sherman Anti-Trust Act. To break up the trusts and restore competition was tantamount to forcing men to wear skins and wield clubs. A new system of politics based upon the developed and domesticated corpora-tion could be achieved by casting out politics altogether, and turning government over to neutral experts who could make decisions free from bias. For many intellectuals this was the goal of reform; for a few it was the fundamental meaning of socialism; for still others it was the means by which society could be saved from the excesses of working-class radicalism. As Robert Sellars wrote, "Socialism stands, then, for something of the nature of the extension of civil service to industry. There will be tenure of position with good behavior; there will be advancement from below upward in accordance with tested capacity; there will be a stress upon both knowledge and experience."

The principle of a neutral bureaucracy, if applied to busi-ness, many writers believed, could revolutionize the industrial world. As a writer for *Twentieth Century* magazine advised in 1895, "The perfect form of the trust is the state. . . ." In the same way, new forms of managerialism could be used to re-structure government. To Charles Ferguson, scientific-manage-ment expert and a friend of Woodrow Wilson's adviser, Col-onel House, "Business everywhere has sucked the life out of politics. . . . The business system is at bottom a revolutionary government, so valid in its ground-plan that nothing can finally withstand the march of its insurrection." Other writers were determined to find the economic laws of progress. James Meyers, one of the promoters of company-oriented Industrial Democracy, wrote after World War I that previous decades had demonstrated the primary importance of scientific studies in industry to "discover *a law of industrial relations,* conform-ity to which will result in a workable, scientifically adjusted industrial civilization." Politics, concluded municipal expert Frank Parsons, could never halt industrial progress: "No law that Congress or legislature can make has so powerful a sanction as the law of industrial gravitation—the progressive integration and cohesion that form essential elements of industrial evolution."[23]

The attack upon politics under the banner of science was not entirely a disinterested crusade for reform. It was also a function of the elitism of collectivist intellectuals, an elitism that had little to do with traditional forms of self-conscious superiority. Rarely, if ever, did these individuals see themselves as a hereditary aristocracy, though Harry Thursten Peck of the *Bookman* declared that the second-generation Robber Barons might become such a beneficent group. More often, intellectual arguments against traditional politics were made in terms of efficiency. "Administrative efficiency . . . can only be secured by the adoption of a method of selecting departmental chiefs which will tend to make them expert public servants rather than politicians," wrote Herbert Croly. "They must be divorced from political associations." In the minds of some intellectuals, America suffered not from too little but from too much democracy—or, at least, the wrong kind of democracy. Political decisions were really *technical* choices. As City College Professor Maurice Parmelee wrote in *Poverty and Social Progress,* "It is obvious that the average citizen is not and can never be competent to perform many of the governmental functions, especially the more important of these."[24] And reformer Edward Devine suggested in his book *Economics* that the greatest obstacle to reform heretofore had been "the lack of directive intelligence." This political elitism compelled some intellectuals to propose a government by institutions beyond the reach of politics. Technicians, efficiency experts, arbitrators, scientists, and bureaucrats—the social service classes—were best prepared to understand the controversial questions that divided American society. These men alone seemed able to translate such questions into solvable scientific equations. Thus one impulse for reform before World War I was far from democratic in the ordinary sense of proposing more political control over social decisions. The issue was to make not representative decisions but correct ones.

This view of society was the essence of an industrial democ-

racy, but it was not generally broadcast in the guise of political slogans because it was inherently anti-political. It meant,
in the words of economist John R. Commons, the creation of
objective social laws out of the best existing practices. Sometimes collectivist intellectuals warmly supported programs
such as the referendum and the legislative initiative because
they accorded with plans to substitute commissions or panels
for elected representatives. But there is nothing substantial in
their writings, nor in the structures of the organizations they
formed, to suggest that they wished to involve people in the
day-to-day decisions which affected the course of their lives.
Even those intellectuals who seemed willing to sacrifice the
rights of private property for the sake of social control over
production were unwilling to surrender their belief in a hier-
archical society. Many wished only a more truly meritocratic
class system. The very nature of reform, directed as it was
toward efficiency and problem-solving, militated against citizen involvement in the minutiae with which self-government
is inevitably preoccupied.

Those movements that directly touched immigrants or the
working man, such as labor unions, the settlement-house movement, the industrial efficiency movement, the Industrial Democracy craze, and, to some extent, the socialist movement,
were concerned not so much with better working conditions
as with the individual's psychological reaction to work. Often
even this interest betrayed a desire to manipulate the work
situation to achieve better production standards or industrial
peace. At other times, proposals by members of these movements were simply too general to deal with problems of democracy within the new managerial community. They were
bare-boned and utopian plans, too anti-individualistic to concentrate upon social divisions smaller than class or problems
less than national in scope. Often the enthusiasm of collectivist intellectuals for the laws of social development led them
to see society as no more than a machine or an organism. They
acted as lawyers for the defense of an abstract common law
of reform.[25]

Although many intellectuals themselves proposed democratic
solutions to the problems of economic inequality and social

dislocation, they were often extremely hostile to anything that suggested revolution from below. They certainly did not welcome proposals that promised to harness social violence and ride it through to social revolution. Class struggle was not the way to social regeneration, they argued. If anyone should stray from the norms of accepted behavior, it should be the social service classes in search of social equilibrium, not the proletariat.

Scenes of social violence, strikes, free-speech crusades, and anarchism figured darkly in the theorizing of collectivist intellectuals. These images were harbingers of permanent social violence. In the years of rapid change before World War I, violent disruptions were common. The apparent social dangers of vagrant youth and irresponsible laboring men were epitomized by such events as the bombing of the *Los Angeles Times* in 1911. Few intellectuals were as extreme—or candid—as Brooks Adams in expressing their fear of social violence. Nor was there always such a cataclysmic fusion of theory and social reality. "If I live forever," Adams recounted, remembering the year of 1893, "I shall never forget that summer. Henry and I sat in the hot August evenings and talked endlessly of the panic and of our hopes and fears, and of my historical and economic theories, and so the season wore away amidst an excitement verging on Revolution." More often it was not fear but the general malaise of industrial turmoil that intrigued and disturbed intellectuals. "My interest has been," Jacob Hollander of Johns Hopkins admitted, "that of all political economists, a study of the causes of modern social unrest."[26]

Social violence worked on the theories of collectivist intellectuals in two ways. Violence was, first of all, a vivid reminder of the social problems of the day and of portending disaster for an unregenerate society. Not surprisingly, many collectivist theories were designed to sublimate such social discord and to eliminate class antagonisms and hostilities. Even prominent socialist intellectuals denounced the theory that class hatred was a progressive force in achieving a new society. Instead they distinguished between class hostility and a kind of proletarian destiny—one reactionary and dangerous, the other capable of transforming society peacefully.[27] Sec-

ond, the threat of violence was used by intellectuals in an altogether opposite direction—as a prod to convince unbeliev-
ers. They accused old-fashioned conservatives of courting
disaster through their opposition to reform. They charged
Social Darwinism and laissez-faire economics with instigating
class struggle. Indeed, such theories, when acted out in the
industrial system, were thought to be the primary reasons for
the creation of a divided society, and not simply the symptoms
of potential hostility. Both radicals and conservatives disrupted
society with their plans of violence or class supremacy.

The Industrial Workers of the World often provided a symbolic challenge to favored plans for social harmony. The
Wobblies represented an attempt to redirect society from below, an organization of marginal elements and ideas which
threatened the very institutions that collectivists—whether
they claimed to be socialists or not—were trying to establish.
The IWW, to their view, stood against institutions themselves,
the very forces which intellectuals thought to be the binding
element of a new society. Modern society, collectivists argued,
could only be organized according to manageable laws and
predictable behavior. In a mass democracy there was either
the freedom of groups or the kind of freedom that led to the
tyranny of the unorganized mob. The Wobblies were visible
proof of the results of ruthless capitalism—disorganized, chaotic, and exploitive industrialism which produced a revolution
of the disinherited.[28]

Like their contemporaries, collectivist intellectuals were
certain that the most significant aspect of American life was
the rapid growth of the trust and the giant industrial organization. But, unlike many of their contemporaries, they believed that this unwieldy monster, if given the chance to
evolve and reform, could be the source of new life forms for
an industrial utopia. With a sense of destiny, a scientific confidence, and a readiness to deal with the economic dilemmas
of their day, these intellectuals offered themselves and their
ideas to American social reform.

2

Outlines of a World View

THE NEW INDUSTRIAL ORDER suggested to many intellectuals the
outlines of a potential mass society—one smoothly organized,
efficiently centralized, and undivided in its attention to social
justice. Perhaps it was the threat of social violence that made
some men look to see how their society was organized; perhaps it was technological progress that initiated a belief in
coming social perfection. Surely the source of such thoughts
was in many instances also a matter of personal vision, as reformers and social scientists saw the possibility of a new social
cohesion growing out of their own efforts as social problem-
solvers. Whatever the source, the tendency to think of society
as a fluid mass of competing groups—not as islands of individuality—was the basis of a new collectivism. This distinct
attitude toward social organization was the basis of an important literature about modern American society, a literature
which focused on a series of problems relating to the adjustment of older institutions and beliefs to the new economic
organization symbolized by the corporation. The heart of
collectivist thought lies in the assembled solutions to these
problems.

America had changed enormously since the Civil War, and
the intellectual tools needed to understand those changes had
altered accordingly. Responding to the rise of the new indus-

trial society, intellectuals developed a new sociological epistemology. This new way of looking at society focused upon the
institutions of development, not upon isolated economic man
but upon the behavior of economic types such as entrepreneurs, workers, managers, and owners, and the larger actions
of social classes and nations. Two movements in the social
sciences helped to push intellectual interests in this direction.
One was a reaction against the theories of Social Darwinism
and English economic individualism. The other was a similar
impulse in American philosophy, sociology, economics, and
anthropology which sought community values and social cohesion in the new industrial society.[1] In part, also, the new
interpretations of sociological data were a result of intellectuals' experience in reform organizations and their belief in a
scientific neutrality that could be politically relevant.

Whatever their plans for social regeneration, collectivist
intellectuals believed in a form of progress. Their conception
of change was almost always expressed in terms of economics
or sociology. In its most vague sense, progress was for them
the continued refinement—even perfection—of the new economic and social institutions. Progress could also mean the
extension of middle-class life to all classes in society. With
economic abundance in sight, society could at last imagine
ending poverty and all its associated problems. The elimination of waste could mean the saving of souls.

To the collectivist intellectual, the economic revolution that
many writers foresaw had already occurred. This belief was
no different from the guiding principle of evolutionary socialists—that the economic institutions of the good society had
already appeared, and that a change in men's hearts and, consequently, in their politics, would suffice to create a new
society. It is no wonder, then, that intellectuals tried so ur-
gently to understand the newly emerging forms of economic
organization. The economic revolution had touched off a
welcome intellectual crisis.

The old ways of organizing the data of political economy
now seemed irrelevant. Thus collectivist intellectuals looked
to the origins and first principles of organizing social knowledge. Henry C. Adams wrote of this dilemma in the late nine-

teenth century as though it were a crisis in the public philosophy: "The collapse of faith in the sufficiency of the philosophy of laissez-faire, has left the present generation without principles adequate for the guidance of public affairs." Social change far outstripped understanding of that change, and sociological methods lagged behind the technology of progress. As the economist Simon Patten wrote, "The economic revolution is here but the intellectual revolution that will rouse men to its stupendous meaning has not done its work." The task for Patten's generation was to understand the laws that governed the new industrial civilization in order to manipulate them for the public good.[2]

Intellectuals blamed the excesses and violence of the new industrial civilization on the reluctance of conservative politicians and businessmen to make scientific knowledge the guiding force of politics. Conservatives seemed to cling mindlessly to the unworkable ideology of laissez faire, while science, which could be ethical, neutral, and progressive all at the same time, offered ready solutions. As the eugenicist Charles B. Davenport wrote when asked to describe the greatest task of Americans, ". . . The greatest national duty is to support all kinds of fruitful investigations in the pure and applied sciences, conducted by those who are capable of adding to the sum of human knowledge." Such gathering and classification of social data was used identically by the social scientist and the muckraker, both of whom appealed to a kind of scientific detachment. But the results of popularized muckraking and the more speculative thinking of collectivist intellectuals were quite different. The difference was clear in a letter which the publisher S. S. McClure wrote to the socialist Charles Edward Russell, instructing him on the distinction between writing an exposé and more detached theorizing: "The work for McClure's Magazine suits me best when it is objective, showing no implications or theories, or what the French call "Tendenceaux"; that is, to Anglicize it, I don't want an article to be tendentious except in presenting facts."[3] That McClure identified theoretical writing with Europe is evidence of how alien speculative thought must have seemed to those in the popular press. It helps explain why collectivists, in their writings, were sometimes self-consciously aware of two kinds of publics and two levels of knowledge.

Perhaps the most dramatic influence on styles of social theory proved also to be the most difficult to apply. The argument over the proper use of Darwinism and of the social meanings which could be derived from evolutionary theory was the framework within which collectivist intellectuals sought new equations of social development. Many of them accepted Darwinism as a kind of universal scientific method, a perfect example of scientific thought. But at the same time they deplored its misuse in the hands of Social Darwinists, and they rejected conservative versions of social evolutionary theory.[4]

The empirical methods of Social Darwinism intrigued collectivists because they suggested that scientific patterns of social behavior were possible, and that natural law could be translated into social law. Often, collectivist intellectuals stood Social Darwinism on its head, using the biological metaphor for their own ideological purposes. At times they were no more adept at moving from biology to politics than their conservative rivals. They were, in fact, no closer to understanding the difficulties that Darwin had left to his enthusiasts than were the conservatives, no closer to realizing that they confused analogies and metaphors for the universal laws of social development. Nor did many go beyond thinking of social laws as more than metaphors to describe habits.

The question of its intrinsic validity aside, reform Darwinism provided an immensely important range of arguments in favor of altering the social environment. It lent the prestige of science and the pose of objectivity to reform, but it was not itself the source of broad social goals. The source of these goals lay in the emulation of progress and in the idealized conception of those forces which seemed to be behind social development. The means chosen to achieve the collective society would be those exhibited by the new economic system, though now harnessed to organize the chaos of laissez faire.

The use of the Darwinian metaphor almost always implied two deeper sociological assumptions. One was the insistence that history developed dialectically, through a process of contradiction and struggle.[5] Progressive evolution seemed the surest way to demonstrate that society was at any given moment simultaneously changing and fixed in a complex system of internal relations and divisions. On this basis it was argued that society had entered a new phase, a development beyond capitalism (or laissez faire). The relation between property and ownership seemed distinctly different with the development of the corporation, and it followed that the social system would be different as well. A fourth phase of civilization, beyond slavery, feudalism, and capitalism, had appeared. Collectivist intellectuals frequently placed contemporary events at the end of a long history of property relations. Like Marxism, this approach froze the economic and social relationships of a historical period into a system—almost a metaphoric one. But, unlike Marx, collectivist intellectuals did not generally concern themselves with class struggle, except to deplore it, nor did they believe it to be the dynamic element in social progress. Instead, they linked technology to the new forms of economic life and political institutions. Evolution had brought what appeared to be a new civilization based upon the corporation. True, this was just the beginning of a new historical period, and not all social and political forms as yet reflected the new economic structure. But for the collectivist, convinced of the importance of his new theories, the image of the future was clear. The social critic must discover how to manipulate the environment in order to transform the social order, for society could now for the first time be guided with conscious purpose. As in Darwinism, historical evolution brought more complex and desirable social relationships. Biology and history demonstrated, above all, the importance of change and the constant renewal of species and social institutions.[6]

The Darwinian metaphor also suited the collectivist desire that any law of social behavior be as comprehensive and as flexible as possible. Standing, as they thought, on the brink of a new social order, intellectuals needed and used metaphors of colossal change or unending development. The more flaws they discovered in the classical order of laissez faire, the more that old theory fell apart and the more compelling reform Darwinism came to seem. The more disorder that could be found in modern economic relations, the more important it became to discover a new, comprehensive theory of social behavior. As Arthur Morrow Lewis argued in his book *Vital Problems in Social Evolution,* the sciences had finally understood the process of change and codified their mechanics: "The discovery and application of the theory of evolution has solved the riddle. In the light of that theory we are able to think of things in their motion. . . ."[7] Social scientists could be optimistic about the future because they thought they now understood the science of social behavior, which they could use to alter the tendencies of history.

The very intensity of struggle itself satisfied some writers that social peace would ultimately triumph. The sociologist Franklin Giddings wrote in 1900 that the human struggle for existence would resolve itself into harmony: "I therefore make no apology for submitting the proposition that the struggle for existence itself tends to being about a human brotherhood in which the non-resistance of evil would be a successful working rule." The principles of Darwin and Tolstoy could be reconciled, he theorized, in a democratic empire guided by the discoveries of modern social science.

For attorney Clarence Darrow, evolution, no matter how brutal its history, proved the inevitable brotherhood of man: "Is there any doubt with anybody who believes in evolution," he asked, "that as the human race evolves it will leave war, murder, and bloodshed out; and that it will cling to co-operation, peace, and harmony, and love? If it does not do this, it will not evolve. That is what evolution means." If one followed Darrow into the center of his tautology, evolution meant progress. A different version of this argument was advanced by the civic reformer Edmond Kelly. Social organization, he felt, had evolved beyond the point where the individual took precedence over the community. Society was now able to end the conflict between individuals, for men had internalized community controls and had accepted the organic nature of the community to the point where external sanctions were no longer needed. The proofs of Kelly's vision already existed in nature. "It follows nature closely," he wrote, "for it follows the plan of the ant-hill."[8]

By understanding nature and society, man could triumph

over both and put an end to unregulated development. The struggle for existence as well as similar patterns of socio-biological behavior which had ruled men's lives could be replaced by new patterns based upon the exercise of human intelligence. Thus Simon Patten could write: "The final victory of man's machinery over nature's control of human society was the transition from anarchic and puny individualism to the group acting as a powerful, intelligent organism." The end of the reign of individualism was implied in the discovery of the laws of human development. The search for the causes of social drift marked—to use Walter Lippmann's language—the beginning of mastery.[9]

Besides its genuine contributions to intellectual argument, Darwinism was also used as a popular rhetorical device. Though it might explain nothing, intellectuals found that an allusion to the theory of evolution was an interesting way to say something quite ordinary, or to provide a scientific explanation for change. In his fascinating essay *Individualism and Collectivism*, for example, Charles W. Eliot of Harvard used the concept of a biologic sport—a departure from predictable heredity—to explain how an intelligent student might have poorly educated, lower-class parents.

Armed with the language of science and a fairly sure understanding of what they were looking for, reformers sought answers about society by studying its most glaring failures. The slums of Lower East Side Manhattan or the South Side of Chicago became their Galapagos. Along with individual forays, research bureaus invaded such areas in an effort to understand poverty or violence. The enormous growth of fact-gathering organizations and the publication of their research helped to support the intellectual revolution which the collectivists preached. The Russell Sage Foundation, the Brookings Institution, the National Industrial Conference Board, the National Bureau of Economic Research, the Twentieth Century Fund, and similar organizations were all founded during the decade before World War I.[10]

Just as the work of individual social scientists was generally accepted as objective, so institution-sponsored research was for the most part assumed to be unbiased. The results of this work, it was argued, had one further benefit: its objective facts about sociological and political behavior seemed almost revolutionary at a time when special-interest groups or great fortunes appeared to rule America. To some observers, this socially objective research could provide the foundations for a true democracy. Thus one writer based his proposal for a national foundation for reform research on the grounds that research was the key ingredient for reform: "Potentially," he concluded, "the greatest producer, recorder, interpreter, and user of social fact is an efficient democracy." Studies done under the auspices of a wide variety of organizations became part of a common pool of knowledge used by socialists, conservatives, and Progressives alike in their struggle against industrial disorder.[11]

Whatever the supposed neutrality of research, its practical applications nonetheless provoked charges of unfairness and bias. Labor organizations and their defenders were particularly sensitive to the early research of private foundations. When Samuel Gompers testified before the United States Commission on Industrial Relations, he warned that some research foundations were dominated by class interests. The Russell Sage Foundation as well as the Rockefeller and Carnegie foundations, he argued, could not be neutral in their work, and their findings would therefore carry very little weight among workers. Before the same commission, the sociologist E. A. Ross made much the same point, opposing the work of foundations set up by private businesses. Paradoxically, Gompers was himself involved with the National Civic Federation which initiated a good deal of controversial research—controversial at least to those who saw in its findings a pro-capitalist bias. Socialists and some other labor leaders had long criticized Gompers for belonging to the Federation, which they considered a propagandist for big business and conservative unionism. Even in his position as critic, Gompers did not challenge the possibility of neutral social research; he merely disliked the results that anti-labor organizations published.

Testifying before the same industrial commission, Louis Brandeis made a point more characteristic of collectivist thought when he suggested that the neutral expert could be made the keystone of labor arbitration. A scientific neutrality could be achieved if all parties to a decision helped to select the mediators. Labor unions, Brandeis concluded, "have found in many instances that some men were available and were as loyal to their cause as anybody could possibly be to a cause. . . . The expert who is to be selected may be selected by the unions with quite as much intelligence and with quite as much certainty of loyal service as if it were the employer." Brandeis was in one sense defending the activities that brought him a national reputation as a labor expert. In practice, the theory of scientific neutrality worked as a sort of compromise between contending forces. Bias thus represented imbalance; scientific neutrality approximated justice. In part this definition derived from a number of agreements between capital and labor accomplished in the era before World War I. The growing importance of the contract between labor and management was more proof of the usefulness, even the necessity, of the mediator and the scientific expert. Collectivism extended this practice into a larger plea for a national state which would mediate the contending forces in society. Like the scientist, the state would be able to avoid the pressures of political and economic interest groups. Its true function would compare with the function of modern social science—passing judgment upon disagreements, reconciling competing interests, and constantly pushing social discord away from confrontation and toward arbitration.[12]

Investigators were enthusiastic over the possibilities of their research. The examination of isolated problems almost always led to social issues that were familiar to every contemporary writer. Researchers were aware of, and constantly searching for, the relation between poverty, class struggle, social violence, alcoholism, prostitution, and other problems. Inevitably, this stream of social problems seemed to flow from the mechanics of the new industrialism; specifically, the ills thrived on uncontrolled social progress and rapid economic change. Society was clearly out of balance; only the precise use of sociological knowledge could bring social custom and practice to an equal level of sophistication with economic practice. As the sociologist Arthur James Todd wrote, "From Comte on-

ward sociologists have pretty much agreed that the only justification for a Science of Society is its contributions to a workable theory of progress." Lester Frank Ward agreed: "I would
never have taken any interest in sociology if I had not been
convinced that it had this mission." Behind the interest in such
administrative theories as scientific management and industrial psychology, behind the utopian proposals for social
peace, lay the splendid possibility of making progress malleable. H. G. Wells, describing scientific study, epitomized this
attitude: "It is the denial that chance impulse and individual
will and happening constitute the only possible methods by
which things may be done in the world. It is an assertion that
things are in their nature orderly; that things may be com-
puted, may be calculated upon and foreseen."[13]

The new collectivist epistemology thus molded itself to two
demands of the day: a system of knowledge ought to be re-
ceptive to scientific generalization, and it ought to be useful
in discovering the laws that govern human behavior. Such a
system would facilitate an understanding of the predominant
economic and social institutions of the day. But, much more,
collectivism called for a pragmatic attitude toward knowledge
and toward social objectivity that made sense in a society best
described by its large units of economic power—the trusts and
corporations. Thus prepared, intellectuals were ready to confront the institution they felt was responsible for the progress
and the poverty of industrial society. As *McClure's Magazine*
put it, and as a whole generation understood it, the cause for
modern distress was quite clear: "The problem of the relation
of the State and the corporation is now the chief question of
the world."[14]

The solution of the problem was not as clear as its cause.
Progressives, socialists, and conservatives were all uncertain
about the precise value and future role of the modern corporation. Even when they seemed to agree, and to say the same
thing, intellectuals were often deeply divided over the social
function of the corporation as an economic institution. Few
saw it as a temporary business form; rather, they were convinced of its potential as a model for society itself. Few failed
to see the corporation's double image: one, the trust, con-

ceived out of legal wedlock; the other, the corporation, the most efficient form of economic organization ever to appear. One form carried the destructive tendencies of the present, the other the creative possibilities of the future. Thus the corporation embraced the paradox which made economic institutions both an embarrassment and an essential element for progress.

This view of the present was extended to historical analysis as well. In the most controversial history of the period, Charles Beard's *An Economic Interpretation of the Constitution,* the same ambiguity appears. Beard pictured the framers of the Constitution as an eighteenth-century special-interest group—but critical as he was he still admired the institutions they erected. His implied interpretation was enormously presentist; self-interest and hardheaded economics led to progressive institutions, and economic centralization meant social progress.

Intellectuals were greatly angered by the excesses of the new corporations, and many were first attracted to a study of reform economics by the publicity that accompanied the appearance of these concentrations of power. Yet few wished to abolish the corporation.[15] Some of the most aroused critics of monopoly, stock manipulation, and low wages were optimistic about the long-run value of the increasing size and complexity of business corporations. They were also sanguine about their own role in reforming business and about the benefits of their advice to the future of the industrial world. Such optimism must have puzzled the owners and managers of corporations. In turn, intellectuals felt that businessmen had not thought out the implications of their great organizational invention. The dean of the Northwestern School of Commerce thought the finer historical meaning and potential of the corporation were beyond the immediate comprehension of businessmen: "In the interpretation of ideals in business, it has not been assumed that business men are as a rule conscious of these ideals." He continued: "It has been our purpose to present the most important underlying ideals which whether business men be conscious of them or not, dominate in business life."

Tarnished or not, the key to social reform was the modern corporation. Collectivist intellectuals clearly understood the kind of division which Theodore Roosevelt discovered between the good corporation and the bad one. They were not surprised to find corruption and poverty as the trail markers of progress, and when they spoke of the corporation they often referred to industrial organizations of uncertain reputation, such as the massive Standard Oil complex. From examples like this they were able to construct models which they could conveniently analyze and describe as the ideal industrial forms of modern society.

This pervasive, often abstract sense of what the corporation represented is striking when compared with what businessmen thought of their own creation. Few businessmen would have agreed with Talcott Williams when he wrote in 1904 of the omnipresence of the corporation: "No one of us, not a tramp, but has at some point, corporate relations, and it is probably that a majority of Americans today, directly or indirectly own corporate Property." Nor would many businessmen have agreed that the corporation had all of the characteristics seen by intellectuals. Certainly, few would have suggested plans for extensive government regulation of business, or the larger need for government management of progress. Yet this was precisely the lesson that leading reformers derived from their own observations of the business world, and which they systematized into theories of the collective nature of modern society.[16]

As industry's largest organization, the corporation was the object of reform for writers of different political commitments who nevertheless shared essentially the same larger view of society. To Charles Edward Russell, the trust provided the strongest evidence for the coming of a new civilization. "Clearly," Russell wrote, "the next stage in the evolutionary process is the substitution of the community for the individual as the beneficiary of consolidated and economized production." The trust itself, wrote Jeremiah Jenks in his report to the Commission on Industrial Combinations in Europe, was instituted to end the chaos of "ruinous competition." By World War I, intellectuals were no longer merely theorizing; many of them had become part of the administrative end of corporation life. As the economist John R. Commons recalled: "One would think that the capitalistic system was crumbling, that the employers had lost the power of discipline. In some cases we found that they had actually abdicated and turned the labor end of their business over to professors." Collectivist intellectuals proved to be a good deal more optimistic about the corporation as an institution than many of those businessmen who actually guided it. These intellectuals argued that with slight changes, or by strengthening certain aspects of business organization, the corporation could become a leading force for social reform. They even found relationships in the corporation which could become the basis for new concepts of community. Few businessmen were able to envision such a future.[17]

Reformers were sometimes as unsure about captains of industry as they were about the companies they, the entrepreneurs, guided. Almost everyone could agree that a large class of industrial barons had devised complicated systems to consolidate their own personal wealth and power. At the same time, intellectuals could see a new kind of businessman emerging in reaction to the very excesses of corporate behavior. As there was now a distinction between ownership and control in business, so there were two kinds of businessmen. Collectivist intellectuals based their optimism about the corporation on their perception that the managerial function would ultimately dominate massive economic institutions, while the function of ownership would continue to atrophy. Management, they felt, would welcome industrial reform, especially because this would achieve an efficient justice. Running a corporation required scientific knowledge and the application of scientific principles, qualifications which would insure the progressive character of managers. Thus the men who actually ran the corporations could be convinced to act upon scientific premises.[18]

The need to understand the corporate form in all of its guises was compelling because intellectuals agreed that it would be the dominant economic form for a long time to come. Even the conservative sociologist William Graham

". . . It is essential to recognize the concentration of wealth
Sumner considered such forms of organization inevitable:
and control as a universal societal phenomenon, not merely as
a matter of industrial power, or social sentiment, or political
policy." Lyman Abbott, a reformer who shared few assumptions with Sumner, agreed: "Combination both of property
and of industry, of capital and labor, is inevitable, because it
is the divine order of human development." Jane Addams told
a conference of sociologists in 1908 that the trust had been the
"great educator of us all." In the end, she said, "its unimpeded
growth must at last include all of us." To Charles R. Flint,
writing in the *Independent,* there was a natural tendency
toward the concentration of economic power. "It is an axiom
in physics that motion follows the line of least resistance," he
wrote describing industrial combinations.[19]

Samuel Gompers quite naturally opposed many aspects of
the trust, particularly those which lay heavily upon labor, but
he had no wish to abolish industrial combinations. On the
contrary, Gompers thought the growth of large businesses
would inevitably breed massive trade unions. His defense of
the corporation stemmed not from viewing it as the ideal organization of work relations, but from a belief that workers' organizations of similar dimension would arise to combat the
power of capital to regulate work conditions. In the end, however, even Gompers looked upon the corporation as much
more than a convenient field for industrial struggle and unionization.[20] It was the natural form of industrial organization
for the twentieth century, he argued; only its policies might
be challenged. Thus Gompers' AFL, the leading American
labor organization, far from being openly hostile to the new
form of industrial consolidation, often welcomed it as an advance over small, ruinously competitive companies. Not surprisingly, in 1905 Charles J. Bullock, surveying an amazing
diversity of attitudes toward trusts, could find almost no one
calling for the abolition of the corporation. Nor were intellectuals concerned about its size. The important distinction in
attitudes toward the corporation among collectivist intellectuals lay in the question of its uses, not its existence.

The great attraction of the corporation was that it combined the best of two worlds—the imperfect present and an imagined harmonious future. Within its embracing economic and social relations were seen possibilities for new definitions of community that were the very antithesis of the passionate class hatreds stirred by an irresponsible laissez-faire system. The corporation represented the opposite of ruthless competition and exploitative monopoly.[21] James MacKaye's *Americanized Socialism* contrasted the wastefulness of the competitive society to a civilization whose parts worked as a single unity, one which could best be understood by analogy with mechanical engineering. For Vida Scudder, teacher, reformer, and writer, the end of the competitive state would bring a reconciliation of opposing social and psychological sentiments. Socialism, she wrote, "proposes to translate into terms of social efficiency the deepest and most mystical law of spiritual being, and to achieve a true harmony between two spheres of life which have always appeared hopelessly incompatible. Renunciation! Sacrifice!"[22]

If collectivists could agree that the benign corporation was the vehicle of an industrial utopia, the precise outlines of this utopia were harder to define. To argue that social relations would reflect dominant economic forms was to argue for economic determinism. Yet determinism by no means meant agreement on the terms of the future. Professor William M. Sloane, for example, in an address to the University Settlement House in New York in 1904, argued that the corporation would create a new form of feudalism in which society would grant protection to workers in exchange for their labor. To others, the factory could become an industrial republic in itself, including all the necessary countervailing elements of community and social hierarchy. Upton Sinclair suggested that all the elements of a new civilization existed in the new economic institutions. The trusts, he believed, were the basis of the centralization and systematization necessary for an industrial utopia. Within them labor unions represented embryonic industrial self-governments. Thorstein Veblen, who bitterly criticized much about modern industrial society, nonetheless was encouraged by the new corporate experts and engineers. The economic institutions of his day, he thought, still suffered from man's ignorance, poverty, and superstition; but science and progress might clear social thinking.[23]

Guided by their theories of sociological knowledge and by their enthusiasm for efficient economic organization, collectivist intellectuals searched for a program that would make social progress more orderly. If society were really driven by ruthlessness and individualism, eternally divided by decentralization or regionalism, then the possibility of creating a just society would remain beyond man's ability. It is no wonder, then, that collectivist intellectuals once more turned to the biological metaphor, describing society itself as a process just as they had defined social knowledge as the description of the process of evolution and change. Their assumption that natural law operated constantly through history suggested the possibilities of environmental manipulation. This assumption also explained why competition had created social progress at one time in history and had promoted social chaos at another. Permanent change and constant progress formed the foundation, as the economist John Bates Clark put it, of a "progressive paradise." The way to utopia was through constant development: "The capacity for further improvement is the essential trait of the best condition now in sight." Brooks Adams mixed this metaphor into an even more striking characterization of society, calling it an organism "operating on mechanical principles." For Charlotte Perkins Gilman (whom the *American Fabian* called the American "George Bernard Shaw"), the biological and mechanical metaphors could describe almost all human actions. Work, for example, she called the "swelling current of social energy discharged through social action." The goal of reform, according to her, ought to be the equal division of the "flood of energy."[24]

Conservative or radical individualism challenged this view, and therefore intellectuals regarded any plan that atomized society as reactionary. As John Graham Brooks wrote, the IWW was dangerous because it represented an anachronistic individualism and because it refused to accept the organic nature of modern industrial and political life. The IWW glorified impulse, "direct action," and class-consciousness. It identified itself with the ancient and now useless individualism of the past. Conservatives made the same error, but in their own interests. They supported absolute laissez faire, claiming that only individualism could bring social mobility and creativity.

To some writers the organic nature of society was so obvious and so real that even disease could not be treated individually. Each sickness must be treated in its social causes because of its effects upon the "community of fate." "It would thus be futile to plan the welfare of one human being without planning for all," wrote Edwin Bjorkman in *World's Work*.[25] As Van Wyck Brooks expressed it, such a view of society was total: "Society is a colossal machine of which we are all parts and . . . men in the most exact sense are members one of another." In all of its guises, the argument that society resembled an organism or a machine was nothing more than a postulate for reform. It advocated the elimination of poverty or the alleviation of work conditions by altering social relations.

Conservatives, too, had traditionally described the mechanics of the economy in terms of iron-clad natural laws, and collectivists accepted part of this description. But collectivists radically changed the idea of natural law by writing their own opinions on it. The objective of society was not merely the enrichment of individuals, they argued, or even the maintenance of property. Society ought to eliminate poverty and more justly distribute income. Natural law, they argued, had important similarities to social law. Descriptions of the operations of the economy and of society were tools to be used in the organization of social progress. By understanding the whole, one could rearrange society's discordant parts. To understand the causes of social struggle was the beginning of peace. Thus Lyman Abbott wrote that he agreed with Herbert Spencer that society was in a process of rapid transformation, almost to the point where social institutions would interfere with the smooth workings of the struggle for survival. But Abbott greeted this change with pleasure, hoping for a "reorganization on a socialistic basis. . . ."[26]

Aside from the fact that it failed to define aims, the great difficulty with the biological metaphor as a way of describing society was that it offered few real insights. It did not ask who would control progress, or toward what purpose. It did not begin to do justice to problems of classes or hierarchies. In an age of industrial malaise and rapid economic change, it was often wishful thinking to describe society as an organism or to stress a community of interests above social divisions. To some intellectuals, the argument for an organic state bore the added burden of being an attack on a class interpretation of society. A few intellectuals considered even the mention of class divisions as equivalent to a sanction of class struggle or socialism.[27]

Yet, as William James Ghent, a prominent socialist intellectual, observed, it was difficult to overlook the existence of classes in America. And most collectivist writers made this problem of social division a principal element in their consideration of modern industrial society. In *Masses and Classes,* Ghent echoed Edward Bellamy's use of the stagecoach to symbolize the onward rush of a society in which existed a fierce competition for the best seats. Instead of a stagecoach, Ghent chose a raft to represent society, a raft loaded with people who over the years had built shelters to keep out rain and cold. Inevitably, some individuals appropriated more goods and shelter for themselves. Ghent argued that such competition would end some day, and classes would disappear. Still, his treatment of class struggle was at least half exorcism, and in this sense Ghent was typical of many intellectuals who talked about class struggle. As the municipal socialist Frank Parsons wrote, "The whole history of human advancement is simply the story of getting rid of conflict." Parsons looked forward to a time when the competitive power centers in society would cooperate instead to create an "all-including union and the extinction of conflict."[28]

Although class struggle clashed with the ideals of social peace, it could also be turned, in the view of the collectivists, to progressive ends—and without raising the spectre of Marxism. Nature provided an attractive example: in the struggle for survival, organisms had grown in complexity and adaptability. So too could competition between classes lead dialectically to a more complex and progressive form of social justice.[29] John R. Commons used precisely this argument, which suggested a positive re-evaluation of class struggle, in remarks before the American Sociological Association in 1908. Commons blamed ruthless competition for class conflict, low wages, and exploitation. Waiting to take advantage of social discontent were unprincipled and dangerous men who were the first generation of Americans not affected by the "great outlet for agitators, the frontier." This dangerous situation was all due to intensified social divisions. Commons, however, was not interested in an egalitarian society, and he rejected any attempt to push class struggle in this direction. Instead he proposed a kind of socialized common law, demanding that society ensure justice to whole classes of men in much the same way as civil justice was guaranteed to all individuals. Society itself would act objectively as judge and jury, without bias toward any class. Conflict would subside. "Gradually," Commons concluded, "back and forth, the different elements of the struggling classes will have their grievances mitigated somewhat, and in the gradual appeal back and forth to this great jury of the people, grievances which cause the class struggle will be gradually eliminated. . . ."[30]

Commons assumed, as did many collectivists, that there were three major groups in society, just as there were in the corporation—workers, capitalists, and the public. Balancing these groups was the key to social harmony. While workers and capitalists operated narrowly within the framework of their economic roles, the "public" represented, variously, the interests of the consumer, or the nation, or society, or science. The experts, officials, scientists, and academics who staffed the national reform institutions, mediation boards, and government agencies were the principal figures in this politically neutral public. They had no direct stake in the corporation, no strong ties to the economically determined world of class struggle. In the end, one's relationship to the corporation determined the presence or absence of class bias. Consumers, as representatives of the whole society, were by definition neutral, though not uninterested in the struggle between workers and capitalists. As John Eliot Ross stated in his book *Consumers and Social Reform,* consumers were the dominant segment of society, "the most powerful element of the industrial world."[31] It was hoped that class struggle might be confined to the industrial sectors of society and not allowed to infect politics, for it could in no way relate to general social ideals. Intellectuals, scientists, government officials, and lawyers could consider themselves the leaders of the third great estate in society, the public. In the frozen dialectics of such a state, the intelligentsia and the technical experts seemed to be the natural rulers.

The state, which was the most important political institution for collectivists, was thus described almost by default— that is, from assumptions about other elements of society. Among collectivists it was rarely separated from its functions, even for the sake of discussion, and rarely considered as an entity existing apart from other institutions. When intellecuals proposed to expand its power, they compared its meager influence to that of state governments or private institutions. But they denied they were creating a massive national bureaucracy. Thus when Herbert Croly proposed a centralized, civil-service state, he misleadingly couched his proposals in terms of "Hamiltonian democracy." Most collectivist intellectuals in fact defined the expansion of state powers as a shift of power from the corporations to the people. The result was a democracy, so named for the reforms it proposed.

Much discussion about the state began by suggesting that it take a firmer hand in guiding economic life, promoting reform legislation, and administering social justice. Intellectuals rarely entertained the Marxist assertion that the state was the political manifestation of a class interest. Rather, they argued, as a supervising institution it could be a center of merit. The best sort of men would naturally be attracted to work in government. As the socialist John Spargo wrote in 1918, the best men would enter government rather than stay on in industry, despite the higher compensation there.[32]

To create this administrative state, reformers promoted the idea of centralized national power and the removal of control over the economy from the local to the federal level. The social implications of centralization were thought to be inherently beneficial because of the disastrous effects of laissez-faire decentralization. Robert Hunter, chief resident worker at the University Settlement House of New York, voiced a common sentiment when he declared that one of the greatest obstacles to ending poverty was state sovereignty and the power of states' rights. A stronger national government was an effort, as reformers saw it, to end the political rule and power of special interests, and to substitute in their place rational political procedures. Charles Steinmetz was quite explicit about what this meant and the sort of changes it would require. He proposed a "powerful, centralized government of deeply competent men, remaining continuously in office, and no political government of this kind can exist in the America of today—nor in the America of tomorrow."[33]

No intellectual was naive enough to think that a simple transfer of power from one administrative body to another would suffice, nor were intellectuals arguing against representative democracy. The new commission form of government would be superimposed upon the old. Charles R. Van Hise, the Wisconsin reformer who championed the commission form, thought the political system needed to expand to meet the concentration and power of industry: "Concentration and cooperation are conditions imperatively essential for industrial advance; but if we allow concentration and cooperation, there must be control in order to protect the people, and adequate control is only possible through the administrative commission." Less enthusiastic, Jane Addams wrote that the trust could be controlled only by a state composed of "all the citizens, a universal class." Herbert Croly's vision, as usual, was more grandiose: "The central government is to be used, not merely to maintain the Constitution, but to promote the national interest and to consolidate the national organization."[34]

At the same time, most collectivist intellectuals were reluctant to give the state unlimited power. The economist Jeremiah Jenks voiced the misgivings of many reformers when he advised against the overexpansion of the state to assume control of the economy. This uncertain vision clouded discussions of the state, as H. G. Wells had perceived.[35]

To find the attributes of community in the political state necessitated the same kind of mental leap that was involved in discovering all of the other elements of society in the factory. As Randolph Bourne wrote, the merging of community and state was a striking by-product of America's entrance into World War I. The war had created a revolution: "Citizens are no longer indifferent to their Government, but each cell of the body politic is brimming with life and activity. We are at last on the way to full realization of that collective community in which each individual somehow contains the virtue of the whole." Yet Bourne finally condemned the creation of such a state, for the "virtue of the whole" that each individual pursued was really a deference to the wishes of the upper class.[36] Bourne's fear of the comprehensive state was typical of collectivist ambivalence about government expansion. But Bourne went further than most writers when he warned that the state represented class interests.

On the other hand, collectivists distinguished between the political and the administrative state, and this distinction rescued them from Bourne's pessimism. The state was most clearly viewed as a kind of interlocking directorate of functional economic and social groups. It was the individual's relationship to the industrial system, not his political citizenship, which finally mattered. The state was merely an industrial arbitrator. When Arthur James Todd, professor of sociology at the University of Minnesota, defined the great changes of modern society, he had little to say about politics. The rise of social reform movements, the increasing use of expertise, and the tendency "toward collective control over all the conditions of community life" were not reflected in a new political system for the nation. Collective control meant the elaboration and extension of many national institutions, including political and economic ones, but primarily it indicated a rise of a national spirit which would suffuse the activities of all men.[37]

If collectivists were unable or unwilling to admit to the statism implied in their theories, other observers were not reluctant to point it out. In *Servile State,* the British writer Hilaire Belloc made a sour prediction about the evolution of capitalist society, in sharp contrast to the hopes of many reformers. Belloc imagined a state which resembled the new feudal society pessimistically predicted by Ghent. In Belloc's and Ghent's books, security was the hostage for which political rights and individuality were traded. To Belloc, everything in modern life, every important political tendency, was aimed at this same bleak end: "The generous reformer is canalised toward it; the ungenerous one finds it a very mirror of his ideal; the herd of 'practical' men meet at every stage in its inception the 'practical' steps which they expected and demanded. . . ." This attack on the swollen role of the state was almost identical to the criticism of state socialism and collectivism that William English Walling made the cornerstone of his political ideas. Belloc's critique would be echoed again, decades later. In the 1930's such men as James Burnham would point to the terrible centralization of government and rampant bureaucracy that had accompanied the "managerial revolution." But to the collectivist intellectual of 1910 there seemed little danger from a bureaucratic state. He was not, after all, talking about the political state. Collectivism was primarily a sociological theory, and the political vision of the future was suggested only in some of the utopian writings of the day.

Taken together, the writings of reformers, sociologists, socialists, and journalists formed the broad outlines of a collectivist theory of American society in which the corporation dominated. Yet few intellectuals could be considered "corporatists." Plainly, their theories were too incomplete, too wrapped up in individual panaceas, to create the kind of tight and complex system that corporatism suggests. These men were much more interested in the simple but profound discovery that the collectivity of society was more important than its parts, and that the institutions which expressed this wholeness were growing more important. Although some of them looked back fondly upon the corporate society that had been achieved under feudalism, most of them were far more fascinated by the future. And the future which most of them saw—at least until 1917—looked very much like socialism.

3

An Ideology Without Borders

COLLECTIVIST THEORY was far broader than any of the specific movements that shared its perspectives. It was, in fact, the common intellectual foundation of two large and vital American political movements which have heretofore been considered distinct: those American socialists who wished to "Americanize" Marxism, and that even larger group of reformers who sought change in American society outside the frame of socialism. The relationship between these two admittedly vague movements has had a number of important consequences for the meaning of collectivism. As uneasy comrades in political theory, their shared assumptions have often been ignored because of the intriguing organizational paths which their various representatives have followed. Considering them separately has also confused the essential thrust of both movements, and hidden their common choice of the collective model of social organization. It is therefore important to understand how socialism and nonsocialist reform thought shared the hypotheses of collectivism as well as the talents of those intellectuals who moved in and out of organizations that appeared to be committed to very different kinds of social reform.

The search for community in economic terms inevitably led some collectivist intellectuals to the brink of socialism, where the view was breathtaking but troublesome. A gulf of indistinct problems appeared between the socialist ideal and the long, steep path which led in its direction. Yet few collectivist intellectuals failed to see the relevance of at least some form of socialism, and some indeed set out on the socialist path. Clearly there was great confusion. While intellectuals watched and helped to build two traditions—American reformism and liberal politics, and American socialism—they were not always sure in which of the two camps they properly belonged. Nor, early in the game, were they certain that either tradition was fundamentally distinct from the other. Of course there were reformers who vehemently denied that their thought had much in common with socialism, or even that both socialism and liberal reformism had emerged from the same intellectual traditions. E. R. A. Seligman of Columbia University said as much, but his denial was largely argumentative. ". . . Notwithstanding the ordinary opinion to the contrary," he wrote, "there is nothing in common between the economic interpretation of history and the doctrine of socialism, except the accidental fact that the originator of both theories happened to be the same man." A more tenuous argument could scarcely be imagined. The shared origins of socialism and other variants of collectivist thought could not be severed by such simple rhetorical strokes.

Modern American reform, as found in the settlement houses, universities, and reform clubs, shared a greatly similar vision of society with the socialism of an influential group of radical intellectuals. Many intellectuals of the period paid lip service to socialist programs or borrowed ideas freely from them for their own purposes. Others formally joined the Socialist party or one of its affiliates. Although there were many related movements—socialist, reformist, Progressive—the ideological distinctions between them were not always clear in the thinking of their respective members. The Socialist party in its heyday was itself a union of contending ideas. And socialism had nothing in common with rote Marxism, anymore than liberal reformism implied a specific set of firm political allegiances.

The affinity of socialism and liberal reformism before World War I was possible for precisely this reason—because both streams of thought were internally diverse and externally sloppy. Intellectually, the socialist movement was not simply a recording machine set to play only the words of Marx, as some later radical organizations became when the textual analysis and ritual use of Marxism signalled the destruction of creative thought; purity was the by-product of living out someone else's revolution. One of the most striking characteristics of socialist thought before World War I was its diversity and the fluidity of its constantly evolving doctrines. American socialism then reflected the impact of the ideas of such living theoreticians as Karl Kautsky in Germany, Sidney and Beatrice Webb, George Bernard Shaw, and H. G. Wells in England, and, to a lesser extent, such men as William English Walling in the United States. At least two broad strains of socialist thought were distinguishable in the writings of Americans: one descended directly from Marx (and was strongest among foreign-born intellectuals and parties more sectarian than the Socialists), and the other more closely resembled liberal reformism. This latter element proved to be more important in the development of American political thought. Known as "state socialism" or "evolutionary socialism," it became the left wing of collectivist thought before World War I.

The beginning of World War I and the emergence of bolshevism in the Soviet Union in 1917 caused the common ground under reform movements to shift, and provided another confusing episode in political history. The pro-war Socialists—including such men as Walling, John Spargo, J. G. Phelps Stokes, and Charles Edward Russell—suddenly found themselves in an extremely uncomfortable position as members of the American Socialist party which opposed the war. When they and many like them quit the party to find a home within the AFL or Wilsonian democracy, they discovered themselves in the middle of the Progressive reservation. Looking backward, it seemed to them that the socialist tradition to which they had contributed so much of their energy was now completely alien to America. Walling, Spargo, and others testified to the foreignness of the Socialist party, dominated, they thought, by Germans and other Central European immigrants. The embryo of communism, which grew within the party and broke off in 1919, taking with it an important segment of the socialist movement, was only further proof that radicalism in general had little to do with the dominant assumptions among intellectuals about the nature and goals of American society. Which is not to say that socialist or even communist influence upon collectivist thought disappeared after the war, but only that it became more obscure.

As seen through the impact of the war, the Russian Revolution, and the events of subsequent decades, the history of political ideas appears to be marked by profound differences between the socialist and liberal wings of collectivist thought. But before the war, in the confusion of shared beliefs, such distinctions were not always clear or significant. In the long run it was the liberal reformers and socialists themselves who counted up the differences between each other's movements. Before that, reform intellectuals acknowledged the common heritage which they understood they shared with American socialism. A good many men moved easily between socialist organizations and those which emerged out of nonsocialist reform impulses. Had the Socialist party not suffered paralysis in the early 1920's, their shared assumptions of the collective nature of modern society might have remained intact.

During the prewar years, while both movements accepted each other as unofficial partners in the subversion of the old order, each also strove for definitional purity. Hostility between socialist and liberal reformist organizations was not infrequent, and it made intellectuals wary of asserting what they shared with their fellows across the fence. But charges that socialists were un-American or that reformers were futile tinkerers were not really significant until Wilson separated those who would or would not join his crusade to save the world.

Because socialism alone seemed capable of putting together the vision of a just future with relevant plans to reform the present, the Socialist party was perhaps the single most important organization to influence collectivist thought. This influence was partly due to the party's resources. But many intellectuals saw reflected in the party their own preoccupation with institutional reform, and found in socialist programs the equivalent of their own thought. Evolutionary socialism and reform capitalism shared a common theory of a vanguard, whether of experts or political leaders, who would lead the way toward a radical alteration of American society. Both movements relied upon Darwinian metaphors and the predictions of modern social science. Both defined the trust or corporation as the central problem and the primary force of progress. And both, feeling that modern society's problems were universal, appealed to an international reform community.

For socialists, the vanguard was often by implication the Socialist party. To reformers, the vanguard was sometimes a group of intellectuals or even an institution such as the settlement house or the university. In practice, however, the intellectuals saw *themselves* at the leading edge of civilization. Their writings often reflected a familiarity with the past and the future, as if both were familiar terrain. This sense of predicting the future course of society fed an almost irresistible urge toward utopianism. The "discovery" of sociological laws, the belief in rapid change, the interchangeability of knowledge from one broad field to another, suggest a carelessness which is often the mark of excessive enthusiasm. However sure or unsure intellectuals were about where society was going, they felt certain that it was on the verge of immense change which they could influence.

Progress would inevitably rest, they believed, upon the emergence of an intellectual vanguard which could articulate the half-hidden laws of social development. As John Corbin wrote in his tract about the fate of the middle classes, the industrial revolution had created a new species of man with a potential for service and with a power beyond what anyone had imagined: "This new middle class of technicians, managers, professional men comprises the creative brain force, the power of guidance and command, without which civilization will crash about our ears. . . ." Charles Ferguson, the scientific-management enthusiast, sourly differentiated between types in this new class. There were, he wrote, utopians like Theodore Roosevelt and Morris Hillquit of the Socialist party, and statisticians like Richard Ely and Samuel Gompers. The truly creative men, Ferguson concluded, were those engaged in scientific-management reforms.[1]

The scientific experts, the corporation managers, the skilled civil servants, even the socialist intellectuals, though they might appear to be neutral arbiters, were at least highly biased in favor of continued social evolution. Because social progress seemed to them so certain, they were in a sense only servants of the inevitable. Nonetheless, the concept of a vanguard was ultimately a political one. If such men saw themselves as composers of social laws which could harmonize progress, they might become a new ruling body, as socialist James MacKaye described them in the *Economy of Happiness*. They might become a "pantocracy," "chosen by the President to serve the nation, from those who have worked their way up in industry."[2]

The translation of political positions into such terms as forward-looking or backward-looking—the measurement of a man's opinions in relation to the idea of progress—was a recurring habit of all collectivists. For example, Bernard Baruch, in a letter in 1920 to Charles Edward Russell, by then an ex-socialist, commented on the enormously important federal experiments in economic planning undertaken during the Wilson administration: "As you know, the entrenched interests—not always so I believe, entrenched with sinister purpose, but more often with the sincere feeling that they are right—attack a man like myself. In their entrenched position, they feel that any change is bad. I do not think of these men as reactionary, but rather as static forces in the community. They seem reactionary because they stand still while the flow of human progress is going on."[3] Baruch's choice of language may seem casual, even commonplace, but his words are charged with connotations of science and progress. If nothing else, they prove that the language of science could be transformed into convenient political formulations, and society schematized into a kind of energy pattern.

Among socialist intellectuals the theory of a vanguard was important and explicit. To John Spargo, the socialist movement had the clearest vision of the future, and within that movement, he argued, intellectuals were the foremost element, an elite within an elite. To early socialist intellectuals, especially those who had come from the ministry or who were Christian Socialists, a particularly strong sense of mission was grafted onto the broader Marxist notion of proletarian destiny. A few of these socialists simply transposed their ministerial function to the movement and acquired a new laity. In *Principles of Scientific Socialism,* Charles H. Vail described the socialist as a kind of priest-scientist: "Socialists, and Socialists alone, have correctly diagnosed the cause of the present evils and prescribed the true remedy. It is their mission to carry the gospel of emancipation to others—to be the missionaries of progress and civilization." Socialism was, for Laurence Gronlund, the "coming religion."[4]

Socialists considered the vanguard as the means to articulate the theory of revolution and the historic destiny of a particular class. This vanguard's existence was implicit in the assumption that some, but not all, men could break the bonds of class ideology to see a clear future of social harmony. To some interpreters the concept of the socialist intellectual as a scientist or even a priest was reinforced by the millennial side of socialist theory. Socialist organizations, or sympathetic groups made up entirely of intellectuals, helped to give an institutional basis to the belief that society contained an elite whose privilege it was to understand the future, and whose duty it was to force society to act in favor of progress. These organizations implied that intellectuals as much as the working class might be the agency of social change.

Beginning with Christian Socialism, and to some extent before that in the Bellamy Nationalist movement, in the American Fabian Society in the 1890's, in the enormous variety of reform leagues and clubs, through the Inter-Collegiate Socialist Society, and, later, in the League for Industrial Democracy, intellectuals had their own organizations for the discussion of collectivist and explictly socialist ideas. These groups, to which an extraordinary number of important reformers and socialists at one time or another belonged, were neither very exclusive nor doctrinally pure. They were, in a practical sense, universities for a generation of reformers exposing their members to the widest variety of American and European reform ideas. In doing so, they reaffirmed the privileged and very special sense of themselves, that intellectuals were developing to explain their own role in the shaping of the future.

The explicit elitism of the intellectual vanguard was not without its problems for writers during this period. The social investigations of such men as Robert Hunter, Charles Edward Russell, and Lincoln Steffens almost always had a dual purpose. The first was to shock middle-class readers into understanding, or at least sympathizing with,ʹthe victims of progress. The second was to influence power groups in society toward reform measures. As Theodore Roosevelt's hostile reaction to muckraking indicates, these two purposes were sometimes contradictory. It was difficult to shock the people without offending politicians.

In addition to the theory of the vanguard, liberal reformers and members of the socialist movement also agreed generally about the nature of society and the mechanics involved in historical change. As collectivists, they perceived that American society, as well as world society, was moving toward the creation of an organic community. Even all shades of Marxist opinion could agree that the society of the future would be based on brotherhood. Certainly this was an appealing vision at the turn of the century, and many reformers shared it. Both industrial and social evolution, they argued, would culminate in a great centralized economy and an administrative state. As Henry Demarest Lloyd wrote in 1902, socialism was a worldwide movement, "but it is the same old democracy. . . . In the civilized countries people are organizing themselves co-operatively, and side by side with this are coming to see that government is the greatest and best of the co-operative societies. They see that they can make their political powers a part of their business capital and an instrument of economic welfare."

Marxism seemed also to depend in part upon a Darwinian concept of evolutionary change, a point which was reiterated again and again. As Arthur Morrow Lewis pointed out in his book on social evolution, Marx was the first economist and philosopher to base his theories upon evolution: "It is because he did this successfully that he is justly regarded as the real creator of sociology and the founder of that historical philosophy which has its roots in evolutionary materialism."[5] The use of evolutionary metaphors by Marx, as well as by almost every socialist intellectual who followed him, confirmed what many collectivists believed: there was little difference between their aims and those of international socialism of any variety. Only the *means* chosen to achieve social transformation could be divisive. The possibility of revolution alternately intrigued intellectuals or frightened them, and ultimately drove many away from a commitment to socialist movements.

Behind the doctrine of evolution lay the desire to make order out of geological shards and to classify the rubble of natural history. Behind the assumptions of collectivism was a similar compulsion to understand the mechanics of an orderly progress. Socialism offered one such well-considered approach. As H. G. Wells wrote, the fundamental ideas of socialism were derived from the same premises that characterized all scientific work: the denial of chance and the discovery of a fundamental order. Thus socialism could with some legitimacy claim that the discoveries of nineteenth-century science enriched its potential. Morris Hillquit's *Socialism in Theory and Practice,* for example, pointedly used modern sociological writings to press the argument for socialism. Early socialists were influenced by such theories as the reform evolutionism of Lester Frank Ward. The determinist nature of some of these new theories of economics, sociology, and anthropology nourished the view that society could be explained in terms of scientific laws, laws which resembled the kinds of economic systems described by Marx and others. By moving the center of historical motivation from the innate ideas of individuals or the guiding hands of a benevolent God to the social and natural environment, social scientists directed their attention to such questions as the conditions of work, mass actions, and standards of living. As Marx had done before them, they sketched a world of resilient individuals existing in a society which tried to bend or break them into industrial categories.[6]

To the large group of American intellectuals who are best described as evolutionary or state socialists, the great interest in reform in the United States at the turn of the century was proof of a general movement toward an industrial commonwealth. Like other collectivists, these men were inspired by the corporation. For the civic reformer Edmond Kelly, the industrialist Andrew Carnegie was unconsciously contributing to the rise of socialism, astonished as Carnegie might himself be at the thought. "He deserves to occupy a front rank in our Socialist army," Kelly wrote, "for having put his finger upon the real evil—competition; and for having pointed the way to the real solution—the substitution of cooperation for competition all through our industrial system." The socialist publisher Gaylord Wilshire agreed with Herbert Spencer that socialism would grow out of the administrative revolution that was occurring in industry, though he criticized Spencer's specific analysis: "When the trust appeared as the great regulator of industry, and a fulfillment of his prophecy, he refused to recognize it as a fulfillment, but persisted in looking at it through the blind and prejudiced eyes of an American politician. He called the trust an unnatural phenomenon which should be suppressed by the police powers of the State." To Charles Steinmetz, the movement within the economic system to alleviate class struggle and to create single-purposed, self-regulating corporations was a "first step toward socialism, and the industrial government of the nation by the united corporations . . . a preliminary and crude form of socialistic society."[7] The logical and inevitable results of rational economic reform would be equivalent to socialism.

Socialists who placed their faith in the new industrial society were as convinced as collectivist reformers that the trust could be the future basis of the good society. In some ways, the socialists were even more sanguine. To Charles Vail, for example, the "trust is simply Socialism for the benefit of the few. The trust, however, has come, and come to stay." The Christian Socialist William D. P. Bliss defined socialism in his *New Encyclopedia of Social Reform* as "the great trust of the people." Charles Edward Russell believed that evolution would inevitably substitute community for individualism and spread democracy to industry. Socialism, he concluded, was "business for the Common Good."[8]

Although a great deal of socialist writing condemned the Robber Barons, some acknowledged their important role in social evolution. Thomas Kirkup, in his influential *Inquiry into Socialism,* wrote that "socialists regard these colossal corporations and the wealthy capitalists that direct them as the greatest pioneers of their cause. By concentrating the economic functions of the country into large masses they are simply helping forward the socialistic movement." Daniel DeLeon of the Socialist Labor party argued that the trust occupied the highest rung on the ladder of progress. The socialist must accept this new form of industrial organization, perfect it, and open its benefits to everyone. Jack London was just as confident in celebrating the centralization of industrial power. The socialist believed, London said, that "everything is moving in his direction, toward the day when he will take charge. The trust? Ah, no. Unlike the trembling middle-class man and the small capitalist, he sees nothing at which to be frightened." And John Spargo, who wrote extensively on Marx for the Socialist party, argued that Marx's theories needed revision precisely because of the appearance of corporations.[9]

To a great many evolutionary socialists, the inevitability of socialism was akin to the unfolding of the American tradition —a spiritual fulfillment of long-standing principles. Thus Vida Scudder defined socialism as "democracy pushed to an extreme." James MacKaye argued that socialism was implicit in American history: "A brief glance at the development of American institutions will show genuine socialism rationally follows from universally accepted American traditions familiar to every American school-boy." The evolution of spiritual principles seemed also to indicate the coming of socialism, and the effort to unite socialism and the kingdom of God on earth was not uncommon in the period up to 1910.

Interest in collectivism was abetted by a number of Protestant ministers, many of whom adopted a form of Christian Socialism in their efforts to combat the individualistic Protestantism of the nineteenth century. Socialism was for them a portrait of the spiritual community that would emerge from the industrial society of the future. Just as Darwin had based evolution on the hypothesis of geological continuity and the slow differentiation of species, so Walter Rauschenbusch, the Social Gospel theologian, looked for the historical growth of community. The kingdom of God on earth would be the sum of mundane, continuing historical events. Christ, like the modern scientists, had recognized this organic development.[10]

Within the Socialist party there was of course a major element which strongly opposed evolutionary socialism, Christian Socialism, or any optimistic portrayal of the corporation. William English Walling, one of the most perceptive of these men as well as a leading socialist theoretician, made opposition to state socialism the starting point of his writings. Yet, as we shall see later, Walling's best insights remained undeveloped, and he too, in the end, joined the celebration of American institutions.

Generally, more traditional socialists were wary of a corporate socialism. One widely read European socialist, Emile Vandervelde of Belgium, quite accurately saw the identity between state socialism and the larger assumptions of collectivism. In *Collectivism and Industrial Evolution,* translated into English in 1901, he wrote: "When the socialists, basing their position on the progress of capitalist concentration . . . proceed to the socialization of the industries already ripe for collectivism, they are only, after all, continuing and generalizing tendencies which show themselves even in the heart of present bourgeois societies." The American socialist Louis Fraina made much the same point, charging that "The larger part of Socialist propaganda and practices in the past have been making for State Capitalism, often euphoniously and misleadingly designated as state socialist." Fraina condemned as "state socialists" a whole class of reformers and intellectuals, especially collectivists. As Nicholas Paine Gilman warned in *Socialism and the American Spirit,* teachers, philanthropists, men of leisure, ministers, men of business, and educated women, "the great body of thinking people in this country who more or less incline to adopt State Socialism must use their reason and avoid the mistakes of writers like Bellamy and others." Clearly, American socialism was surrounded by a growing body of thought which assumed that American society was already evolving through technology, reform, and centralization into a democratic commonwealth, and that its present institutions, through historical modification, could be the basis for a good society.[11]

The ties of collectivist thought to the socialist movement extended beyond the fascination that intellectuals had for the

American Socialist party or for what were regarded as the shared goals of socialists and collectivists. The internationalism of the socialist movement was also a point of similarity. Collectivists identified their own efforts to change society with the works of an international movement that was strongest in England and Germany. Both revolutionists and reformers saw their work as part of a world-wide attempt to solve problems that existed in every industrial country. Before World War I, many Americans were enthusiastic observers of reform efforts in England, New Zealand, Australia, Japan, and especially Germany to solve the crisis that industrial progress had created. Many of the programs undertaken abroad seemed relevant to the American situation. Not only were problems the same, but, as the single-tax advocate and urban reformer Frederic Howe wrote, America simply epitomized the problems of industrial change all over the world: "In the development of America may be seen the development of Western civilization. Here as elsewhere evolution has followed a sequence as orderly as it was inevitable." Charles Edward Russell also believed that the industrial crisis was universal. "We need not suppose," he wrote, "that we are alone in confronting these problems nor that they are in any way unique or peculiar. They exist around the world; they are faced, or have been faced by every civilized people." Everywhere the corporation, or variations of this massive new economic institution, had touched off speculation about the future. It is no surprise, then, that many intellectuals traveled abroad searching for the means by which other nations were attempting to end class struggle and regulate their economy. Nor is it surprising that the United States government financed several such studies.[12]

Before 1914, Germany was most commonly cited by American reformers as a great example for study, and Germany indeed exercised a profound influence upon the unfolding of American socialist thought. A large number of social scientists went to Germany for training, and many of them returned fired with a new sense of the social uses of history, sociology, and economics, determined to inject these new ideas into the budding American social sciences. Germany had taken some highly original measures toward solving industrial problems, and even to those who disliked the heavy bureaucratic hand that had been placed upon German industry, the measures themselves were worth considering. To Frederic Howe, the manner in which German cities were managed seemed quite likely to head off the kind of disaster which he felt was imminent in America's urban areas before World War I. The German city, he wrote, "has demonstrated to the world that the city need not be the despair of civilization. Rather it is an agency of great possibilities for its upbuilding."[13]

One sign of the enormous interest in Germany was the visit paid there in 1913 by a party of three hundred American engineers led by H. L. Gantt, former vice-president of the American Society of Mechanical Engineers and an important advocate of scientific management. Earlier an industrial commission headed by Jeremiah Jenks had been sent to Europe by the United States government to study industrial combinations and their relation to the state. Although the commission spent two months studying the legal and economic systems of England, France, Germany, and Austria, only in Germany did they find industrial progress comparable to that in the United States.[14]

Other reformers were wary about copying German programs for industry and social justice. Socialists, particularly, were extremely suspicious of anything resembling Bismarckian reforms. At best, wrote James MacKaye, the attempt to adapt the German experience in this field ought to be highly selective: "Let us adopt the good, while opposing the evil, in German institutions."[15] But even during World War I, when anything of German origin was anathema to the patriotism of American intellectuals, German examples still were relevant. Morris L. Cooke, a member of the Federal War Industries Board, addressed the Frederic Taylor Society in 1917 on the need for centralized economic authority in the United States. ". . . Let us put our house in order," Cooke said. "Let us build a democratic organization of these industries, let us build something that will at least compare favorably with the German structure; let us get our industry in such shape that it can be considered almost a part of the Government, and the Gov-

ernment can come to us and do business with us feeling that
we are almost a coordinate branch of the Government."[16]
Taken together, German socialist thought and the practical
steps in economic reform begun by the German state provided
American intellectuals with the same sort of ambiguous experimental model as the Soviet Union would do in the 1930's.
Internationally, each seemed to be the contemporary avant-
garde of the collectivist movement; each contained the contradictory possibilities of the future.

Reform movements in other nations also impressed American intellectuals. For example, William Demarest Lloyd was
interested in the political and social system of New Zealand.
After a trip there in 1899, he wrote two favorable books, *A
Country Without Strikes* and *Newest England,* describing the
new society he had discovered. To a few intellectuals, even
Japan offered relevant examples for solving some of America's
problems.[17]

The willingness of American reformers and socialists to look
to foreign examples of reform and revolutionary experience
was one function of their belief that the crisis at home was a
part of larger world developments. Intellectuals often assumed the universality of social centralization and industrial
poverty; everything in their experience with industrial society
reinforced such an interpretation. They refused to accept a
theory of collectivism in one country. At the same time, almost
all American intellectuals believed that the United States was
unique in the intensity of its problems and in its willingness
to deal with them without resorting to violence or revolution.
The European experience was nevertheless looked upon as
highly important before World War I. And to argue the international nature of America's problems was to attack indirectly
the conservative assertion that America's uniqueness meant
that it could rely upon the old individualism to solve its social
problems.

Ultimately, war and revolution worked to limit this particular form of internationalism and to emphasize instead the
uniqueness of America. From the new vantage point of 1917,
in fact, a good many intellectuals, several former socialists
among them, suggested exporting America's national interests

as if they coincided with the highest good for the whole world —a very different kind of internationalism indeed. By 1917 the position of the American Socialist party against the war was denounced by some former Socialists as mere propaganda for the German side. The rise of bolshevism along with a strong international communist movement directed from inside Russia made foreign internationalism of any sort suspect. Some lines of international exchange closed down, at least temporarily. As Franklin Giddings wrote, German theories of the state had been indicated and condemned by the disastrous adventures of militarism: "The thoughts of sober-minded men have turned anew to theories of political life because a Teutonic philosophy of authority has incited, has directed, and has sought to justify the most diabolical collective conduct" the human race had ever committed. To John Spargo, who quit the Socialist party because of its stand against the war, the Socialists had by their actions proven their subservience to German philosophy. They did not support American participation in the struggle, Spargo commented, because Germans completely ruled the American Socialist party. Socialists were "un-American in the sense that their methods are not in accord with American ends, American conditions, and American political psychology."[18]

It was easy and popular during the war for ex-socialists to accuse their former comrades of treason; still, this could not wipe out the interchange of two decades. Too many ideas, too much information, had passed between the two camps. Data gathered by reformers became source material for socialist tracts, and some of the methodological and even the ideological assumptions implicit in such data survived the translation into socialist terminology. More important, much of the influential literature produced by American socialism was based upon non-Marxist sources, just as much reformist thought had been influenced by the writings of Marx and other socialists. In their younger days, intellectuals who later became leading socialist writers had often learned most of what they knew about radicalism from reading Richard Ely's *Socialism and Social Reform,* Edward Bellamy's *Looking Backward,* or Laurence Gronlund's *Cooperative Commonwealth.* All three of these works based their criticism of the present and their plans for the future upon a foundation that was much more Christian or Protestant than it was Marxist.[19]

In the period after 1900 the most important works in socialist literature (aside from translations from the German) were those of a group of intellectuals whose primary experience had been in reform organizations. Morris Hillquit, one of the leaders of the New York Socialist party, related how he had organized this group for the purpose of creating a specifically American socialist literature. It included Robert Hunter, William James Ghent, William English Walling, Algie M. Simons, Charles H. Vail, and John Spargo. Each intellectual brought his own special reform background to the task. Hunter and Walling had been workers in New York's University Settlement House, and Charles Vail had been a minister. As Hillquit must have realized later, this journalistic effort meant that an important body of socialist work would be based, in part, upon nonsocialist traditions. It meant, in fact, the appearance of a number of books in which reformist, collectivist ideas were freely and uncritically mixed with Marxist theory and language.[20]

The other body of literature produced in the Socialist party was much closer to European sources, reflecting the influence of Marx, Engels, Kautsky, Bebel, and others. Written by such men as Victor Berger, Louis Boudin, Louis Fraina, and, to some extent, Morris Hillquit, these works represented another stream of socialist consciousness. As if to confirm this division between socialist intellectuals by denying it, Jessie Wallace Hughan, in *American Socialism of the Present Day*, ridiculed the notion that there were two brands of socialist literature. "There is a prevalent impression," she wrote, "that the American Socialist forces are divided into two camps: the one, known as the Marxist or revolutionist, adhering in all respects to the letter of the Marxian Law, and the other termed revisionist, constructivist, or opportunist, consisting of a band of social reformers who cling to Marx merely as the liberal Churchman still clings to the creed of Calvin."[21]

Some socialist intellectuals, such as William English Walling, tried to steer a course between these tendencies, while others tried to combine them. The implications of this attempt to marry two different views of socialism were unclear until the beginning of World War I, as were the effects upon socialism of the ties between reformers and socialists. When the pro-war intellectuals quit the Socialist party in 1917, they took with them part of the heritage they brought to socialism—their involvement in practical reform movements. The very men who in 1911 had set out to create an American socialist literature now denounced the party. The literature remained nonetheless, and similarly the socialist vision remained a part of the assumptions of collectivism. If anything, it became stronger as former socialists brought both their ideas and goals to the mainstream of reform collectivism.

From Fabianism to
Industrial Democracy

THE SOCIALIST VERSION of collectivism depended in large measure upon the existence of the Socialist party. It provided the institutional security and visibility needed by intellectuals who sought a firm foundation for social reform. But the Socialist party did not survive World War I with much life or influence. After the war new institutions, particularly the labor union, seemed far more promising as resources of reform for many intellectuals, some of them ex-socialists. The theory which was developed to justify this reliance upon labor, and which elevated unionism to a national reform movement, was that of Industrial Democracy. Less ambiguously than socialism before it, it became the vehicle for the expression of collectivist assumptions.

Industrial Democracy appeared at the end of a long line of reform schemes proposed by collectivist thinkers from the 1880's to the end of World War I. In this succession of proposals, one can trace a shifting institutional base as well as a logical development and refinement of ideas. Political clubs, the Socialist party, and the labor movement, each in their turn, seemed to be the most practical base for working out reform plans. As intellectuals became more specialized in their roles —as labor arbitrators, for example, or in new positions in universities, on government commissions, and in business itself—

they became enamored of new ideas and organizations. Together with other changes in intellectual life, these factors helped to shape the direction of collectivist thinking. Industrial Democracy, especially, became the principal legacy of collectivism for subsequent generations of intellectuals. In the 1930's it occupied the attention of Reinhold Niebuhr as he sought to modify and update the principles of the pluralistic society, and it intrigued James Burnham and other contemporary thinkers as well.

Before World War I, the collectivist intellectual looked upon himself as an educator and a teacher, as someone who had determined the outlines of history and was anxious to communicate his vision of the future. However grandiose his sense of possibilities, the intellectual nevertheless was often faced with his own practical lack of power. Whatever future one could predict for American civilization, it remained conjectural because it depended largely upon economic events which were beyond the intellectual's control. This situation sharpened the intellectual's sense of isolation from real power. How could one know the future and not play an important role in its realization? Instinctively, as a solution, many intellectuals turned to their ability to communicate ideas. Behind the rush of political literature and propaganda published during the years before World War I, there often lay at the edge of the intellectual's imagination the suspicion that it was all in vain. In 1883 Henry George had written that "the great work of the present for every man and every organization who would improve social conditions, is the work of education—the propagation of ideas."[1] This straightforward statement rested upon an unproved belief that ideas were effective and that the nation could consciously change its mind. Deep within collectivist assumptions also lay a contradictory notion that the agencies of change were, and ought to be, the impersonal forces of history.

Some writers have pictured intellectuals in the Progressive era as men who swept away the confusion of old ideas, and whose great contribution to American politics was to introduce modernity and science into social thought. Intellectuals not only brought light; they doomed the old gods of other-worldly speculation. Ideologies were destroyed, and society was liberated from the grip of tradition. Working through the most up-to-date sociological and scientific assertions, these men came to synthesize pragmatism, a reform ethos purportedly based upon human experience, which did not require detachment for understanding. As the historian Eric Goldman has written: "The progressive thinkers had not failed the progressive activists. Reformers of the early 1900's who were producing an appealing workaday program were simultaneously being provided the ideological means to dissolve away conservatism's steel chain of ideas. For Reform Darwinism, with its overarching pragmatism, made the whole progressive program quite consistent with human nature, enticingly scientific, thoroughly democratic, Constitutional, and moral."[2] The intellectual is pictured here as a kind of propagandist-scholar, sitting at the right hand of the reformer, justifying his ways to men. But the fact is that many intellectuals were unaware they were forging an ideology for popular social reform. Others were disturbed, or at least uncertain, about the political direction the United States was taking. Collectivists, particularly, searched for an outlet for their intellectual energies in almost every direction except the justification of Progressive politics. Only after World War I was there much agreement among the various wings of reform thought, and this was the result, more than anything else, of the war and the strictures it placed upon independent thought.

The evolution of collectivist thought often had little to do with the practical side of reform—at least until the war. Those intellectuals who developed the collectivist stance were never a unified group, nor did they subscribe to the same programs or join identical reform organizations. There was, nonetheless, among such intellectuals from the 1890's through World War I and into the 1920's, a growing self-awareness and the search for an institutional context for reform. Although they began by relying almost exclusively upon the participation of middle- and upper-middle-class urban Americans in politics, collectivist intellectuals gradually began to define the solutions to reform questions more broadly. They sought a theory of society which would draw all elements of society into equal participation. This purpose appeared in a scattering of organizations and programs until World War I, when it was best exemplified in the slogan of Industrial Democracy.

From the 1890's to the 1920's, intellectuals joined scores of reform organizations and supported an odd variety of social panaceas. They did so in search of general ideas which would explain the rapid and upsetting social change that could be seen everywhere. They sought in countless different groups for a power base from which to initiate reform, but no institution quite matched their purposes. Despite the resulting confusion of organizations and the faddishness of certain ideas and projects, there was a pattern and meaning to the activity of reformers who began their work in the municipal leagues, then joined socialist groups and discussion clubs and intellectual societies. At the turn of the century, many reformers were still committed to local reform through clubs, settlement houses, or municipal reform leagues. After 1901, many of these same men and women shifted their attention to national matters, and some even embraced socialist internationalism. To the enlarged scale of their analysis, collectivist intellectuals added a constantly changing view of the reform potential of different groups in society. Until 1915 they were inclined to see socialism or the Socialist party as the adhesive force that would bind the working class to their plans and perceptions of the future. After 1917, with the demise of American socialism, and even somewhat before this, the labor union began to emerge in their writings as the institution upon which they could base a successful reform movement.

By 1918, as Industrial Democracy became the focus of so much of collectivist thought, the enormous variety and confusion in the ranks of collectivism became more evident. In the discussion of Industrial Democracy, collectivist intellectuals encountered, for the first time perhaps, a rich potential of seemingly contradictory but related plans for social reorganization. The subsequent discussion between radicals and conservatives demonstrates the usefulness of examining the general forms and institutions proposed by different kinds of reformers, rather than looking to their practical political efforts. The substance of agreement on fundamentals made political discussion possible.

The organizational development of collectivist thought to 1920 may be seen in three periods: in the municipal reform clubs of New York City during the 1890's; in the intellectual discussion groups of the early twentieth century, and the Socialist party; and in the organizations that later promoted Industrial Democracy. In each kind of reform group, intellectuals tried to construct a workable model of power and a source of energy for a reform movement that would give them the credentials to enter the cockpit of social evolution. By the end of World War I, it was clear that such attempts could no longer assume a boundless potential for industrial evolution; rather, reform would have to build upon the existing institutions and functional roles of industrial society. Yet even in that period of wartime exhaustion, the vision of a great new society did not vanish. To some writers, the war meant an opportunity for everyone to absorb the lessons and experiences of twenty years. As the financier Frank Vanderlip wrote in 1916, the war would be a "vast experiment in State socialism," whose lessons the United States should not ignore.

The long march of reform began in efforts to overcome the power of corrupt city machines. The impetus for the development of municipal reform clubs in the 1890's came in large measure from ministers, settlement-house workers, and businessmen who realized their personal helplessness and lack of political power in such cities as New York. The quiet detachment and voiceless apathy of the "better classes" was to some of the early urban reformers the best explanation for the rise of political machines.

At least these were the thoughts behind the organization in 1882 of the City Reform Club of New York, which was begun principally by the future President, Theodore Roosevelt. At first the club spent much of its energy opposing the Tammany machine; it was successful, in any event, in attracting members. But by 1885 the number of active participants had dwindled to around fifteen or twenty, and the group was reorganized to work for more immediate political reforms, among them liquor regulation and better police protection. When interest continued to wane, a further reorganization occurred in 1892, largely through the efforts of the lawyer Edmond Kelly. A new club was organized out of the sagging City Reform Club, and took over most of the defunct group's activities. The new City Club, however, moved vigorously into political reform. It established a series of Good Government clubs located throughout Manhattan, which became known in the New York press as the "Goo-Goos." The purpose of the Good Government movement was primarily political—to elect an honest mayor and municipal officials, and to establish clear and permanent city laws to deal with the problems of a new industrial society.

The means to these ends were suggested by Kelly in the form of a political alliance between wealthy reformers and the city's workingmen. This alliance was to be accomplished by establishing local meeting places throughout the city. The first such clubhouse was started in 1892 on the East Side of Manhattan. More clubhouses opened throughout the city in the next two years. Reflecting their makeshift political alliance, these clubhouses most resembled two earlier city institutions —the ward clubhouse once used by the Tweed machine, and the elegant urban gathering places of New York's cultured classes. The purpose of the "Goo-Goo" movement was to provide a political meeting hall where the reform-minded well-to-do might influence large numbers of voters, and where the workingmen might find a healthy place for social activities. As Kelly reported, "It has been demonstrated that if the amusement fund which the workmen now dissipate in saloons were converged into a clubhouse, they would amply suffice to make that club self-supporting."[3]

Since the purpose of the Good Government movement was to provide a counterweight to the political machinery of Tammany Hall, its success hinged upon a permanent alliance between the leisured classes and the workingmen. The founders hoped the urban club might provide a workable substitute for the Tammany ward headquarters. Like Theodore Roosevelt, Kelly and his City Club friends felt strongly that good government was the responsibility of the wealthy, and that this responsible element must secure a popular base. In 1892 the best solution was a democratized club, an aristocratic gentleman's organization thrown open to the voters. As Kelly explained, "The organizers of the Club proceeded upon the theory that the present condition of our government is not all the fault of the workingmen, but that if our men of leisure would sacrifice as much time to the interests of the city as workingmen do to the interests of their political machine, our city might secure the government to which its place in the country entitles it." The City Club also tried in several ways to separate urban politics from state and national matters. It proposed, for example, to weaken the power of the city machine by changing the dates of elections so that they did not coincide with national voting days.[4]

By 1894 the Good Government clubs had thrust themselves into the New York mayoralty contest. Together with other urban reform groups, such as the New York Committee of 70, they succeeded in electing William Strong. The victory over Tammany was quick but of short duration, and organizers of the Goo-Goos soon realized how shallow had been their triumph. Mayor Strong's administration stumbled when it tried to create a nonpartisan government, and Strong himself refused to run for reelection. Nor, it turned out, was the local meeting house forging a permanent political alliance between the "leisure" classes and the workingmen. Discouraged, the City Club lost interest in its fledgling Good Government movement, and the clubhouses were gradually abandoned. The parent organization became an urban interest group which lobbied for better snow removal, against carriage highways through park land, and for a more honest and humane police force. The effort to involve the workingmen of the city was also abandoned, and by 1900 the City Club was primarily a gentleman's reform organization.[5]

Despite its ultimate failure, the City Club's early years helped to shape reform thought in the 1890's and reflected the assumptions of many intellectuals who participated in its works of social regeneration. Wealthy and educated reformers were greatly disturbed by the chasm they felt existed between themselves and the lower classes. Because the "better classes" had failed to provide leadership, they argued, city bosses had been free to indulge in corruption and to create political machines to institutionalize their power. Obviously, a new tactic was necessary, along with some form of appeal to an alliance with those who regularly followed Tammany. Thus the City Club tried to provide a physical setting for workers to meet reformers. Following the lead of the urban machines, but in the name of honesty and efficiency, reformers tried to make politics into something nonpolitical and nonpartisan—that is, to monopolize it for their own ends. Quick victory and then quick defeat led some of the members to realize that there was no easy way to end the isolation between classes. The leaders of New York society could not attract the masses of urban voters to programs of honest government by appealing to virtue, honesty, and sobriety. Unlike the settlement houses, after which the Good Government movement was in some respects patterned, the urban political clubs failed to attract members on a lasting basis.

But the organization did provide a different and important experience for those intellectuals, reformers, and businessmen who were attracted to its debates of larger social issues. The City Club elevated the intellectual consciousness of its members and their awareness of their common commitments. It involved a cross-section of intellectuals who were doing important thinking and writing about the modern industrial state and its problems. Men whose names recurred throughout the next two decades at the head of reform movements—including Washington Gladden, Franklin H. Giddings, Jacob Riis, Edward T. Devine, Richard Ely, Richard Welling, Felix Adler, Nicholas Murray Butler, Stanton Coit, John Jay Chapman, and Elihu Root—were officers, members, or speakers of the club. Businessmen J. P. Morgan and James Loeb provided occasional support for its projects.[6]

Another wing of the "civic renaissance," and a contemporary of the City Club, was the Social Reform Club of New York, begun in 1894. This group took a different direction than its predecessor, toward a deeper or at least a more speculative radicalism. Rather than trying to educate the lower classes to their civic responsibilities, the Social Reform Club was a meeting place for the discussion of contemporary reform movements and the practical aspects of socialism and cooperation. The group was less willing to advocate electoral paternalism and more interested in pragmatic schemes for social reconstruction. Beginning with Tuesday evening discussion groups, the club organized formally in 1896 and drew up a reform program for New York City. Among its proposals were home rule for the city, direct legislation, civil-service reform, compulsory education, a minimum wage, shorter work hours for women, town halls for public political meetings, the advancement of organized labor, and a whole series of minor civic improvements. Club members met to discuss these programs and to listen to guest speakers at the clubhouse at University Place in downtown New York. As the *Annual Report* of the organization declared: "Advocacy of any school of thought, any dogma or universal solution, is immediately ruled out of order. The aim is to secure expert statements on both sides of subjects under popular notice, and then a free discussion of the rights and wrongs of the matter." The invocation to be pragmatic implied sufficient agreement among members to make discussion possible. Thus proposals by socialists, municipal reformers, and labor leaders, among others, were discussed as the practical means to implement the kinds of reforms and create the type of society that most members desired.

After its first active year, the Social Reform Club boasted a membership that was divided among men of the organized trades, professionals, settlement-house workers, and businessmen, while about one-third of its members were women. Beyond discussing political and sociological issues, the club lent its facilities to other groups interested in the cultural aspects of social reform, for example, the "People's Singing Classes." Labor unions were also encouraged to use the club's facilities and its sizable library of books and pamphlets devoted to social reform. Like the City Club, the Social Reform Club included in its ranks a good many important New York intellectuals and reformers, among them Lyman Abbott, Felix Adler, Samuel Gompers, William Dean Howells, Albert Shaw, Ernest

Crosby, Julius H. Cohn, Robert Hunter, Edmond Kelly, William James Ghent, and J. G. Phelps Stokes.

While some of its membership overlapped with that of the City Club, the Social Reform Club attracted intellectuals and reformers who were more active in ongoing reform movements. It gave tentative support to organized labor, sending, for example, a delegate to the AFL convention in 1896. After 1896, under the presidency of Edmond Kelly, it sought to investigate and mediate labor disputes, and to educate public sentiment about industrial conditions. The club, as Kelly wrote, "was formed to take 'the next step' in social reform." In 1898 that apparently meant the active support of labor unions through the raising of money to support a strike of spinners and weavers at New Bedford, Massachusetts. In the same year the club organized a short-lived Ladies' Cooperative Tailor's Shop and made plans for a cooperative store.[7]

Weekly club meetings caught the time's spirit of reform—the optimism of reformers and their willing consideration of a whole range of programs. Indeed, their interest in a kind of culture of reform was reflected in discussions and in the activities of the members. The plans for a meeting in January 1897, for example, announced a typical program: "Songs, poems and prose will occupy the first hour, telling of the social enthusiasm, needs and hopes of our own day." The members, who represented reform and business leadership throughout the city, heard a wide range of subjects discussed and debated by socialists, academics, labor leaders, and journalists. In 1897 and 1898, for example, the club discussed socialism and reform in New Zealand, the possibilities of municipal ownership, the state of working conditions in the American merchant marine, schemes for arbitrating labor disputes, solutions to the vagrancy problem, the Russian Doukhobor sect, and the philosophies of John Ruskin, William Morris, and Tolstoy. They heard such speakers as Ernest Crosby, Samuel Gompers, Andrew Furuseth of the Seaman's Union, Leonard Abbott, Laurence Gronlund, and E. R. A. Seligman. They held meetings to memorialize such figures as Edward Bellamy, and later held a reception for the poet Edwin Markham, whose poem

"Man with a Hoe" became an inspiration for socialists and reformers. The interest in radical schemes for social regeneration grew in the first decade of the twentieth century, when Robert Hunter, a future Socialist party member, became president of the organization.

The importance of the Social Reform Club lay not in its few successful reform projects, nor in its small and sometimes half-hearted efforts to help the labor movement, but rather in its impact upon the intellectual tone of modern social reform. The club became a kind of trade school for reform ideas, where reformers joined with businessmen to talk (and sometimes harmonize) about socialism, cooperation, labor unionism, and a whole variety of practical programs. This catholic interest demonstrated a vague but growing agreement about the general nature of industrial society, the meaning of its institutions, and the role of reformers in the agitation for progress.[8] And it suggested the deepening self-consciousness of an elite of reformers and intellectuals interested in social change.

The reform spirit of New York's urban clubs was captured in the theoretical formulations of the short-lived American Fabian movement. Ties between Fabianism and municipal reform seemed very close in 1898, when an editorial in the *American Fabian* praised the Social Reform Club for electing Edmond Kelly its president. It went on to predict that the club would become the center for a growing American Fabian movement. William James Ghent, who was both a member of the club and a writer for the *American Fabian,* sensed the same direction in the club's activities. Fabianism failed to attract much attention as a movement in the United States, but the magazine was quite correct to identify its own spirit with the aims of much of contemporary reform. As one of its most active supporters, William D. P. Bliss, remarked, the purpose of Fabianism was "to unite social reforms and lead the way to a conception of Socialism, broad enough, free enough, practical enough to include all that is of value, no matter whence it comes. . . ."

As a movement, Fabianism never achieved its ecumenical goal of uniting reform movements, but it did give temporary expression to some of the scattered notions of social reformers.

Like Industrial Democracy which came after it, Fabianism provided a theoretical justification for what the Social Reform Club and other organizations had in fact begun to do. It explained and rationalized the important role of intellectuals and middle-class reformers in the coming social transformation, and it depicted that transformation in the broadest evolutionary sense.

The American Fabian League and its publication, the *American Fabian,* were founded in 1895 by the Christian Socialist William D. P. Bliss. A reformer of inexhaustible energy and innumerable projects, Bliss had traveled to England in 1894 where he became deeply impressed with the work of the British Fabians. When he returned to Boston, he founded his own magazine, the *American Fabian,* using the British name to designate his own efforts to create unity among scattered, local reform groups. Bliss, like many of his contemporaries, was careful to mark out the left-wing boundaries of his activities, and thus rejected the Socialist Labor party and its emphasis upon class struggle and the proletarianism of Marxist theory. True, he admitted, social reform must include the working classes among its allies, but it should temper their violence and prevent disruption of the inexorable process of social evolution.[9]

The *American Fabian* and the movement it inaugurated was frankly reformist, drawing ideas from many different philosophies and organizations. The magazine was primarily an educational organ, and only secondarily concerned with politics. The movement sought to establish a mediating position between middle-class reformers and trade unionists. It rejected the fixation of single-cause reform projects, such as Prohibition and the single tax, but only in order to subordinate the best ideas from each to a broader program. Quite naturally, the rough-edged, self-sufficient Marxism of the Socialist Labor party was alien to such a conception.

In 1895, Bliss took a few steps toward organizing a national Fabian Society, but he was able to found only scattered groups in California, New York, Boston, and Madison, Wisconsin. At the same time, the American Fabian League set up an ambitious correspondence school which promised courses in economics, sociology, and political science based upon the works of Edward Bellamy, Bliss, and the English Fabians. But these plans outran Bliss's abilities and interest. By 1896 he had tired of the magazine and proposed to move it to New York, where a group of his friends could continue publishing it.

Once in New York, the *Fabian* drew new energy from a different group of writers. Among the most important of these was Charlotte Perkins Gilman, whom the staff proudly called the "American George Bernard Shaw." At the same time the magazine found an ally in the New York Social Reform Club. It devoted time, as did the club, to exploring the ideas of such European reformers as Mazzini, Ruskin, and Tolstoy. Prospects for both movements seemed momentarily bright in 1897 when the magazine proclaimed: "The Fabian movement—at present the most rational and moderate of all reform movements—is . . . destined, perhaps, to assume more and more a position of commanding importance in our social evolution." With the election of Kelly in 1898 as president of the Social Reform Club, that group seemed on the verge of performing the mission for which Bliss and the other American Fabians had prepared themselves: "As might be expected," the magazine advised, "the club will enter at once upon a task distinctly Fabian in character, the first move being toward the painstaking accumulation of trustworthy data on matters of municipal importance."[10]

Despite these high expectations and promises, the *American Fabian* folded in 1900, and other small Fabian journals were dead by 1902. Perhaps one reason for the movement's failure was the vagueness and indecision that Bliss took for ecumenism. Bliss's mild socialism, really a form of municipal ownership which he called "voluntary socialism," was nothing very new or striking in reform circles. His extraordinary optimism was belied by the times: who could believe with him that the socialist commonwealth would come with virtually no struggle? Yet he wrote, "Socialism simply needs a knowledge to be accepted."

The Fabian movement was not wholly without influence, for it did examine some of the most important assumptions of middle-class intellectuals. It represented one of the first positive statements of collectivist theory, and articulated the collectivist bias of a number of important reformers. Typical of this bias was the Fabians' emphatic belief in social evolution, their fascination with economic determinism, and their willingness to precipitate a reform philosophy from a mixture of contemporary movements. Fabianism emphasized the peaceful transformation of society and the extension of middle-class styles of life to others. It aggressively separated Marx—when it cited him—from that part of Marxism which counseled revolution. It welcomed the growth of government centralization and economic monopoly as beneficial and necessary. Above all, it centered attention upon the reformer as a member of a social intelligence corps, one who could muster the facts of industrial crisis and lead the charge for reform. The Fabian movement illustrated the ease with which Americans adapted British reform terminology to describe what was clearly their own movement. (They would do so again in 1918.) Finally, both Fabianism and the urban reform clubs provided links to earlier reform impulses, for example, to Bellamy's Nationalist movement (Bellamy was a contributing editor to the *American Fabian*).[11]

No permanent organization remained from this phase of urban reform activity. Yet these first groups established patterns of organization and conceptions about the role of intellectuals in reform movements which were not lost. Early failures were perhaps inevitable in the face of rapid change and new problems. The general effect of early reform activities was more self-edifying than anything else, and provided an initial exchange of ideas among businessmen, intellectuals, and professional reformers. The American Fabians represented a small intellectual movement with an uneasy and disappearing constituency, for they appeared during a hiatus in the history of radical movements, in the pause immediately before the founding of the American Socialist party. Nonetheless, in the name of Fabianism, Bliss, Ghent, and Charlotte Perkins Gilman did much to summarize the connections among Christian socialism, Bellamy's Nationalism, municipal reform, and

a highly elitist version of socialism. In doing so they anticipated the later relations of collectivist intellectuals to the
American Socialist party.

By 1900 the municipal reform clubs had become less important as centers for reform activity. Intellectuals and reformers
gradually turned their attention to national organizations, and
especially to the Socialist party. They did so as they realized
the need to stretch beyond their own resources and their own
middle-class world. This new phase of activity had, of course,
an enormous impact on the development of collectivist
thought, so much so that the relationship of intellectuals to the
Socialist party is almost a self-contained story.[12] But while
they looked for more substantial bases for reform, intellectuals
and reformers continued to come together in discussion clubs
to debate the larger issues of social evolution. And so this device continued beyond the active life of the municipal reform
clubs.

One of the new reform discussion clubs was the X Club,
founded in 1903 by William James Ghent. It continued to
meet until 1917 when the issue of the war split its membership
into hostile camps. (Later, in the 1920's, Ghent revived the
club.) Among its early members were some of the leading
American socialist thinkers, including Ghent, Edmond Kelly,
Algernon Lee, William English Walling, and Leonard Abbott.
At the club's meetings they talked with prominent reformers
and writers, including John Dewey, Charles Beard, Franklin
H. Giddings, Walter Weyl, Norman Hapgood, and Hamilton
Holt. Socialism and reform were the topics most frequently
discussed. The club invited visiting European socialists such
as H. G. Wells and Emile Vandervelde to address its meetings.
As Charles Beard recalled of the group: "What fine times and
what daydreams (or deliriums) we once had!"[13]

Another discussion and propaganda group organized by
New York reformers was the Collectivist Society. Founded to
promote Christian Socialism, the group retained a distinctly
Fabian outlook with the goal of propagating the broadest
ideals of social reform. The society was officially formed in
March 1902, primarily by William James Ghent and Rufus

Weeks, an insurance executive and later a Socialist party member. Included among its original members was Owen R. Lovejoy, secretary of the National Child Labor Committee. Other reformers who participated were Hamilton Holt, Albert Shaw, John Spargo, J. G. Phelps Stokes, Edwin Markham, Josiah Strong, W. D. P. Bliss, William Dean Howells, and E. R. A. Seligman, all familiar names in reform circles.

In explaining the group's choice of the title "Collectivist," one of its educational pamphlets remarked: "Collectivism is the newer word, first used by French writers, and later by German and English, to denote the economic side of socialism." In terms of economic ideals, the pamphlet continued, laissez faire was dead; in its place were the rudiments of a socialist economy. Yet a terrible gap separated economic reality and social organization, for the rush to industrial oligarchy continued. The Collectivist Society saw its function as working to "swerve the movement aside," and to "make the transition from competition to public industrial ownership, or Collectivism, a peaceful transition. . . ."

As Ghent remarked, the organization had been founded to popularize the premises of "scientific socialism" and to propose a reorganization of social and economic structures. "The members of the Collectivist Society," he recalled, "were of all sorts —party members (Socialist party), near members, and others of various degrees of closeness to the regular organization." At its first annual banquet, held at Peck's restaurant in Manhattan, the group was addressed by former Fabian Charlotte Perkins Gilman. At subsequent gatherings, members heard such speakers as John Spargo, Morris Hillquit, and West Coast publisher Gaylord Wilshire.

Although the Collectivist Society had little national impact, along with the X Club and the earlier reform clubs it passed on the tradition of the *American Fabian* to the twentieth century. More important, perhaps, it renewed ties which were firmly established in those early years among the various segments of urban reform movements.[14] Such organizations as the Collectivist Society and the X Club reinforced the friendly interchange among social reformers, a burgeoning socialist intelligentsia, and an interested business community—and illustrated the ties among Christian Socialism, Fabianism, and American Marxism.

Much more will be said later about the role of intellectuals in the American Socialist party, and about the collectivist assumptions that guided many of its prominent members. But one event in 1906 underscored the importance of a growing, self-conscious reform elite, as well as illustrating the divergent traditions from which the most important socialist intellectuals emerged. It was a conference of reformers, businessmen, and politicians held at Noroton, Connecticut, at the estate of Robert Hunter's father-in-law, Anson Phelps Stokes, a gathering that devoted its energies to finding a common ground for modern reformers.

The guest list showed an impressive array of reform talent, consisting of reformers, politicians, and radicals from a wide variety of organizations and commitments. Among those invited were Populist Tom Watson, J. G. Phelps Stokes, Ernest Crosby, Franklin Giddings, John Spargo, Seth Low, Jacob Schiff, Victor Berger, Charles Edward Russell, Morris Hillquit, and publishers Joseph Patterson and S. S. McClure. Phelps Stokes and the other organizers of the conference assumed these men had something to say to each other, and that there ought to be an intelligent interchange among the countless varieties of reform thought. The papers and discussions thus considered a wide range of problems and solutions, from municipal ownership to socialism to the single tax, and provoked diverse opinions represented by the socialist Berger, the Populist Tom Watson, and the social worker Robert Hunter.

Perhaps the most striking result of the conference was its bringing together a small group of individuals who eventually became the intellectual core of the American Socialist party. From their own experiences and from their new commitment to socialism, these men set out consciously to create an American socialist literature. Thus Hunter, Phelps Stokes, Russell, and Spargo took with them into the politics of revolution all of the ties and relationships that had called them to Noroton.[15]

As the avocation of reformer-intellectual became more acceptable and familiar after the turn of the century, and as the growing socialist movement impressed its version of the future upon the reform consciousness, groups of intellectuals naturally organized themselves into discussion clubs devoted to socialism. The most important such organization was to be found in the universities, the emerging habitat of the modern intellectual. This was the Inter-Collegiate Socialist Society (ISS), founded in 1905 by Upton Sinclair as a discussion club for young intellectuals interested in the socialist transformation of American society. It represented a step beyond the urban discussion clubs in the organization of intellectuals interested in reform.

When Sinclair thought of organizing a group of young socialist intellectuals, he did not invite them to join the American Socialist party. He wanted a more inclusive group of reformers and social scientists who could challenge the broad intellectual problems raised by socialism. Thus the list of intellectuals consulted in the formation of the ISS was a cross-section of the existing reform intelligentsia. With its different purpose in mind, however, the campus-based society, with chapters at a number of Eastern and Midwestern universities, developed outside the restrictions of locally oriented civic clubs, settlement houses, and urban discussion groups. It reflected the rapidly growing importance of the university as an intellectual base of operations and a recruiting ground for converts to reformism among the very people destined to occupy important positions in the new technical and bureaucratic sectors of society. It signaled the convergence of academic social science, in the names of Franklin Giddings and Richard Ely who gave it support, with the practical reform activities of men like Ghent and Lincoln Steffens. The Inter-Collegiate Socialist Society was nominally a socialist organization, but it did not place any real political demands upon the intellectual in the manner of organized political factions. Instead it most resembled a broadened version of the earlier discussion clubs, but now explicitly devoted to examining diverse reform impulses from a socialist perspective and weighing the great variety of plans devised to transform America into an efficient industrial republic. In updating the concept of the urban discussion club, it also strengthened the intellectual's awareness of his unique role as a reformer.[16]

On the basis of its membership and activities, the ISS was

probably the most successful Fabian-like organization in America before World War I. But its similarities to British Fabianism do not rest as much upon the direct influence of that foreign movement (though there was some) as upon the simultaneous development in the United States of similar attitudes toward socialism. Because of this parallel development, the journal of the ISS, the *Inter-Collegiate Socialist,* often reproduced works by the British Fabians, and during and after the World War it carefully examined the proposals of the English Guild Socialists, who represented one tendency of Fabianism.

The most important contribution of the Inter-Collegiate Socialist Society during, before, and after the war was to popularize among intellectuals the idea of Industrial Democracy in its various guises, and to congeal the hopes of reformers, among them socialists, around one or another version of it. (In the 1920's the ISS changed its name to the League for Industrial Democracy.) The Industrial Democracy proposed by the ISS represented a functionalist, or pluralist, definition of collectivist assumptions. It was a major step in collectivist thinking because it came close to accepting the business version of the division of labor within the corporation, as opposed to a class view. It also made political options relevant to radicals, who could now define their form of Industrial Democracy as favoring unions, while conservatives argued for greater influence for owners and management.

Industrial Democracy shared the collectivist definition of modern industrial society, and it promised labor unions and other working-class organizations a pivotal role in the social balance required for democracy. In pushing for this general formulation of social reconstruction, which was obviously far different from traditional socialist solutions, the Inter-Collegiate Socialist Society became a bridge between the urban clubs and those organizations working behind the labor segment of the economy. The ISS steered attention away from the middle classes and toward organized labor. At the same time, however, it reinforced the ambiguity intellectuals felt toward the American Socialist party, which was still openly hostile to conservative labor unions (no matter what their role in industrial bargaining), and which still relied upon ideas of class-consciousness and revolution. Moreover, the ISS, while it strengthened the self-consciousness of radical intellectuals, also contributed to their estrangement by casting them in a theoretically passive role, behind the leading wedge of the trade union. It emphasized and continually sought a neutral social-service role for intellectuals, as arbitrators, mediators, and supporters of unionism. This was ultimately its vision of the coming social democracy and the supportive role of intellectuals in it.

The interest in Industrial Democracy at the end of World War I, to which the ISS contributed extensively, illustrated the pervasiveness of collectivist thought. It was now so well accepted that it could be used to embrace widely divergent plans for social reconstruction. Industrial Democracy was a temporary culmination of several years' search for a language to describe the functional relationships of an industrialized America. It provided the Guild Socialists, the pro-war socialists of the Social Democratic Federation, Christian theologians, labor spokesmen, independent reformers, government commissions, liberal as well as conservative businessmen with a shared view of the structure of the American economy, and the key assumption in almost every plan for Industrial Democracy. Essentially, the view was this: that social forces and even ideas could best be described in terms of functional groups—of workers, owners, managers, or consumers. What animated the discussion of Industrial Democracy was the question of how to balance the interests of this economic quadrangle.

Franklin Giddings remarked upon the spirit which had emerged at the end of World War I, the tendency on the part of intellectuals, and occasionally of government officials, to seek a reorganization of society. Perhaps this spirit is nowhere better illustrated than in the discussion of Industrial Democracy. Aside from its vigor, the discussion revealed the great range of collectivist proposals. As Walter Lippmann wrote in 1919, despite the great variety of plans for reorganization, all had a common element: "This, it seems to me, is the difficulty of the whole federal problem whether it appears in the form of a Soviet, or industrial self-government, or the

League of Nations, or the United States of America. It is extraordinarily puzzling to know how to prevent the coagulation of power at some one point in the Federal system. . . ."[17] This was the dilemma of any working theory that defined human activities solely in terms of functional roles, and the divisive point between pro-union and pro-management writers.

Early on, in 1903, John Graham Brooks had noted a "remarkable consensus of opinion among able writers, economists, business men, labor leaders, and socialists trained by experience." This was even more true briefly during World War I, with its new and intense experience of national effort. The war broadened the consensus into an accepted sociology of the new industrial state. At least temporarily, a great many different plans were proposed for postwar reconstruction, all of them thought to be variants of Industrial Democracy. Despite their obvious differences, each was based upon the collectivist scale of values.

The term Industrial Democracy had several distinct origins and meanings. But by 1918 both radicals and conservatives agreed that their argument centered not on the term itself but on the relative power which each would grant to the various economic groups in society. To many intellectuals this practical question was a relief from the rigors (and sometimes the metaphysics) of socialism and its disturbing call for revolution. Industrial Democracy was an attempt to preserve what ran smoothly in the economic system while shifting its internal power relationships.

With Industrial Democracy came a further waning of the role of the middle-class intellectual, the public-spirited private citizen, in collectivist thought. Paternalism remained, but in a new guise, with the citizen's role determined not by birth or fortune but by what amounted to a new version of class, defined by education and occupation. Those functions in society which were derived from industry became more important. The intellectual was still to be the handmaiden of a new industrial sociology; but now the impractical dreams of a single-tax revolution, municipal socialism, and similar programs were relinquished in favor of a society to be reconstructed out of its organized economic sectors. Thus the labor unions—perhaps even the conservative AFL and not some vague concept of workingmen—now seemed to hold the potential balance for the good society.

Conservative versions of Industrial Democracy of course had little to do with this revision in the tactics of paternalistic reform, being more directly based upon the revolution in managerial tactics and attitudes within the factory. This revolution was widespread but often incomplete, depending upon local attitudes. It was widely heralded nonetheless. A number of well-known experiments in reform capitalism, which suggested the idea of Industrial Democracy, were tried by the Filene Store in Boston, the National Cash Register Company, Ford, and, more promising, in legislative attempts to regulate work conditions which created the Wisconsin Industrial Commission. As the muckraker Ida Tarbell, who had done so much to condemn Standard Oil in the public mind, wrote in 1916, progressive manufacturers had come to realize the importance of reform within the factory. Many would soon see the "factory as a school." The result, she concluded, was a revelation to the employer: "His industry has become an important link in the chain of human institutions which minister to men." The benefits to his workers were sobriety, safety, and social creativity, for they would find in themselves new powers, impulses, and enthusiasms to give "work a new meaning, to moral issues a fresh reason." Tarbell's optimism and her complicated moralizing over programs designed precisely to end worker independence and transform men into more willing employees was typical in intent, if not in tone, of many management-inspired plans for Industrial Democracy. Beyond a docile and happy labor force, the real benefits, as she implied, went to the owners, who could enjoy almost a Christian sanction for their programs of involving workers in extracurricular programs, company baseball teams, picnics, and social events.[18]

To be sure, some conservative programs for Industrial Democracy recognized the need for a better balance of power in industry. One early attempt along these lines was that of the *Mediator* magazine, which began publication in Cleveland in 1910. Although it was a management-oriented journal of Industrial Democracy, the magazine attempted to rationalize an unbiased attitude toward workingmen. Like the social reform clubs of the 1890's and many of the popular magazines of the radical and reform press, the *Mediator* also seemed partly committed to the culture of reform thought. Thus in its early issues it alternated serious articles with poems by James Oppenheim, Louis Untermeyer, and Edwin Markham, all writers who celebrated the integrity and the natural humanity of workingmen.

The *Mediator* was founded by C. B. Bartlett, an advocate of industrial education and vice-president of the National Association of Industrial Education. Its initial issues proposed a "Square Deal" for business and labor. This Square Deal (literally a four-sided diagram of modern industrial functionalism) sketched the balanced relationships of labor, capital, employer, and public. Writers for the *Mediator,* following the diagram, proposed that each point in the industrial quadrangle be represented and considered in industrial planning; that all the social divisions of labor created by modern industry have a hand in deciding questions of working conditions and wages.

The magazine also sponsored annual conventions held outside Cleveland at "Mediation Woods," and made a few tentative steps to organize a national Square Deal Club. Still, the magazine made little impact, though it managed occasionally to attract important writers such as Louis Brandeis, John R. Commons, and Samuel Gompers. After 1912 its editorial position stiffened, and it began to follow a pattern characteristic of other management plans for Industrial Democracy. From its first issues it had spoken of self-improvement plans for workers and admonished against laziness and idleness. After 1912 it began to repeat such advice more seriously, denouncing socialism and the dangers of nationalized industry at every opportunity. Simultaneously, the importance of the Square Deal diminished. The magazine became a pro-management, anti-radical journal. Nonetheless, in its heyday the *Meditator* had attempted to provide an answer to industrial dissension and alienation from a managerial point of view. It demonstrated the desire of some businessmen to achieve industrial peace by asserting an identity of interest among the functional parts of the modern corporation. It was one of several local movements which helped to lay the groundwork for the enormous, though short-term, interest of businessmen in Industrial Democracy at the end of the First World War. And it raised business Industrial Democracy above the mere mechanical adjustment of plant conditions to consider the larger issues of social development.[19]

A more sophisticated and widely hailed management plan for achieving a new industrial democracy was the efficiency movement. Scientific management, as explained by Frederick Taylor, was a short-cut to increased production and industrial peace, and a plan for harmonizing antagonistic interests in the factory through a better use of space, time, and work. Taylor's plan, in other words, would place a boundary of science between corporate owners and managers. The special terms of this separation would benefit the managers and prevent the inefficient exploitation of factory labor. Although it was most famous for its time-and-motion studies—an anti-labor tool disguised as scientific objectivity—the idea of scientific management often received the sanction of high reform circles who saw it, theoretically at least, as a benefit to the workers.

Louis Brandeis, who did much to popularize Taylor's theories, expressed the highest hopes of many Taylorites before the United States Commission on Industrial Relations. To Brandeis, Taylorism was simply the transfer of scientific and sociological methodologies from an abstract academic setting to the practical problems of factory management. As in science, methods of organization, classification, and experimentation could be applied to create rationalized work conditions: "It presents in respect to existing industrial discontent, the same sort of solution that the opening up of immense western lands presented to the problems of civilization fifty years ago. It was not any solution at all for the ultimate problem, but it gave a way out, and it seems to me that this is just what scientific management does here." Brandeis denied that scientific management sought to promote an industrial speed-up, as some unionists claimed. Instead, he argued, it was a way for the worker to assume a role in the management of business.[20]

Robert Hoxie, an economist and a special investigator for the Industrial Commission, disagreed with Brandeis about the possibilities of scientific management. But in his sarcastic portrayal of Taylorism he noted the ideas that intrigued Brandeis and a great many other intellectuals, including some prominent ex-socialists: "Mr. Taylor conceives of the industrial situation as one in which the relations between employers and workers are governed by a fundamental harmony of interests. This being assumed, perfect equality between them and complete democracy in all their relationships is to be sought in sweeping aside the personal authority of the employer and the arbitrary rules and regulations of the workmen with all the machinery for negotiations and enforcement of decisions created by both, and substituting in all matters the impersonal dictates of natural law and fact." Although some labor unions strongly opposed scientific management before World War I, a number of intellectuals, some quite pro-labor, were attracted to its abstract promises. Among these were socialists William James Ghent, Algie Simons, and Ordway Tead, and Walter Lippmann, John R. Commons, Herbert Croly, and Howard Scott, one of the founders of the Technocracy movement which briefly aroused the interest of intellectuals in the early 1930's.

The efficiency enthusiasm lasted only a few years, but it had a great influence upon intellectuals who were designing plans for social peace. Scientific management demonstrated the possibilities of scientifically reordering social relations inside the factory. It was a plan which aimed to reform management and to hasten the final split between old-style laissez-faire capitalism and Industrial Democracy.[21]

Before Taylorism became a popular movement, the possibilities of intrafactory cooperation had been suggested in one of the best-known practical applications of the principles of Industrial Democracy—the settlement of the New York cloak, suit, and skirt strike of 1910. The strike had been called over a wide range of issues, not merely a simple question of wages. As it progressed, it attracted the support of New York socialites and, ultimately, of a number of liberal businessmen such as Edward A. Filene of Boston. A solution to the complicated situation was negotiated after the appointment of several joint regulatory boards representing management, the unions, and the public. The result was an impressive, if temporary, demonstration of the fruits of cooperation. Workers, management, and the public (in this case represented by reformers Lillian Wald and Henry Moskowitz) could apparently reach agreement on work conditions and procedures in the manufacture of clothing, and institutionalize the proposals of groups like the Social Reform Club—proposals also advocated by such powerful bodies as the National Civic Federation.

Labor frequently saw in such round-table solutions a great victory for the unions. The New York experience was to be repeated in the regulatory bodies created by Woodrow Wilson during World War I, a move which some labor leaders would greet with even more enthusiasm. Yet not everyone was pleased about such arbitration plans. As Carl Mote wrote in his book *Industrial Arbitration,* there was little in the experience of industrialized nations to warrant great optimism about plans for industrial peace.[22]

Aside from these concrete experiences, a very different impetus for Industrial Democracy came from the proposals of radical and socialist organizations. The British, particularly, developed a variety of schemes for industrial reorganization, many of which centered on unionization and political laborism. One of the first discussions of Industrial Democracy was published in England in 1897 as a Fabian tract. This early examination of the structure and function of workingmen's organizations was the source of inspiration for the later Guild Socialist movement, which made much of the trade union as a prototype for future society. Although the Guild movement was not officially launched until 1912, there were earlier expressions of its major ideas in, for example, Arthur J. Penty's *The Restoration of the Guild System,* published in 1906. In the United States, too, the union organization was sometimes regarded as the basis for Industrial Democracy. As Charles Vail wrote in 1897 for the *Twentieth Century* magazine: "The unions furnish us the skeleton of the future commonwealth." Yet American intellectuals, by and large, did not elaborate this concept until much later, partly because unionism was distasteful to them, partly because other tasks such as socialism occupied an important body of reformers, and partly because the American Socialist party and the major American craft unions were hostile competitors rather than allies. The important discussion of Guild Socialism in America came after the demise of the Socialist party, when the union, not the party, seemed to offer the firmest base for reform.[23]

A more general antecedent of Industrial Democracy was the new industrial sociology from which the major assumptions of collectivism were derived and which had been developed over several decades of discussion. By the end of World War I many intellectuals felt an impending call for social reintegration and industrial reorganization in terms of functional definitions of social status and balance within the corporation. As Charles Beard wrote, the slogan of Industrial Democracy and the "collectivist drift in legislation and administration" were two of the most important postwar developments.

The war had created an organizational vacuum for collectivist intellectuals. The Socialist party began to splinter in 1914 because of the war issue and later fell apart over the matter of supporting the Communist Third International. As American Socialists became politically irrelevant, so their already tempered version of proletarian revolution became less attractive. Intellectuals who had once viewed the socialist movement as a weight to restore the balance in society now found themselves searching for a new set of reform methods. To such intellectuals, the labor movement seemed immensely attractive. Labor had always been a principal element in the reconstruction plans of collectivists, but now, without socialism and its revolutionary theories, the established unions looked increasingly like the best representatives of labor within the pluralistic structure of Industrial Democracy. Moreover, there were now concrete proofs of labor's potential. AFL representatives had been invited during the war to sit upon commissions that ruled over labor conditions, profits, and the distribution of raw materials. A version of Industrial Democracy had apparently become a weapon of war. Convinced of such arguments, ex-socialists John Spargo, William English Walling, and J. G. Phelps Stokes made the transition from socialism to Industrial Democracy.

The career of William James Ghent well illustrates the development of collectivist ideas from Fabianism to Industrial Democracy. In the 1890's Ghent was a Fabian socialist and worked hard to help waken the middle classes to their social responsibility. Committed to a broad and eclectic version of social reform, he pursued such efforts in the Collectivist Society and the Social Reform Club. By the second decade of the twentieth century, Ghent had become an important intellectual in the American Socialist party. His faith in reform now shifted to the proletariat and to workingmen's political and economic activities. But at the end of the World War, Ghent was vehemently opposed to the Bolshevik Revolution—and to the American Socialist party for its anti-war stand. He then became a devotee of the Taylorite efficiency movement. The early 1920's saw him move even further from socialism as he entered into a dispute with Harold Laski and Walter Lippmann over their idea that the state consisted of multiple sovereignties—that is, legitimately competing automonous groups. Ghent had drastically changed his perspectives. Through him and others like him, the Fabian impulse matured into Industrial Democracy. The purpose and the vision of social reform remained much the same; only the terms of the struggle were seriously altered. Thus Industrial Democracy contained all the ambiguities and cross-purposes of its diverse supporters.[24]

By the end of World War I, Industrial Democracy, in its various versions, embodied three of the most important assumptions of collectivism. First, it defined people in terms of economic roles, and specifically by their work within the factory—not in terms of their ideas or commitments. Thus human consciousness, when it mattered at all for social analysis, was primarily an economically determined factor. Politics was ancillary to questions of working conditions, income distribution, and even social alienation. Thus all social questions could be posed within the context of corporate economic institutions.

The second assumption was that each functional group in society—capital, management, labor, and consumer—ought to be allowed and encouraged to express its interests in an organized fashion, inside the web of an industrial pluralism. Cooperation between contending groups would then replace competition, because all elements of the economic model desired the harmony of industrial progress.

The third principle was that the corporation and its attendant centers of power signaled the creation of new kinds of social classes. They could be harmonized by a new science of society. Thus, for those intellectuals who supported it, Industrial Democracy was a general plan to reorganize the nation on the basis of scientific law, and therefore to begin the final evolution toward the good society.

Within this very general context of agreement, there were vast differences of opinion about how much power should be allotted each group in the new industrial pluralism. Many businessmen planned to use some weak form of Industrial Democracy to prevent independent unionism. This is clear, for example, in the profit-sharing movement so warmly supported by men like Harvard's President Charles Eliot. As he told one correspondent in 1914, the purpose of such programs was to escape "the deplorable effects of trade-union teachings. . . ." At the other extreme, Syndicalists and IWW "Wobblies" hoped to redress the power within industry completely in favor of the workingman. In the middle, where most plans for creating a new collectivist society were proposed, the issue was one of balance.

A closer examination of some of the programs for Industrial Democracy reveals the practical uses of collectivist assumptions. The end of World War I brought forth a flurry of plans for social reconstruction. From every political persuasion came tracts, books, and articles published on the new industrial system. The very rigor of the demands of war—now loosened—seemed to encourage a willingness to experiment. As the Progressive party-backer George Perkins wrote, the European war was "striking down individualism and building up collectivism."[25]

Among the more persuasive advocates of Industrial Democracy were such corporation leaders as John D. Rockefeller, Jr., and, behind him, a whole group of business writers. To Rockefeller and other important executives, the internal politics of industry demanded reorganization. If the movement for industrial cooperation failed, Rockefeller told a meeting of the

American Chamber of Commerce in 1918, industry might have to suffer more radical changes outside the control of management. The "Rockefeller Plan," as it became known, was little more than a superficial delegation of representative powers to the corporation's functional units. The management of a company would be shared—in certain minor ways—by representatives of capital, labor, and the community. Rockefeller's plan, which repeated some of the suggestions of the *Mediator,* also recalled the strike settlement of the New York Garment Workers and even the organization of the National War Labor Board set up by Woodrow Wilson as a war efficiency measure. No doubt Rockefeller's larger purpose was to ensure peace within his own business empire, prevent violent strikes, defeat independent unionism, and discourage the growth of radicalism among workers. But he found support for his program among the growing body of professional experts of industrial peace. Often their plans were even more abstract, or based upon simplistic gimmicks and public relations schemes.

Walter Gordon Merritt, for instance, in a pamphlet reprinted from *Iron Age* magazine, argued that the twin perils of absentee ownership and radical unionism could be avoided by reorganizing industry. "In industry," he wrote, "it is believed that this is largely avoidable through making each company itself a kind of industrial republic." Paul Litchfield's book *Industrial Republic* made much the same point, though it worked the "republic" analogy into a complete theory for industrial peace. Litchfield, a vice-president and factory manager of the Goodyear Tire and Rubber Company, proposed a series of checks and balances to govern industry. Each factory would resemble a federal republican system, with a house of representatives and a senate. But beneath this mock-syndicalist political apparatus, Litchfield clearly intended that management preserve its rule, and in the process impede the growth of independent unionism.[26]

Litchfield's plan was similar to proposals made by John Leitch in his book *Man to Man.* Leitch was a risen factory worker who had become an industrial relations and efficiency expert. His idea for industrial peace, he wrote, came from observing the practice of political democracy and adding a large measure of the Golden Rule. Most of his book was an account of modifications in factories that had instituted Industrial Democracy plans. But Leitch's own plan, carried out in a Brooklyn pipe factory where the workers represented a mixture of nationalities, was the most interesting. He reorganized the factory according to "a kind of constitution, a government on the same lines as that of the United States. We formed a Cabinet consisting of the executive officers of the company with the president of the company as president of the cabinet. The legislative bodies were a Senate made up of department heads and foremen, and a House of Representatives elected by the employees."

James Myer's *Representative Government in Industry*, published in 1924, summarized important business proposals for Industrial Democracy into a compendium of progress. After citing the enormous variety of plans already in effect in private industry and governmental agencies, Myer argued: "Industrial democracy if sincerely set forward by the owners of industry may result in avoiding a violent transition to the new industrial order." Significantly, Myer did not deplore the new industrial order, only a proletarian path to it. His proposals went beyond the simplicities of many other Industrial Democracy advocates. He included, for example, the findings of the new industrial psychologists Ordway Tead and Carlton Parker. He argued also that the worst aspects of old-style business had created rebellious psychological types: ". . . All of the socially objectionable features of labor union policy and action, and the sometimes unfortunate types of labor leaders, are directly attributable to the rebel mind which is one of the two possible mental reactions to the autocracy inherent in the master and servant industrial relation of capitalism."[27]

The common theme of all these books, and what united all advocates of a business-style Industrial Democracy, was the assumption that reorganizing the factory to give workers some formal control over production, or at least to give them the illusion of such control, would profoundly alter the terms of work and perhaps even increase production. F. V. Goodwin, the general secretary of the American Chamber of Commerce, explained to Edward Filene of Boston why he felt that business and labor must plan together. "Neither party has the decision," he argued, and thus each must appeal to the state for judgment. Given this standoff, the application of the scientific methods of industrial sociology and psychology might ease the transition to a new economy based upon politicized units of mass production.

Corporation presidents and business writers were not the only ones who proposed to tilt the balance of Industrial Democracy in favor of management. The work of A. B. Wolfe, who prepared an extensive report on Industrial Democracy for the wartime United States Shipping Board of the Emergency Fleet Corporation in 1919, explored the potential impact of worker self-adjustment through the creation of representative functional units within the factory. To Wolfe, the solution was a "square deal," and a "city manager" form of industrial government in which workers could gain a feeling of power in participating through committees. "Co-operative management," Wolfe wrote, "involving the ownership of industrial equipment and no abolition of the final responsibility of the present owners and managers of industry, but at the same time giving the worker a real voice in industrial government, may be regarded not only as an avenue to a square deal, but as an insurance against the spread of ideals and demands which would threaten both the present ownership of industry and the measure of productive efficiency and order which we have achieved under 'capitalistic' ownership." Although Wolfe denied that his plan was similar to proposals of the IWW, or even of the Soviets, he felt compelled to answer such a charge, thus leaving the impression that he had considered all forms of Industrial Democracy and then chosen the one that would work best. To him, the proposals of the Socialist party in 1918, of the AFL, of the United States Chamber of Commerce report of the Committee on Industrial Relations, and of other groups, were all variants of the same idea.[28]

Like other writers who were interested in Industrial Democracy, Wolfe thought one of the most impressive statements of industrial organization came from England. The Whitley Report, published there in 1917, was a widely read statement of the principles of Industrial Democracy. In this official document the British government suggested that industries reorganize themselves to provide workers with more self-government. Organized workers (trade unions) and organized management would then meet within the framework of a permanent and continuous committee system in each industry to regulate conditions of work and wages. The purpose, according to the report, was to return enthusiasm to the workers, apply their intelligence and creativity to production, and stop the acrimonious and destructive pattern of strikes and confrontations. The Whitley Report was often discussed and widely cited in articles and books in the United States during 1918 and 1919. The interest in British plans for industrial reorganization was so keen that one American author, Charles Fenwick, called England a testing ground for the theories of Industrial Democracy.

The American government made no formal commitment to Industrial Democracy as the British had done, but the proposal of the Plumb Plan in the United States provoked important discussion in the government and the press and made Industrial Democracy a political issue. The central notion in the plan created by Glenn Plumb, legal counsel for the railroad brotherhoods, was to nationalize the railroads, or, rather, to continue the operation of the industry which the government had assumed during World War I. In 1923, Plumb and William Royland wrote a book which called for the reconstruction of all industrial life on the premises of Industrial Democracy. Plumb was perhaps more interested in cooperation—in redefining the terms of ownership within the corporation—but he was also anxious to increase the efficiency of the entire industrial system and to experiment with the granting of managerial functions to workers. In the end, the authors wrote, this system could be initiated by instituting a new form of ownership. Workers would receive stocks and wages paid from the gross revenues of the corporation.[29]

In several ways the Plumb Plan resembled the English theory of Guild Socialism which was discussed by a number of American intellectuals in 1918 and 1919. This form of Industrial Democracy shifted power in the internal order of industry away from the managers and owners to the workers.

Guild Socialism had been built upon several movements. In part it was encouraged by the handicraft and feudal revival begun in England by John Ruskin and William Morris. It also drew from the theory and practice of the French Syndicalists and the American IWW who advocated worker-controlled industry, direct action, and the general strike. Guild Socialism took account too of anti-statist theories, such as that of Hilaire Belloc, and it was strongly opposed to the state socialism of the Fabian movement at the same time that it accepted the Fabian interest in union organization.

Like American Industrial Democracy, Guild Socialism defined social roles in terms of economic functions within the corporation. And, like most of collectivist thought, it argued the need to bypass politics so as to avoid overburdening the state with the regulation of economic and political life. As Savel Zimand, the American bibliographer of Guild Socialism and a member of the Bureau of Industrial Research, wrote: "The theory of national guilds is the unification of the syndicalist plan for the supremacy of the workers as producers, with the supremacy of the state as advocated by collectivists. The guildmen wish to make the state the organization of the workers as consumers, which shall own the means of production as trustees for the community." While many English Guildsmen opposed the bureaucratic version of state socialism which they detected in Fabianism and other socialist movements, their theories were not incompatible with the developing American sense of the collective society. Americans were also skeptical of the state as such. Thus the Guild movement was often accepted in America as another variation of the broad plan for Industrial Democracy.

American intellectuals did not seek to reproduce Guild provisions on American soil. Rather, they used them, and other such ideas, to increase the options of Industrial Democracy. Several writers recognized that Industrial Democracy and British Guild Socialism were parallel movements. Leland Olds, for example, saw the influence of Guild Socialism in the Plumb Plan. Others, such as Norman Hapgood, wrote of the connection between the theories of state socialism, radical syndicalism, and Guild Socialism. Ordway Tead, then a mem-

ber of the Inter-Collegiate Socialist Society, was particularly
enthusiastic about the Guild emphasis on what he considered
an important modern development: the new functional role
of the working class.[30]

Although the Guild Socialist movement was seriously discussed for only two or three years, a number of collectivist
intellectuals were impressed with its merits. Three ideas in
particular made the Guild movement relevant to Americans.
The first was the description of a functional democracy based
upon new industrial roles. Guild Socialism, like collectivism,
assumed that group sociology could be used to create a balanced industrial democracy. Industrial specialization in the
corporation, the Guild Socialists argued, had depreciated the
value of old political forms. The highly differentiated problems of managing a corporation could not be regulated by
geographically representative parliaments. In fact, parliamen-
tary politics could be irresponsible and dangerous because they
did not comprehend the fundamental activities of modern society. Democracy would have to advance beyond the advocacy
of certain negative individual rights to include broader economic rights. The Guild Socialists argued that the old rules of
private property or the rights of ownership were archaic in a
society of corporations where managers ran industries and
ownership was limited to the accumulation of dividends.

A second appeal of Guild Socialism was its anti-statism. It
wished, for a start, to reduce the power of the state, to eliminate its abstract justifications, and to substitute for politics the
limited and necessary prerogatives of guidance and administration. Collectivist intellectuals in the United States had long
proposed to modify the functions of direct political rule in this
way and to substitute administration for policy, replacing politicians with experts and commissioners. Behind this proposal
lay the idea that the state could be transformed from the political arm of a class, or the representative of a complex system
of practices, traditions, and ideas, into a democratic meeting
place and a center for the adjudication of outstanding social
questions. Some critics were quick to see that this administrative state would probably mean more government than less,
and one in which political citizenship would be traded for a

kind of functional belonging. The administrative revolution was as often as not proposed as a substitute for solving genuine political problems.[31]

A third important premise of the Guild Socialists was their belief that the trade union was the most effective force for reform, a guild society in miniature. This same potential intrigued American intellectuals. After the demise of American socialism, the unions loomed more important. This represented a distinct ideological evolution from the early years of the 1890's, when municipal socialists and American Fabians had seemed to favor the existence of trade unions but had done so only to emphasize the necessary voting alliance between the middle and upper classes and the workers. Their programs had been as much aimed at the lethargic middle classes as at working-class organizations.

The general position of the American Socialist party toward unions had been at best ambiguous, though Socialist leaders were unfailingly critical of the American Federation of Labor. But after 1914 a good many ex-socialist intellectuals as well as a number of more moderate thinkers began to consider trade unionism on a different basis. Industrial Democracy and Guild Socialism were programmatic incentives to this new view, for both described the labor union as the organized workers' component in the new industrial pluralism. Thus many reformers and even socialists came close to accepting the basic terms of the argument stated by the more astute conservative exponents of Industrial Democracy, whose purpose was either to disarm or limit independent unionism. These reformers did not dispute ownership, except to argue that the managerial function was now more important, and they did little to prove the truth of this key contention. Nor did they oppose the form of industrial organization that had emerged under private capitalism. Instead, they joined the argument over the question of the distribution of power among owners, managers, workers, and consumers.[32]

Two important theologians, Father John Ryan and Harry F. Ward, demonstrated how Industrial Democracy could also absorb the general notions of Christian Socialism. These two Christian thinkers continued the tendency of optimistic religious reformism to give theological expression to theories which already were largely secularized versions of religious views. They wrote, as Reinhold Niebuhr would do after them, extended dialogues between older and newer versions of Christian Socialism. The works of Ryan and Ward linked Christian Socialism to such secular institutions as unionism. And they refreshed the religious sanction for reform expressed earlier by such men as Washington Gladden.

Father Ryan developed his theory of Industrial Democracy over a period of three years, principally in three books. The first of these, *Distributive Justice,* was published in 1916. In it he proposed a "canon of Human Welfare" which would drastically alter the distribution of social rewards according to need, effort, productivity, and general human welfare. His next book, *Social Reconstruction,* was a discussion of postwar reconstruction plans. At the close of World War I, Ryan, like many other writers, was fascinated by Guild Socialism and similar proposals which promised more democracy in America. His own suggestions for the just society emphasized the role of the labor union. He proposed a mixed economy of co-operative ownership and limited management of factories by workers. A later work, *Industrial Democracy from a Catholic Viewpoint,* updated and extended his earlier views, and mingled the principles of Guild Socialism with his own notion of Industrial Democracy. Ryan's first aim was to end industrial violence and dispute. Collective bargaining, he argued, could never establish permanent industrial peace. Instead, some overall reorganization (such as the Plumb Plan) ought to turn control of industries over to the shared management of workers, owners, and the public. Such a program, Ryan argued, would be entirely compatible with historic Catholic doctrine. The new society would most resemble the medieval guild system, under which the Church had flourished. "The industrial democracy of the Guild system cannot be restored in this day of greater machinery and greater corporations," Ryan wrote. "But the spirit of that earlier and saner period can be made to function again in the modern system."

Harry F. Ward, a theologian at Union Seminary in New York City, also saw a new order which he thought would update the social principles of Christianity. His book, *A New Social Order,* published in 1919, was a demonstration of the compatibility of Christian Socialism and the secular proposals of collectivism. Ward first outlined what he felt was an existing post-revolutionary society which still possessed antiquated institutions. It had passed through drastic economic change without needed social and political adjustments. Class struggle was the unmistakable signpost of this lag, and symbolized the need for society to change the nature of its political and economic relationships. Destructive struggle ought to be replaced with the social harmony of Industrial Democracy. The distinct units of economic society should therefore be encouraged to organize themselves and then meet to compromise under the disinterested guidance of the state. The legitimate function of government, Ward asserted, was to represent as well as to oversee economic and social groups and to provide a meeting ground for true industrial cooperation. Although Ward proposed a form of Industrial Democracy for the United States that was not especially radical or new, he did suggest that the Soviet experiment might test the principles of Industrial Democracy. Ward was not here proposing a revolution for American society. He conceived Industrial Democracy (as the Guild Socialists did) as a plan to redress the balance of power in society in favor of the working classes. "The hope of the future," he wrote in justification, "lies in the great undeveloped capacities at the bottom of human society."

Aside from influential theologians such as Ward and Ryan, other elements in the organized churches of the United States welcomed Industrial Democracy. A long report written for the American Episcopal Church in 1919 reviewed the enormous variety of reconstruction plans proposed after World War I. The writers were critical of some versions of Industrial Democracy, especially those which they felt were masks for management power over the workers. They agreed with Ryan and Ward, the English Guild Socialists, and American cooperators that Industrial Democracy ought to favor the workingman.[33]

Another link between the ideas of Industrial Democracy and Christian reformism was the consumers' movement—the organized version of the final side of the industrial square.

Consumerism assumed that the public was as involved in the ownership of industry and in related economic questions as the owner, manager, or worker. As John Graham Brooks, the first president of the National Consumers League, had written: "This is the economic truth. To buy a sweated garment is to have someone work for you under sweated conditions as definitely as if she were in your own employ." This sense of responsibility—especially among women—for industrial conditions lay behind much of the League's appeal to abolish child labor and sweatshop conditions. But the appeal broadened after World War I. As Florence Kelley, one of the guiding spirits of the organization, wrote: "In the past half year the individual consumer has suddenly occupied the centre of the industrial stage. But the most urgent appeal addressed to her is no longer that she take thought for her indirect employees. . . . The issues of tomorrow are collective issues."

Thus moral responsibility had a practical side. The consumer, as a member of an organized group in society, could exert pressure upon the economic and social system because invariably he or she touched the industrial process at some point. It was precisely to this constituency that Ryan, Ward, and many of the Industrial Democrats proposed their plans. If organized, consumers could take their place alongside unions and management. As the manager of industrial relations for the United States Housing Corporation suggested in 1920, society needed an "American Federation of Consumers" to match the organized powers within the corporation.

Curiously, one of the organizations to which all these theories attached the most potential was at first hesitant if not hostile to Industrial Democracy. The AFL under Samuel Gompers had written its own plan for industrial reconstruction after World War I, but it did not suggest Industrial Democracy. Instead, it reasserted labor's rights to collective bargaining. Collectivists reassured themselves that the mechanics of collective bargaining contained all the earmarks of Industrial Democracy. And by 1920, Matthew Woll, a vice-president of the union, had proposed a plan which sounded much like earlier formulations of Industrial Democracy, or at least like a continuation of wartime administrative boards. Whatever

Gompers' public position on Industrial Democracy, he had been a member of the National Civic Federation for several years and had participated in informal discussions which amounted to one variety of Industrial Democracy—that organized from the top down. Furthermore, Gompers had taken advantage of an alliance with ex-Socialist party intellectuals, including Walling, Spargo, Ghent, and Phelps Stokes, to agitate for support of Wilson's entry into the war. For their part, these socialists proposed their own version of Industrial Democracy and, indeed, attempted to organize a new political party around these theories which would advance the goals of the labor movement.[34]

This short-lived political tendency, which was an unofficial ally of the AFL, was called the Social Democratic League and was led by Spargo, Phelps Stokes, and others. Its history is extremely complicated, for its existence depended upon its usefulness to the Wilson administration and the government's efforts to prosecute the war and win the peace. Nonetheless, the organization was also important because it helped to solidify the interests of radicals and ex-radical intellectuals in the general tenets of Industrial Democracy. The program proposed by the League was explicitly called Industrial Democracy—by which the founders meant something like British Guild Socialism. As William English Walling wrote, "The Social Democratic League of America believes that complete 'industrial harmony' can be achieved only through industrial democracy, with the great industries managed and controlled by the associated producers in the interest of all who are usefully employed. . . ." Spargo admitted that his conception of the League was an American version of the Fabian society, and there was more than occasional evidence in public statements that some League members were directly influenced by Guild Socialism. One draft of the first manifesto of the League, for example, contained the following passage, which was later excised: "We therefore intend the abolition of the United States Senate, and propose that Congress shall consist of two equal Houses—the House of Representatives, elected by the people at large to represent them as consumers,—each state choosing its own representatives, and the House of

Labor, elected by the people as workers,—each industry choosing its own representatives."[35]

Yet the Social Democratic League proved to be poor competition for even a weakened Socialist party. The League failed to create any ongoing political movement, though it briefly tried to do so in 1918 when it organized the National party. Its members ultimately scattered to take up other reform business. The organization nevertheless demonstrated the ease with which many socialist intellectuals could jump from socialism to Industrial Democracy. And under the rubric of Industrial Democracy these men could support Gompers as the spokesman for American labor and hence the most important representatives in the politics of reconstructing American industry.

For a short time in the early twenties, some form of Industrial Democracy seemed destined to triumph. The most striking prediction of this victory, which saw Industrial Democracy as a by-product, almost a casual effect, of the growth of labor unions, was Frank Tannenbaum's *The Labor Movement,* published in 1921. Tannenbaum took the sense of inevitability that surrounded such collectivist schemes as Industrial Democracy and stretched it to a final extreme. He concluded that the organization of the working class into unions would automatically destroy capitalism. "The analysis of the work and method of organized labor in the following chapters," he announced at the beginning of his book, "seems to predicate the displacement of the capitalist system by industrial democracy—an achievement which is implicit in the growth and development of the organized labor movement." Tannenbaum's faith in the radicalism of functional organization rested upon the premise that capitalism could not tolerate pluralism, and that the organization of unions would destroy the status quo: "functional representation is likely to become the pivotal force of governmental structure." Thus Industrial Democracy, even in its incomplete guise in such institutions as the Railroad Labor Board, was the advance guard of true industrial government. A new feeling for society was emerging: "A kind of functional citizenship, a kind of industrial patriotism, a kind of pride and interest, a sense of power and with it a sense of responsibility has made its appearance."[36] What a short distance from this statement to the belief that organization itself was revolutionary—that centralism, institutionalism, and government in the largest sense made up the good society!

Ironically, just as Tannenbaum was expounding on the revolutionary nature of pluralism and its potential to burst the rigid unity of the authoritarian state, Harold J. Laski was developing much the opposite theory. For Laski, the state was ultimately less important than the individual. Its nature depended upon those powers and mixed allegiances that it shared with other groups such as trade unions. Individualism, on the other hand, Laski wrote, "implies, from the very nature of things, insistence that the allegiance of man to the state is secondary to his allegiance to what he may conceive his duty to society as a whole." Laski's belief in pluralism was quite flexible and nonrevolutionary as compared with Tannenbaum's simplistic model. And Laski proposed to use this pluralism not to make a revolution but to incorporate diverse allegiances into loyalty to a larger society of countervailing groups.[37]

Whatever their origins and purposes, each of the proposals for Industrial Democracy rested upon shared assumptions about modern society. These assumptions were, in effect, the major ideas of collectivist intellectuals translated into a practical program for social peace. Just as in the first decade of the twentieth century socialism had seemed the best way to propose the collective possibilities of the new industrial society, so Industrial Democracy later became the focus of discussion. The one difference was that the discussion was now openly joined by conservatives and businessmen. To be sure, there had been conservative and even traditionalist socialists; but Industrial Democracy represented a much broader discussion of the practical application of collectivist assumptions.

In the short run, the implications of those plans advanced under the title of Industrial Democracy seemed conservative or radical according to the bias of the writer. But from a longer perspective the drift of these ideas is distinctly conservative. From the 1890's to the end of the First World War, intellectuals had searched for a platform for their developing views, and for organizations that could wrench concessions from industrial development. At the same time a few business leaders—and perhaps more business writers—became interested in the practical application of a similar social and economic analysis, but from their own angle of vision. After the war, the experience of almost three decades of change had been largely educational. Intellectuals always stood upon the shoulders of their reform organizations. They used their own understanding of the industrial system to achieve for themselves a creative role as arbitrators, planners, and interpreters. From their elite self-description as Fabians, many turned to a more tentative role as champions of labor unions. This had little to do with a waning self-confidence, but rather resulted from the growth of organized factions within the corporation that were scarcely visible or predictable earlier. From the cramped but well-appointed quarters of the urban reform club, with its local reforms and narrow vision, to the broad hypotheses of Industrial Democracy, was, ironically, a journey toward a theory of economic determinism.

Once intellectuals had abandoned the Socialist party, dropping plans for the single tax and other such reforms, once they accepted the idea of balancing economic units for Industrial Democracy, many thought that they understood and could harness the forces of industrial society. Collectivist assumptions, it was thought, suddenly became real and practical. But in truth the speculative thought of collectivism had never been unreal or detached; it was often a theoretical mock-up of reality. Ultimately the implicit economic determinism of the theory led collectivists to back down before the forces of history. It was no longer important to change men's minds, only to get the proper representation on an administrative committee. In the long run such a stance was conservative. Industrial Democracy proved to be a gathering of diverse forces around plans for industrial reorganization, where, for once it seemed, everyone agreed on general principles. Thus another phase of collectivist thought was widely propagated in a crucial debate over the strategies for achieving the good society. One or another version of this pluralism occupied collectivists after 1920.

*   *   *

The general theory of collectivism drew its outlines from existing American institutions, especially the new corporations. Mindful of these institutions, intellectuals conceived a new society well adjusted to specialization, complexity, and a mass nature. They half hoped, half expected that such a self-regulating industrial democracy would emerge from the breakneck evolution of American society. Shepherding this drive to social maturity would be the intellectuals themselves, the interpreters of a great future harmony.

To describe collectivist intellectuals in this manner and link their ideas to economic institutions immediately raises the question of motivation. While many of them interpreted the social attitudes of their day with a theory that was iron-clad in its determinism, it will not do to turn such a theory around upon them. Collectivist assumptions were too rich in their variety to admit such an explanation. Thus the lives of individuals reveal the working out of different projects from a shared core of assumptions. Inevitably, men stand between institutions and ideas; in this instance they best illustrate the range and flexibility of the reform spirit. Their relationships to American institutions, spelled out in their attitudes toward hierarchies, their fellow men, human motivation, and, above all, the instruments of reform, often reveal an intense self-projection and a struggle to achieve self-fulfillment through social change. As often as not, the meaning of a reform idea was the story of the person who proposed it and his own adjustment to the leading institutions of his day. Thus the idealized industrial state represented the abstract peace that reformers made with their enormously changing and uncertain world.

The following chapters describe six intellectuals who expressed the central ideas of collectivism, but who gave these ideas very different concrete forms and called for distinct re-

123

form procedures. Each found a different institutional basis for reform agitation, and each expressed a different mixture of collectivist ideas—socialism, managerialism, Industrial Democracy, corporatism, or pluralism. Each, however, managed to remain well within the context of attitudes toward American industrial society that have so far been explained. Each proved the enormous flexibility of collectivist ideas while preserving an essential compatibility with that larger body of assumptions about the mass structure of the new society.

*   *   *

5

Edmond Kelly and the Socialism of Order

AMERICAN INTELLECTUALS of the late nineteenth century needed a system of metaphors and a syntax to describe their feelings about the newness of the industrial civilization emerging around them. Darwinism, with its derivative images of process, progress, and change, finally proved too malleable and contradictory, even too popular, to fill this need. Language often divided political thinkers who might otherwise have been united if they had had common symbols to communicate their shared reform experience. But no one thinker appeared to provide them with such symbols, despite the efforts of such men as Henry Adams to prepare the way, and so intellectuals stuttered over the complicated "isms" of single-taxism, progressivism, socialism, and countless other solutions.

In the lives of many reformers, these various concepts rarely proved to be of overriding importance; nor, in many instances, were they even sure signs of belief. Often they were simply footholds on the devious climb toward political understanding. Socialism, like its ambiguous relatives progressivism and Industrial Democracy, was both a movement and a network of metaphors. Intellectually, socialism could refer to the broadest set of collectivist abstractions or to specific revolutionary tasks: it functioned both as an abstract intellectual system and as an embodiment of individual longings. The socialist intellectuals of New York City, whose constituency was composed of municipal clubs, liberal businessmen, and the variegated urban reform movement, tended to speak principally to themselves about the condition of other people—the poor, the working classes, tramps, prostitutes, and deprived children. Yet these segments of society also comprised their constituency, though at a considerable remove. The socialist philosophy of reform encompassed radically different priorities; the way in which reformers saw the evil and ignorance around them was often a function of their own intellectual concerns.

Although Marx, Kautsky, Bernstein, Hillquit, Debs, and other socialists had set out to create a revolutionary working-class movement of one sort or another, they had also succeeded in attracting a very different-minded sort of person to the socialist idea. In America, middle- and upper-class intellectuals helped to give American socialism a very special character, much as the Fabians in England had done. Principally, these men turned to socialism because they thought it represented an amalgam of the most progressive trends in modern political thought; to many it expressed their own vaguely examined collectivist assumptions. So it was with Edmond Kelly, an elegant if somewhat austere international lawyer who joined the Socialist Party of America in 1907. Joining the Socialists represented Kelly's final effort to push society toward the reform that occupied much of his fascinating life.

There is nothing in Edmond Kelly's background to suggest his late choice of socialism. He was born on May 28, 1851, in Blagnac, near Toulouse, while his parents were touring France. His father, Robert E. Kelly, was an Irish immigrant who came to the United States in 1830 and had worked his way to ownership of a successful cigar manufacturing company. For the first few years of Edmond's life, the family remained in Europe. Then, after living five years in the United States during the Civil War, the family returned to live permanently in Europe, where Robert Kelly died in 1891. Edmond's two sisters married into the French aristocratic D'Humiere family, and his brother Horace assumed management of the tobacco business in the United States.

Although most of his youth was spent in Europe, Edmond

had a transatlantic education. After several years with a private tutor, he attended Kings School in Dorsetshire, England. In 1868 he entered Columbia University as a junior, and was graduated in 1870. He then returned to England and to Cambridge University, where he took a degree in science in 1875. Finally, he returned once more to Columbia to finish a law degree in 1877. For two years he practiced law in New York with the Coudert Brothers, leaving in 1879 to join a branch of the firm in Paris. There he remained until 1884, when he set up an independent practice. In that same year he married Frances Bacon Bartow. After her death in 1891, Kelly returned to the United States to teach municipal government and legal history at Columbia. Around this time he began to publish three successive books which attacked the principles of Social Darwinism, and, with his friend Richard Welling, he founded the City Club of New York. In 1898 he was elected president of the Social Reform Club. At Columbia, he also found time to coach the crew team. Always active physically, he was an expert fencer, an avid mountain climber, and a hunter.

In 1899, Kelly tired out from what seemed a futile struggle against municipal corruption in New York, returned to Europe to become Counsel for the American Embassy in Paris and to resume his law practice. As chief counsel for George Westinghouse in Europe and a representative for other large American corporations, including the European Vanderbilt interests and the Equitable Life Assurance Society, he soon became a well-known expert on international law. When told by his doctors that he had only a short time to live, Kelly returned to the United States in 1906, at which time he joined the Socialist party and worked on his lengthy book, *Twentieth Century Socialism,* which he completed only a few weeks before his death in 1909. During this last short period of his life, Kelly remarried, published a utopian novel under the pseudonym of Ellison Harding, and worked for a number of Socialist projects, including the New York *Call* and Upton Sinclair's Helicon Home Community, a communal living project in Englewood, New Jersey. This extraordinary career led Kelly from the fringes of the wealthy and cultured expatriate community in Paris during the 1880's to the radical political world of New York City, where he was honored upon his death by a special meeting in the Bowery attended by his Socialist friends and by Ben Radman, "King of the Hoboes."[1]

A highly educated man who belonged to a class familiar with political power, Edmond Kelly took his social position and responsibilities very seriously. His interest in a philosophic analysis of social problems was undoubtedly partly stimulated by his father, with whom he exchanged letters discussing the political ideas of Herbert Spencer and the rules of poetry. Edmond wrote occasional poems to his wife Fanny, as well as aphorisms expressing his ideas on politics, morality, and poetic order. Like other young gentlemen of his class, he was a clubman; he joined the Stanley Club during his early days in Paris, and in later years belonged to similar clubs in New York. His first serious published writing, a short work in 1885 on the "Proposed French Corporation Law and Its Effects on American Life Insurance Companies in France," offered merely the rather judicious insight that the particular law in question would discriminate against American insurance companies.

In Kelly's later, more serious writings, the evidence of his father's influence was stronger. The elder Kelly had retired from business at an early age and had devoted much of his remaining time to philosophy. As Robert D'Humiere, his son-in-law, wrote of him, Robert E. Kelly "enumerated a sublime philosophy of sanctification—a somewhat new form of self-sacrifice, exercizing upon his children in their upbringing a most refined and mystical influence." At the center of the elder Kelly's philosophy was a mystical faith in the human will which he elaborated in a text, *The Alternative,* published in 1882 under the pseudonym of E. R. Clay. Essentially, the book recounted the elder Kelly's version of philosophic definitions—overly precise at many points—but indicative of a desire for ethical certainty. His writings also had strong undercurrents of a deep malaise and a tendency toward self-sacrifice and renunciation. Kelly invented a psychology which in some ways anticipated William James's discussion of the subconscious. Doing away with all fixed or innate ideas, he nonetheless argued that man's life was almost entirely determined by forces which played upon his unconscious mind. Freedom could come only in denying these forces and making the overwhelming effort to act in a moral manner. One must, therefore, recognize the subconscious determinism of the human psyche yet rise above it. Kelly wrote: "My intention in laying bare the objectives and wretchedness of our condition coincides with that of the Gospel without its supernaturalism and mysticism. It is to stir an insurrection against the Infernal in Nature, for the subversion of the reign of Instinct and the substitution of that of Wisdom and Will."[2] Much the same uneasiness with the world existed in young Edmond, as did a desire for psychological order and control over life's loose ends and desultory passions. But Edmond turned these tendencies to politics instead of psychology, and argued that society, not nature or man's mind, inhibited his freedom. He erected a theory of a good society based upon social and political renunciation, rather than willful dominance over the subconscious.

In 1885, Edmond Kelly published a second book on French law which demonstrated a very different kind of interest in legal matters. Indeed, it represented the first statement of a theme which was to interest him for the next twenty years. In this short tract, *The French Law of Marriage,* Kelly compared the Anglo-Saxon and French concepts of marriage. Addressing the American and English audience for whom the book was intended, he argued for an understanding of the more rigid Roman law, and even for some sympathy for the concept of *patria potestas,* which granted legal power to the head of a family to enforce his will upon wife and child. The attraction of French marital codes was not, he felt, their rigidity but their undying commitment to preserve the family structure. Kelly wrote: "If the Roman theory of *patria potestas,* tempered by modern civilization, is to be admitted in our age, and if the conservation of the family as the basis of social stability be deemed of primary importance,—if, indeed, that importance be considered so great as to overshadow the benefits to be derived from the early development of a sentiment of individual responsibility which appears above all precious to the Anglo-Saxon, then the provisions of the French law . . . appear a necessary part of a wise dispensation."[3] Two assumptions commingled here. One was that society could be best preserved by a strong family system; the other was that Anglo-Saxon freedoms and individual liberty could disrupt such higher social values as social stability.

While building a successful legal career in Paris in the 1880's, Kelly was apparently also thinking of returning to the United States for a career in politics. In 1888, for example, he wrote to a friend: "My political plans in America are taking shape. You'll find the field too encumbered here. True self government is possible only on a virgin soil—at least for a century or more—America's the place for it today!" In the same period, certain autobiographical remarks in his various writings indicate a growing feeling that he was destined to make a political mark. In 1889, for example, he began to keep a political journal during travels in Italy and France. Several entries offer tentative answers to questions about the nature of political power and political corruption in modern society—concerns that impelled him toward his political career.

In an odd entry in 1889, there is an inkling of the seriousness with which Kelly had already begun to take himself as a political writer, when he compares himself to Thomas Carlyle. As he recalled, his wife Fanny wished to interrupt him during a work period one morning, but he insisted that she wait. "This suggested to her," he recalled, "the injustice of the publication of Jane Carlyle's journal. She felt that had she kept a journal she might have often set down incidents by way of complaint, that subsequent events had entirely explained or cast into the shade—a busy overworked man must necessarily sometimes disappoint a loving wife, but his companionship when it can be freely given more than makes up for it afterwards. So was it clearly with the Carlyles."[4]

In this same journal there are several passages comparing American and European political institutions. Not only were institutions such as marriage important to consider, but Kelly found that the political corruption he deplored in America was very much a part of British and French government as well. Only a political theory that offered a strong system of political unity could overcome these excesses of self-interest, which he argued were the basis of political evil. Only unity, coherence, and power, if properly enhanced, might shake off the corruption of greed and compromise.

The attempt of the French to rewrite their constitution in the late nineteenth century provided Kelly with the occasion to speculate, in his notebook, about the meaning of government itself. In doing so, he turned to the model he knew best and admired most, the Federalist Papers, particularly those attributed to Alexander Hamilton which expressed the need for a strong central government.

The first principle of good government, Kelly concluded, was that it be separated from politics, for government was concerned with rule, order, and justice, and politics only with self-interest and corruption. The object of reform, therefore, would be to make this drastic separation between government and politics wherever possible. Kelly noted: "Inasmuch as the budget is today the stone of contention on which ministries split—why not take it out of the domain of politics except in so far as economies and extraordinary expenses are concerned?" In his view, a committee of experts could deliberate over necessary expenses and allocate a budget, with politics never bearing upon these decisions except in rare cases.

Another way to purge corruption from government would be to strengthen and more precisely define the role of the executive and the Supreme Court, and to lift both beyond the passions of greed and political influence. Government, Kelly concluded, should be clear in the separation of its functions, but universally committed to the broader interests of society. The greatest evil occurred when this prescription was reversed, when government was captured by special interests and the rights of the citizenry consequently destroyed. The French political system was crippled, Kelly commented by way of example, because of the weakness and vulnerability of the French premier, and because the rigidity of the all-too-logical French mind drove Frenchmen to propose extreme political solutions. The English—more sensibly, if less efficiently—had created a powerless royal family who suffered the follies of pomp and wore the "purple of ridicule" without possessing the ability to rule.[5] But in Kelly's view neither the French nor English systems had solved the problem of corruption.

At this point in his life, Kelly was not particularly interested in popular democracy. His disapproval of government by referendum suggests his position: "People can vote on men not on measures," he wrote. The lower classes should not be absent from politics, he felt, but they were presently so deeply enmeshed in urban political machines that their good intentions were invariably distorted. Kelly had, early on, developed an extraordinary animus to the urban political machine because of what he felt to be its moral corruption. Many of the aphorisms that he jotted down amidst his political notes reveal an interest in corruption of nearly obsessional dimensions. "Corruption," he remarks in one entry, "makes an atmosphere; we cannot breathe it in one place without exhaling it in another—we cannot become familiar with it in the papers without expecting to encounter it in our lives; we cannot laugh at it in the theatres without domesticating it in our hearts."

Still, Kelly believed that urban political machines did more than corrode democracy. He thought of them as a deeply entrenched enemy more powerful than any tyranny anticipated by James Madison in the Constitution. The urban machine was a class, or faction, Kelly thought; it was so skillful that it could neutralize the best intentions of the Founding Fathers. No matter what institutional obstacles or constitutional checks were placed in its way, the political machine was capable of seizing each wing of government: "It clearly shows that it is quite useless carefully to separate the powers if those powers are all held by the same class." Corruption was the ideology of the new class that controlled political machines—a class worse even than the Venetian oligarchs, who, according to Kelly, were at least divided by petty jealousies. Machine politicians were unified by ambition. The urban machine was "composed of shrewd men who know how to surrender personal claims for the benefit of the organization which is their common purveyor; it is far more likely to survive and prosper." Corruption thus brought a superficial order and even good administration; but all the while, Kelly warned, "the moral sense is rotting at the core."

As Kelly viewed it, the problem was neither a lack of democracy nor the wrong form of government, but an immoral social system. How, then, could one rearrange the political order to make it conducive to good government? "A truly representative body," Kelly answered, "is one that reflects the common sense of the mass." Good government meant the translation of the moral virtue of the people as a whole into political action. Anything which divided citizens from each other into classes or obscure ideological allegiances worked against the ability of government to express this ideal. Kelly never lost sight of this admixture of moral and political principles, even though he was to experience a series of bitter disappointments in his reform projects.

In late 1891, shortly after returning to the United States, Kelly wrote in his notebook: "We have a deep and wide river to cross; some of us, conscious how deep and how wide it is, stand shivering on its brink; others, unconscious of its dangers, plunge headlong in, but unprepared for the struggle in store, as soon as they strike the strong and terrible current turn back either to escape altogether from its embrace or to dissipate energy in a thousand futile efforts." What reformers needed was a vessel: "Let us build a boat; and let us not attempt to cross till the boat is built."[6]

The vessel Kelly chose to negotiate the turbulent politics of corruption was the urban reform club. After the death of his wife Fanny, he returned to the United States to begin a new life as a civic reform leader and a lecturer at Columbia University. His close friend Richard Welling recalled Kelly's mood when he returned to America: "impatient at the resigned attitude of his old Columbia classmates in the face of Tammany misgovernment. . . ." Kelly joined the old and rather lethargic City Reform Club which had been started by Theodore Roosevelt. Almost immediately he suggested a reorganization, then persuaded a number of reluctant businessmen and old acquaintances to join the new City Club.

Soon after, Kelly began organizing a city-wide political structure to compete with Tammany Hall. The result was the Good Government Movement, a series of clubhouses designed to attract working-class votes for honest political candidates, and to entice the "better" citizens of New York to regain their political nerve. During the winter of 1892, Kelly persuaded several representatives of labor organizations to call at his house in Manhattan, and urged them to join his campaign. None, however, was ready to do so. Kelly was noticeably sensitive to this early indifference to his plans on the part of the working class as well of the city's wealthier men. The new City Club, he wrote, "in spite of the brilliant gathering of millionaires at the opening meeting of the club," could not extend its influence unless it were willing to move out of its comfortable clubhouse on Fifth Avenue. Kelly's advice was only half-heartedly accepted by the City Club, and his Good Government Movement always existed in an uncomfortable relationship to the club's trustees. Perhaps this early reluctance derived from the spirit of the City Club's predecessor, the City Reform Club, which had spent much of its time investigating whether taverns were properly closed on Election Day in New York City. Or perhaps, as Kelly implied, the repeated failures of most urban reform projects had cooled the ardor of wealthy New Yorkers to enter politics at all.

Yet Kelly's "Goo-Goo" movement, as it came to be called, temporarily overcame some of these early difficulties, and before long its influence was felt throughout the city. By 1894, it actively supported William Strong for mayor, and it worked during the campaign with such organizations as the Reverend C. H. Parkhurst's Committee of 70. After Strong's successful election, Kelly concluded: "What the Good Government Clubs contributed to the campaign was, in the first place, to bring into the field of politics a membership of over seven thousand men, mostly young, who had never been in politics before, and who entered it for no purpose save that of destroying a corrupt partisan ring. In the second place, these young men were brought together in the closest of all organizations—the social club." In the Good Government Movement, Kelly had created the outlines of an ecumenical reform organization which drew such figures as Washington Gladden to its ranks and which stirred support from the New York settlement houses. Kelly's purpose had also been to confront upper-class apathy: "We have two tasks" a friend recalled to him after the election of Strong, "first to *fight* the bad, intelligent men . . . and second, to educate the stupid ignorant ones."[7]

But even after helping to elect Strong, Kelly was disappointed, for almost immediately after the election the Good Government Clubs fell into conflict over political allegiances and bickered about candidates. From personal preference, heritage, and because of Tammany's hold upon the Democratic party, most members favored Republicans. But Kelly thought the Republicans were often no better than the Democrats. He wanted the Good Government Movement to cultivate its own, independent candidates. Such action would be an important step in detaching local politics from national political fights. Yet this view was obviously unpopular in an organization whose members were often conservative by temperament and loyal Republicans by family tradition. Often political discussions in the club, even when dealing with practical issues, degenerated into squabbles over first principles. In retrospect, Kelly recalled that the constant intrusion of the doctrines of Herbert Spencer was "paralyzing." Social Darwinian arguments, he noted, prevailed among club members and generally served to dampen any genuine consideration of reform.

Kelly's solution was to resign from the clubs and try a somewhat different approach through a different kind of club. The Good Government Movement fell into the hands of his friend Richard Welling, who continued to work with them until he, too, grew discouraged. By the turn of the century, Welling sought other sources of reform, finally concluding that only an early, firm education in civic responsibilities might turn children away from the corrupt ways of past urban politics. To accomplish this he founded the National Self-Government Clubs, which urged the practical teaching of civics and responsible government in the public schools.[8]

Beyond teaching his course at Columbia in municipal government and constitutional history, Kelly continued to work for urban reform, but now as a member of the new Social Reform Club. Begun as a discussion club, the Social Reform Club was formally organized in 1896 to take an active hand in urban reform projects. Unlike the City Club, the Social Reform began on a more friendly footing with New York's trade unions. But there was still much to learn. Kelly recalled that the members of the Social Reform Club were also strongly influenced by Spencer's ideas as well as by economic individualism, just as his acquaintances in the City Club had been. "Under the stimulus of this bias, the Social Reform Club was organized in New York," he wrote, "for the purpose of bringing into social contact men who worked with their hands and men who worked with their heads, and of rescuing the leaders of Trade Unions from what then seemed to be the manifest errors of Collectivism." But, Kelly continued, those who received the greatest education were not working men but the wealthier, more cultivated members like himself. The experience forced him to retrace the path of his own assumptions and to begin "a careful revision of the scientific grounds of Herbert Spencer's individualism on the one hand, and of the economic fallacies of socialism on the other."[9] In October 1898, Kelly was elected president of the club. "I am saddled with this new responsibility," he wrote to his son Shaun; "fortunately it is work that I am very much interested in, but whether I shall have strength enough to do my duty to it has yet to be seen."

Kelly's health, which was not of the fittest, was a constant source of anxiety to him. And he undoubtedly still felt the shock of losing his wife. Such feelings emerged during a strange visit to the famous medium, Mrs. Piper. Possibly at the suggestion of William James, who was studying the work of Mrs. Piper, Kelly and his friend Richard Welling paid two visits to this reputed clairvoyant who claimed to be able to report conversations with the dead. Kelly's description of his visits is a fascinating mixture of belief and disbelief as he retells the conversation he supposedly had with his wife Fanny. The first session was the more successful, for the medium suggested throughout the interview that Kelly's wife had told her an intimate family nickname. Toward the end, Mrs. Piper was seized from the "other side," and blurted it out: "then," Kelly wrote in amazement, "came the most extraordinary incident of the session; there were some convulsive movements which generally indicate a change of control, that is to say, instead of speaking with the hand, she took control as it is called, of the head; by using the voice of the medium; the voice of the medium gasped out as by a supreme effort the name she had been so long trying to get, 'boysie.' I was so confounded that I hardly believed my ears. . . ." Another session followed, but

Kelly became suspicious as the medium floundered and her persuasiveness dwindled.[10]

During the late nineteenth century many people were fascinated by phrenology, hypnotism, and other parapsychological phenomena and research. Such was the confidence in science that it was thought that even the occult could be interpreted and codified by new scientific procedures. Kelly was not exceptional in his fascination with the unconscious and its scientific possibilities. But not far beneath his claim of scientific interest lay the brittle shards of personal tragedy. Kelly was deeply troubled by the death of his young wife. Both his career and his own life exhibited a rootlessness, a lack of family solidity, or even professional stability. He felt a strong dissatisfaction with almost all aspects of his life, as did his father before him. His dedication to reform can thus be viewed not only as the pursuit of certain and clear public goals, but as relief from a private life which was deeply troubled.

As an expatriate and an international lawyer, Kelly had experience with and knowledge of both American and French culture, and traveled easily between the two societies. Perhaps a desire to bring coherence to his own experience reinforced his belief that disorder was a problem of striking social dimensions in every industrial society. When he approached such problems, they seemed to take on the quality of the universality of the human condition itself. Thus questions of marriage, deracination, community, and economics were intertwined in his vision of a new social philosophy. His first choice for a reform institution, the urban social club which provided a meeting place for intellectuals and workingmen, he saw as analogous in its communal ties to the family, which in past centuries had given society its stability. The urban reform club was, in a sense, his own spiritual home, and the institution upon which he based his hopes for reform.

Although Kelly assumed the leadership of the Social Reform Club in 1898, his tenure was short. After the outbreak of war with Spain—a war which he avidly supported—he traveled to Madrid to become an attorney for the interests of the Equitable Life Assurance Society. In 1899 he returned to Paris, where he remained for the next five years. Still, in the few months of his presidency of the Social Reform Club he left his mark. He helped to push the club toward more serious reform than securing clean streets or adequate snow removal. Under his leadership, the organization tried to establish a cooperative ladies' tailor shop and occasionally helped to raise money to support strike participants. Yet Kelly reported finding the experience in general disappointing, for it did not lead to workingmen's votes for clean government. It merely forced intellectuals like himself to search more deeply for appropriate reform projects.

In the midst of this activity, Kelly published a series of works which analyzed his experiences as both lawyer and reformer. During the 1890's he turned out three major books: *Evolution and Effort,* published in 1895, and a two-volume work entitled *Government or Human Evolution.* Each of these represented a modification of his earlier views, and all harkened back to the failure of the municipal clubs. In a sense, each of Kelly's books was also a dialogue with Herbert Spencer containing a denunciation of Spencer's defense of unremitting competition. In general, Kelly concluded that the Spencerian notion of competition was merely a description of urban corruption. But Kelly did not entirely throw off the influence of Spencer, for it was Spencer who set the terms of the dialogue and who raised the questions which Kelly felt compelled to answer. Kelly based his philosophic position upon a sociological translation of evolutionary theory. From biological science and Darwin, he derived the foundation of the method which he used to discover larger laws of social development. Kelly sought no less than to make Darwinian science compatible with a Christian and moral commonwealth. Viewing science and society as two connected fields of study, he wrote of political science in the notes for his lectures at Columbia: "But political laws though varying in time, while they operate are as inexorable as Natural Laws."

Evolution and Effort, Kelly's first book during this period, was taken up with the distinction between scientific law and the laws of social development. Natural phenomena were governed by the order of necessity, he wrote, and nature evolved toward a sort of amoral complexity. Society, on the contrary, was ruled by human effort. Natural law was amoral; social law was moral and Christian. Spencer had been correct to speak of law in both realms, but he falsely assumed a direct analogy between nature and society, thereby missing the more fragile and indirect links between the social and scientific realms. He had been correct to stress evolution as a descriptive tool for writing human history, but wrong to limit the concept of evolution to the progressive chaos of competition and aggression.

Beyond its attack on Spencer, *Evolution and Effort* represented the intellectualization of two deep concerns in Kelly's life: his reform activities in the City Club and the Good Government Movement, and his less articulated but still keen desire for family solidarity and moral order. The first page of *Evolution and Effort* is almost confessional, and clearly alludes to the loss of Kelly's wife, his despair, and his search for a theory of society that would be personally comforting yet still aggressive in the fight against corruption. "When in the lusty vigour of our youth we first discover the logical defects of our creed," he wrote, "it is with triumphant sense of escape from bondage that we enroll ourselves among freethinkers. . . . But when, after calamity has darkened our lives, some ritual of baptism or marriage or death brings us once more within the walls of the church we had in younger days with so light a heart abandoned, our memories are moved by old associations recalling, perhaps, a vanished hand or a silenced voice; the words of Scripture which familiarity had once sterilised for us become alive with new meaning. . . ."[11] This statement did not signal Kelly's return to the Catholicism of his family, which he had abandoned, but it did measure the vigor of his general religiosity.

The task of social philosophy, Kelly continued, was to reconcile Christianity and political community. This could be done only by distinguishing between the structures of science and religion, to the benefit of both. Science, Kelly argued, "is knowledge of the laws of Nature," and as such was deterministic. Although society was also governed by laws, these responded to human endeavor. Thus effort and religious sentiment were the guiding forces of society. In each realm, knowledge was accumulated in an evolutionary fashion. Nature exhibited changing species, whereas in human society evolution was marked by a shift from instinctual behavior toward moral action. Man evolved a mental faculty, almost a religious organ of adjustment to the environment. Thus human beings erected institutions to protect themselves from the cruel reach of the laws of natural survival. Human conduct went far beyond the stir of instincts. In the family, for example, which had once been a propertied relationship, mutual love replaced greed. Any true citizen of the "second epoch of evolution," as Kelly named the 1890's, could understand and employ science and religion to their best purposes: "When religion and science have come together to make up such a man as this, then, perhaps, he may be fitted to undertake self-government on the larger field which, because it is larger, is for that reason more complicated and more difficult, and yet upon which every adult male is now at liberty to break a lance in his own cause as well as in that of the commonwealth—politics." And so the best possible hope of natural and social evolution, for Kelly, was to be found in the appearance of a scientific reformer.

In Kelly's view, a new moral citizenship would be defined by the special knowledge each man should have about the proper uses of science and religion. Spencer, according to Kelly, was a brilliant but superficial thinker, who knew nothing of social evolution and therefore remained mired in admiration for the struggle for survival. Human evolution had an entirely different, though analogous, development, which was not driven by the same ruthless and mechanical laws of nature. Political regeneration, as Kelly saw it, was possible only if the Christian gentleman were returned to politics. Here Kelly's theorizing provided an intellectual wrapper for his own political activities. But deeper considerations were at issue. The anarchy of laissez faire that characterized political society was also visible elsewhere. Society was no longer unified by churches or by the strength of the family. "The family, which is the basis of our civilisation," Kelly noted, "is gradually breaking up." Society was at loose ends, overflowing with corruption at the top and sown with disorder at the bottom.

Kelly was as much fascinated with and fearful of disorder from lower-class elements in society as he was disgusted with corruption among ruling politicians. The roving bands of the unemployed, tramps, and paupers were for him symbolic of an endemic social chaos. For such unfortunate types he proposed rehabilitation labor camps and moral regeneration through work. While in France during the early 1900's, he spent considerable time trying to discover what psychological disorders might drive men to dislike work. In all of his books following *Evolution and Effort,* he returned to discuss the meaning of vagabondage; and in 1908 he devoted a separate work to the subject, entitled *The Elimination of the Tramp.* At the time the book appeared, Kelly was at work to persuade New York State to set up rehabilitation centers for such men and women.

By 1895, Kelly had decided that the responsibility for reform ultimately lay with the state as a representative of the whole society. At this point his writings represented a simpler version of the complex kind of collectivism that he would later devise. He reversed the formulas of Spencer and abandoned social individualism. But for now the theoretical groundwork had been laid. Implicitly, at least, Kelly had already decided that the function of family and church—and their fading communal ties, which had once restrained people from becoming tramps and municipal crooks—ought to be assumed by government. He even suggested a state-subsidized press and an established church, both nonpartisan but unremitting in their preachments against corruption and wrongdoing. Some of these ideas, he obliquely hinted, were related to socialism. To be sure, his own views and the suggestions of the English Fabians were remarkably similar at points. He could scarcely have been unaware of this, for his description of the Fabian Society was practically interchangeable with his conception of the urban reform club: both were based upon the existence of a "large class of citizens who today stand neutral between the employer and the employee."

With the publication of *Evolution and Effort,* Kelly had stated most of the themes that would occupy his intellectual energy for the next ten years. He did so, moreover, in an explicitly Christian context, proposing a new "gospel of effort" to stand in place of the Social Darwinist "gospel of wealth." But his ideas still wanted texture. He was hesitant about the appropriate direction to carry his theories, unsure what to call them, and uncertain about his own activities and his relation to other social movements. Still, he had succeeded in satisfying his own need to blend social solutions that would work in two ways—resolving his own personal disappointments as well as the social disintegration he saw everywhere. In broad terms, he had begun to conceive a revitalized Christianity made possible by the collectivist economic state.

Several muted themes in Kelly's earlier works relating to this collectivist state were more extensively treated in articles published around the turn of the century. Each marked a further development in his reluctant drift toward socialism. One of his articles, for example, compared the physical size of political units in New York City with the much smaller Parisian *arrondisements.* To Kelly, New York's greater size was symbolic of the profound isolation of the modern city dweller in America: "The cult of isolation is destructive of good democratic government, which depends for its success upon collective action for political ends." This isolation, matching the psychological results of individualism, resulted in bad government: "We are in fact a mob, each of us hypnotized by his avocation, without sympathy or communion one with another, and because isolated by the very pressure of the crowd about us, incapable of our own distress."

The solution to this and related problems, in Kelly's view, was municipal control and ownership of utilities and transportation. Only by removing politics from government could corruption be isolated. Urban politics did not just interfere with justice or the setting of reasonable rates for public services; politics legitimized a whole corrupt system, serving the exclusive interests of selfish capitalists. Owners, Kelly wrote, did not run gas companies; experts did. Yet the owners set prices and determined policies. Thus the urban machine, behind which these men hid their true power, was in reality the political armament for a small company of wealthy monopolists. The business of public utilities, Kelly argued, should not be the exclusive domain of owners: "Municipal administration is a gigantic business, requiring as close attention on the part of those for whose benefit it exists as that of the banker or the manufacturer or the merchant. . . ."[12]

Fixing upon the causes of corruption, Kelly repeatedly recalled the failure of his own "brownstone" class to lure workingmen to reform causes. Over the years he became more suspicious of his old assumptions, and more ironically self-aware. Thus he wrote: "To this end we must bear in mind that the members of Columbia University do not represent to the dweller of Five Points [a New York slum] the only source of political wisdom; on the contrary, accustomed as the latter is to seek warmth and society in the liquor saloon, it is not unnatural that he should imbibe with his evening dram some of the moral notions which pervade liquor saloons. . . ."

Kelly's next two books, which formed the series *Government or Human Evolution* (published in 1900 and 1901), brought him much closer to collectivist political theory and therefore closer to the answers he sought. Together with his earlier works these also completed his refutation of Spencer. Upton Sinclair recalled that he had first read Kelly's books at the suggestion of Ray Stannard Baker "who said they made a great impression upon him." Sinclair read *Evolution and Effort* and then the two later books, "which," he explained, "impressed me as being the most satisfactory refutation of the reactionary sociology of Herbert Spencer that I had ever come upon."[13] (As impressive as Kelly's arguments may have been, Sinclair was undoubtedly convinced to begin with by the intensive and widespread attacks on Spencer then being made in contemporary journals.)

Far more important than Kelly's argument against laissez faire was his proposal of collectivism as an alternative to the present system. In his first volume (entitled *Justice*), Kelly restated old ideas. The occasion for writing was once again to point out the failure of municipal reform. Kelly now drew stronger arguments for collective action instead of the more

limited reform efforts he had previously proposed. He reiterated his anti-Spencer stance, citing the difference between the
state of nature and human society. Evolution was a mechanical principle which could develop species differentiation in
nature but was devoid of any moral or progressive content. Yet
Kelly was far from rejecting the terminology of Darwinism.
Questions of progress, development, and human evolution still
very much dominated his own language, even though he rejected the processes of Social Darwinism.

More clearly than before, Kelly felt that man's religious
sense and his family structure were the evidence of Spencer's
errors. The religious faculty and humane family relationships
differentiated man from the animals. Kelly's idea of marriage
was now more important than ever, for it became to him the
key to social progress and, considered by itself, formed the
ideal society in miniature. Kelly implied that society might be
reconstructed so that moral virtue, given practical existence
by such institutions as marriage, could once more determine
social structure. Marriage and its primary virtue, self-restraint,
would thus become a guide to community, destroying the
competitive ethic. Such a transformation would be greatly enhanced, Kelly felt, by the creation of an active state-supported
religion which could become the mediator between humane
values and political and social reforms. A new society would
emerge, not, as Spencer had argued, one governed by the laws
of nature, but a more careful construction built upon conscious and humane effort. The ideal of justice was the driving
force of this complex evolution of ideas and institutions, and
it tested man's efforts to improve life by manipulating the environment. Justice, as Kelly put it, would "eliminate from our
social conditions the effects of the inequalities of Nature upon
the happiness and advancement of man, and particularly to
create an artificial environment which shall serve the individual as well as the race, and tend to perpetuate noble types
rather than those which are base."[14] Thus even his father's
wish for absolute moral self-control might be realized in a new
social system.

Kelly's arguments were not especially original, but they are
interesting for the subversive way in which they sought to

achieve the same end as the Social Darwinists—the evolution of higher types of individuality. Kelly's aims were conservative, for he desired law and stability, the preservation of his own conception of the nineteenth-century family, the obliteration of prostitution and alcoholism, and the establishment of an updated social Christianity. Kelly's position hardly marked him as a radical among intellectuals of his time. Yet his solutions were extremist, and he was reckless in his thrusts against the moral defenses of laissez-faire individualism. His proposals called for a complete reversal of priorities, with an economic system that was subordinated to the more important demands of morality. Society, he argued, ought to reassert control over the twin private worlds of business and politics, and it could do so by positive action on the part of the collectivist state.

Kelly realized that a moral order required an economic order, and he did not avoid the very difficult question of who would control the economy. The economic proposals of his reformed society derived from what amounted to his shadow tracings of existing economic organizations. In a review written in 1903, Kelly discussed the German economic crisis of a few years before and wrote enthusiastically about the effects of modern economic organization. He criticized German cartels, not for their centralism or monopoly but because they were primitive and imprecise institutions. Compared with American corporations, cartels were chaotic and poorly organized. The German experiment was only a halfway house, whereas the times called for a far more thorough economic organization to prevent what William James Ghent had called a "benevolent Feudalism." Nothing could completely end the danger of periodic economic crisis, but "nothing less than such a combination of producers, manufacturers, and carriers as in our Steel Trust can efficiently adjust production and regulate prices."[15] As the state ought to assume the direction of religious and political reform, so it ought to become the guardian of a new centralized economy that eliminated competition.

Kelly's social and economic theories lacked only a name and a coherence, both of which were supplied in his second book, *Individualism and Collectivism,* published in 1901. Like his earlier books, this one began with a confession of failure and an admission that grave misunderstandings lay beneath the urban reform movement. Kelly also disclosed his frustration with easy solutions. A few months of contact with workingmen in the Social Reform Club, he said, had convinced him and a few friends that "we had caught a Tartar." To control this dangerous catch, he proposed to abandon his old means of organizing society. It would no longer suffice to propose political reforms. Society must be reconstructed on a collectivist basis.

Such a view had certainly been implicit in Kelly's writings as early as 1895; it runs, for example, throughout his discussion of the Good Government movement. Although he was tentative, almost sketchy, about the meaning of collectivism and the shape of the future collectivist society, Kelly was nonetheless quite certain that this word contained in it the implications of a solution to the moral and industrial crises of modern society. "At present," he concluded, "collectivism is a creed rather than a programme. But it is a practical creed—one we can take into politics with us as well as into church." This creed implied a new society: "Collectivism is the theory that the production, transportation, and distribution of the necessaries of life can to a certain degree to-day, slowly to a larger degree, and perhaps eventually altogether, be best undertaken by the collective action of the city or State, through the substitution of cooperation for competition and social for self interest." Collectivism, then, for Kelly, was the end of a dialectical process suggested in earlier works. The history of such institutions as the Christian Church and even marriage demonstrated the constant struggle of two moral forces—of idealism, which elevated social life, and of corruption, driven on by self-interest, which lowered it. Capitalism in its competitive stages was based upon greed and therefore inevitably exhibited debased social values. The collectivist state would be based upon the modern trust, the arguments for which Kelly believed to be self-evident. Because men banded together in trade unions and merged businesses into corporations, it was obvious that social cooperation was more important than individualism. Collectivism therefore had a new moral basis: "Collectivism, properly understood, is a religion," he wrote. As his friend the

Reverend Heber Newton of New York enthusiastically commented to him in 1901, Kelly's raising social theory to the level of ethics was surely the greatest single contribution of his book: "There certainly is not in the English language any argument for collectivism approaching this in scientific temper, in philosophic analysis and in what is so admirably expressed in our American colloquialism; level-headedness!"[16]

Individualism or Collectivism was intended to be the economic solution of a social problem, just as the first volume, *Justice*, provided the moral background. Kelly had obviously begun to read widely in socialist literature by this time. There were noteworthy traces of English Fabianism throughout the book, and even a fledgling theory of imperialism based upon overproduction. Significantly, Kelly now agreed with the socialist assumption that personal motives were not, in the long run, the causes of social corruption and inequity, but that a system of institutionalized evils were. Collectivism may originally have been a moral stance to Kelly, one suggested by his study of Spencer, but it was fast becoming a religious movement that implied a particular economic system.

Kelly's collectivism, incomplete as it still was, suggested answers to the questions he had long asked about the organization of society. Once the state had become collectivist and had undertaken the guidance of the social and economic system, dramatic reforms would be possible. Corruption and social dissolution could be ended. In the new society, for example, the role of officials—who would surely multiply in such a system—would necessarily be different. Much like the new experts and technicians in industry, they would be incorruptible because under collectivism no advantage could be gained by bribery or advantage-seeking. Such temptations would simply disappear. Money would no longer be used to reward service; instead, citizens would receive a dividend for doing necessary state work. Such industries as communications and utilities would be state owned, with private enterprise lingering in the back alleys of economic activity. Vagabonds and tramps would be placed on state farms for rehabilitation, and prostitution and crime would evaporate. Kelly's new order most closely resembled state socialism, though he did not call it that. He had built upon a social conservatism the rudiments of a collectivist state. But to call for reform was never enough. His hatred of corruption was so strong and his desire for a new society so great that he was not prepared to halt at mere intellectual analysis. He now sought a movement to embody his goals.

Although Kelly had in effect embraced a form of Fabian socialism in his book on collectivism, he still remained aloof from the socialist movements of the day. His friend John Spargo attempted to explain this reluctance in 1910. The problem for Kelly as well as many other American intellectuals, Spargo noted, was the rigidity of the socialist movement itself. In the first few years of its existence, Spargo continued, the Socialist party had defined its stand on social issues in terms of class struggle, which repulsed Kelly. However: "With the development of a new school of Socialist writers who made it their special task to restate the Socialist position plainly, in ordinary language, without the confusion of a mass of academic verbiage, his [Kelly's] difficulties vanished and he saw in class consciousness, not the sordid thing he had imagined, but a great spiritual force."[17] When Kelly finally joined the Socialist party in 1907, the act confirmed Spargo's view, and indicated that collectivist theories were becoming central to the development of American socialism.

During the last phase of Kelly's career, from his stay in Paris in 1899 through his return to the United States until his death in 1909, he gave each of his political and intellectual interests one final major expression. In this last decade of his life, his health continued to fail, though he remarried in 1906 and managed even to the end to continue his reform activities and writings. His second wife, helped by his son Shaun, edited and published his last and most influential work, *Twentieth Century Socialism*. In these last years, Kelly's life was also encumbered with problems about his son's nationality, a problem aggravated by Kelly himself having been born in France. Kelly relied on his friend President Theodore Roosevelt to intervene in his son's behalf. The irony of this was that at almost the same time Roosevelt replaced Spencer as Kelly's chief antagonist in the realm of social theory.[18]

One characteristic of all four books written in these years was Kelly's sense of urgency, his compulsion to finish the task of social reformation. Robert Hunter was impressed with Kelly's mood of impatience when he first met the lawyer in Paris in 1907. Hunter's record of their conversation is noteworthy. "Could you tell me just how cheaply one can live in New York?" Hunter has Kelly say. "That is to say, just how cheaply can you live? My health requires some comforts, but I will reduce them to a minimum. I have been working for years to free myself. I want to see now if I have saved enough to give the rest of my life to the cause of the workers." The sense of urgency which Kelly's new friends in the Socialist party noticed about him was probably due to his knowledge that he suffered from a fatal disease. He returned to New York, as Upton Sinclair recalled, determined to found "a sort of Fabian Socialist society in this country." He enrolled in the Socialist party and attended meetings of Branch One in New York City, a section which included among its members Ernest Poole, Rufus Weeks, and Charles Edward Russell.

Russell was struck by the incongruity of Kelly's appearance among working-class comrades in the back of Bodenbach's Bar and Saloon in Manhattan—immaculately dressed, with his "scholarly bearing, delicate features, carefully trimmed gray hair, and modish attire." A latecomer to the socialist movement, Kelly was nonetheless a tested warrior for reform. With his own time so short he was impatient. As Hunter wrote: "When the cause lagged or dissension in the party arose he seemed in positive anguish, because it put off the day when something would be done—the something he craved to see, at least to have some little glimmer of before he had to go."[19]

Kelly's version of socialism as a new moral order based upon an economy of collectivism was another name for the views he had already held for several years. As a socialist he reasserted Christian virtues: sobriety, industry, self-control, and family in the context of an economic and political system designed to save these values. Traditional as this was, Kelly's proposals went far beyond simple nostalgia for a disappearing society. His sense of the modern industrial and political crisis, compounded by his own personal failure at reform, made him propose drastic changes. He wanted to provide socialists of every stripe with a comprehensive plan for action, and at the same time to defend his newly adopted movement from the sniping of Theodore Roosevelt, who had denounced radicals for their "looseness of thought." As Roosevelt had it, socialists were advocating and practicing free love, an excess which he claimed had characterized the Paris Commune of 1871. This charge prompted Kelly to respond bitterly, "There is no class in which the looseness of morals more prevails than in the class to which Mr. Roosevelt himself belongs—the self-styled Four Hundred."[20] That Kelly was of the same class as Roosevelt did not stop him from lashing out.

Kelly's reform program was addressed to several different audiences. In 1906, still not a confirmed socialist, he offered workingmen a semi-religious, even mystical version of his reform theories. His *Practical Programme for Workingmen* showed Kelly standing hesitantly and reluctantly before the socialist movement. In a series of short chapters meant to suggest the divisions of the Bible, Kelly asked simply, "Shall we continue to tolerate an Environment that keeps us slaves, or shall we create an Environment that will make us gods?" Workingmen should adopt the "New Gospel," and work to replace the competitive system with a society of cooperation. Man's way would be eased by his natural reflex to oppose and reject the abnormal system of competition that history had imposed upon him. Even in nature, Kelly now declared, competition was exceptional behavior. By no conceivable means could competition support any positive values or natural rights. Private property and the free market were both artificial arrangements, and as such were the hardware of human bondage. Competition must be replaced by a system of "Solidarism."

This new system, as Kelly now described it, could be achieved through the ballot box, which was society's best way to register its ideals. Obviously, Kelly was still suspicious of socialism, and he specifically rejected Marxism for its reliance upon class hatred as a weapon of social change. His practical program for workingmen was, in effect, another call for reform along well-known lines, except that he more and more came to see such lines leading precisely toward the socialism that he rejected. He spoke in terms of creating a national reform movement based upon the nationalization of property. Indeed, he agreed with a great many American socialist intellectuals who shared his collectivist assumptions. What he lacked was confidence in the socialist movement in the United States.

The Demetrian, Kelly's next book, was a utopian novel, published under the pseudonym Ellison Harding. Although certainly his least known book, it is still his most successful in showing the richness of the collectivist society he envisioned. At this time Kelly's interest in utopias probably inspired him to join Upton Sinclair's project for a "home colony" of writers, editors, and musicians. In 1906, Sinclair had purchased an old boys' school near Englewood, New Jersey, and urged couples to join in communal living arrangements there. Although the venture was cut short by a fire which destroyed the buildings, Kelly was among those who had agreed to become a trustee of the colony.[21]

Like other utopian novels of the day, Kelly's utopian work echoed other influential books, particularly Edward Bellamy's *Looking Backward.* Kelly was quite unoriginal in his application of the dramatic mechanics of the utopian novel. His hero, Henry T. Joyce, was a bachelor resident of Boston who fell asleep in his quarters and awoke in the year 2004. Bellamy had, of course, used almost the identical beginning. But here almost all similarities ended. Whereas Bellamy's book had been a tourist's trip through the mechanical and social wonders of the future, Kelly was far more interested in the lineaments and the utility of new social institutions, whose resilience he tested with a plot of intrigue and conflict. For both Bellamy and Kelly, the values nurtured by utopia were similar. Yet Kelly's was the more daring book, and at the same time the more old-fashioned of the two, for he combined a Catholic, even pagan, religious imagery with the symbols and practical institutions of new sexual mores within a collectivist economy. In novelistic form, Kelly could imagine the answers to all that ailed modern life. His anguish over corruption, prostitution, immorality, vagabondage, and upper-class corruption could be laid aside. But he did not assume, as other writers tended to, that all social or political problems would disappear. His optimism extended only so far as attempting to disarm such problems through a series of new social practices.

Like Bellamy's hero Julian West, Henry Joyce fell asleep in Boston and awoke in a new civilization. Like Kelly himself, Joyce was a lawyer and, ironically, a person for whom the new society ostensibly had no use. The paradise which Joyce woke to was a collectivist society, the very future embodiment of Kelly's own platform for social regeneration. Curiously, it was also a Victorian's conception of a Greek paradise. In the opening scenes, Joyce approaches a settlement named Tyringham, noteworthy for its large Gothic Hall. In the fields nearby, workers are reaping grain. Guided by one of the residents of the settlement, Joyce watches the people lay aside their work and break into song which he recognizes as Bach's Fugue No. 7 in C Flat. "Here," Joyce comments, "was the charm of frankness, of gayiety, and of simplicity, coupled with a cleanliness of person, delicacy of thought and manner, culture, art, music—all that makes life beautiful and sweet."[22]

Joyce is quickly accepted into the community and learns of the Cult of Demeter, which is the moral center of the society. The cult, he is told, represents a worship of marriage based upon a reverence and expression of the deepest, truest instincts in men and women. The highest act of worship is the "sacrifice" by marriage of one of the Demetrians (a group of selected women) to someone designated by the priests to be her husband. Once a woman has given herself to the cult, there is no choice in the matter, except that the marriage may be terminated after the weaning of the first child. As Kelly writes, the "highest duty of man was in labor and countenance, and women, fertility and labor." Science had transformed the old ideal of abstinence, and society now gave sexual activity its proper place. Liberated from its historical struggle for wealth and security, religion could now contain and guide man's moral development, anticipating, even regulating his most basic needs.

The economic system of Kelly's collectivist utopia, unlike Bellamy's, was not based upon inventions and mechanical gadgetry. Kelly's future utopia was less organized and less industrialized than even the society of early twentieth-century America. His imaginative world remained largely agricultural, with the state owning land and leasing it to farmers. Unpleasant work was assigned by lot. The division between town and city and farm was eliminated because people shifted their residences to live in different kinds of environments during the year. Although Kelly had already written about the need for a collectivism based upon industrial organization, his utopia paid little attention to industry. This was no oversight. Given the chance to sketch the ideal society, Kelly used modern institutions merely to reorganize and refresh older practices. He had, in fact, spliced a derivation of modern corporate forms onto an essentially agrarian vision of the world, where all citizens, instead of just the upper classes, moved from town house to country house, and labored in the earth as much for love as for necessity.

The prison system in this society reflected Kelly's long-standing proposals for penal colonies in which criminals and vagabonds were reformed through work. Its politics had only a vague likeness to that of Kelly's own day. For one thing, women could vote. For another, political parties represented not men but political principles. It must have been with great satisfaction that Kelly drew the established party of collectivism as the party of conservatism, with the radicals as disruptive elements who wished to reintroduce private property.

The plot of the novel centers around two threats to society by a party of dissidents who attempt to overturn the moral and economic order. These attempts at overthrow come in the form of sexual excesses and economic exploitation, both firmly denounced by Kelly as perils to the new society. In a complicated series of events, Joyce becomes involved in the political struggle, then resists seduction by one of the party of private enterprise, and finally helps save collectivism. In the end the system triumphs, but not without loss and self-sacrifice. As Kelly has one of the cult of Demeter say in the end, "Every institution, human and divine, has to pay a price for the blessings it bestows—*dura lex sed lex.*"

The Demetrian is surely Kelly's most interesting book. Unused and even unsuited as he was to purely literary work, he nonetheless constructed a fascinating moral tale endowed with a private vision of the future that was firmly but oddly shaped by an older set of social values. It was a work which showed a mind willing to stretch itself to extraordinary lengths to conserve and nourish the institutions it most believed in. It was the vision of an austere conservative, who saw that he could save what he treasured most only by proposing almost unending change.

With his novel completed, Kelly in his last two books turned to an explicit development of his conception of socialism. His short work *The Elimination of the Tramp,* published in 1908, contained bits and pieces from his idealization of the agrarian utopian community, combined with a tough attitude toward tramps and toward social charity which echoed Spencer's attacks on ameliorative institutions. Behind this book lay several years of thought about the problem of tramps. Earlier, while in Paris, Kelly had joined the Institut Général Psychologique de Paris. As a member of this group, he presented a paper in 1902 surveying European attitudes toward vagabondage. His conclusions were severe: If a man could not work for some reason, society should help him. If he would not work, then he was probably mentally ill and should be placed on a rehabilitation farm to regain his moral sense through work.

In order to disband the army of American tramps, in 1908 Kelly proposed to place irresponsible members of society on labor farms where they could regain physical and psychological stability. This was necessary, he wrote, because vagabonds were "infesting our roads, damaging our property, assaulting our women, corrupting our youth, and breeding disease, moral and physical, through every city and hamlet in the land." Vagabondage to Kelly was the supreme symbol of the evils of economic individualism. At the time he published this book, Kelly was also working to persuade New York State to begin a program of labor rehabilitation camps.

Much like the Social Darwinists whom he identified as his ideological enemies, Kelly blamed the existence of vagabondage both upon existing industrial conditions and upon the temptations of charity. Vagabondage, he suggested, was not caused by unemployment alone, or even by "mental disorder," but also by the seductions which such a life exercised upon young men, and a life made easy and attractive "by the facility with which they can get free rides on trains and food and lodging from police and municipal lodging houses, wayfarers' lodges, Salvation Army institutions, relief societies, and Church missions."[23]

This stern view went untempered in Kelly's last work, *Twentieth Century Socialism*. To Kelly, socialism was a moral order, and though he was genuinely sympathetic to those whose lives had been damaged and distorted by industrial disorder, he did not question traditional moral institutions in the same way that his contemporaries Van Wyck Brooks or Randolph Bourne or Max Eastman did. Nor would he have sympathized with or even understood their denunciation of American "Puritanism."

Twentieth Century Socialism, published in 1910, appeared one year after Kelly's death. Although his health had deteriorated during his last years, he was able to complete a first draft of the work shortly before he died. His Columbia University colleague Franklin Giddings wrote one introduction to the book, followed by another introduction by Rufus Weeks, a Socialist party friend. Weeks's description of socialism was an apt picture of the enthusiastic attitude Kelly shared about the movement: "An immense revolution, a wonderful revolution, is opening in the mind of the human race; a new driving force is taking hold of the souls of men—the devotion to the welfare of the whole; a new sense, with all the intensity of a new-born feeling, is emerging in the consciousness of men—the sense that one cannot be healthy or happy unless the race is happy and healthy."

Kelly's friend J. Lebovitz at the Library of Congress, with whom he was assembling statistical proofs of the efficiency of socialism, believed Kelly to be a seminal thinker. Lebovitz wrote to Kelly's widow after reading the book: "I am convinced that when its truths finally percolate down to the comrade on the soap box that it will have a profound influence upon American socialist thought and action. And reach them it must, for it represents the findings of a man who had opportunities to see more than any of us and who *did* see more clearly than any of us. In the long run we shall have to come to him as the conservative has to come to us."[24] Lebovitz shrewdly understood the tone and the purpose of this work.

Although intended for more conservative audiences than Socialist party regulars, Kelly's book nonetheless drew widely upon the traditional literature of socialism. Recalling his first favorable impression of socialism, he told how his reading of the Fabian Tracts had made socialism real to him. This version of social reformation was precisely opposite to the vulgar view that aroused Theodore Roosevelt's crude denunciations. Thus, wrote Kelly, his task was to demonstrate the moral acceptability of socialism and its economic practicality, to distinguish it from "the crude ideas that prevailed before Marx, Darwin and the development of the trusts." As the final thrust of moral evolution, socialism would naturally represent the sum of divergent ideas. Thus Kelly felt justified when he cast widely for his sources, and drew upon Huxley's criticisms of Spencer, Kautsky's rejection of violent revolution, Spargo's discussion of socialist productive relationships, Henry George's theories of land value, and, most importantly, his own previous works. *Twentieth Century Socialism* represented a revision of Kelly's earlier collectivism, updated, renamed, and embellished with the arguments of a number of leading socialist thinkers. His model for the good society remained as always the family: "There is too no function of the family more important than that it serves as a model of what the state ought to be as distinguished from what the state actually is." He criticized such thinkers as Edward Bellamy for underestimating the problems that the family had resolved, for, he wrote, "the great obstacle to happiness in community life is sexual instinct," which could only be contained by the guiding institution of the family.[25]

Thus socialism was to be the resting place for Kelly's lifelong commitment to moral reform, his final choice as the most effective agency of social change. Under socialism, Kelly felt that at least in the future a man of his standing and inclination could find a sense of personal usefulness in a system that would bring control and law to production and a new moral order enlightened by science. Unending progress would create an earthly utopia. The evolution of new economic and social institutions would eventually, by the force of their operation, create new definitions of citizenship.

Socialism was a deeply personal commitment for Kelly, impatient as he was at the end of his life to secure the reaffirmation of values which he saw disintegrating all about him. "Socialism presents a simple, obvious and unanswerable solution to the manifold problems presented by the competitive system." Like other collectivist intellectuals, he blamed competition in economics and social practice for the cruel and wasteful economic system which divided men into social classes. Socialism, or solidarity—for him the two words were practically synonymous—defined a society whose reality was already contained in the rough shapes of present institutions. Kelly was conscious that his version of socialism still clashed with the official pronouncements of the American Socialist party. In the last months of his life he wrote in the party press that a radical political organization ought to be devoted not just to workers but to all consumers. The constituency for socialism ought to be all those who would share in an efficient and practical reorganization of the economic system. But the socialist movement which he embraced somewhat uneasily in his last days did not precisely share his ideas of a Christian commonwealth based upon a centralized economy.

Although he had traveled far along the ideological spectrum, Kelly remained much the same sort of person intellectually at the end of his life as he had been when he set out as a young lawyer in Paris. There was even a symmetry to one of his last actions. His first reform ventures had been associated with the urban club, and so were his last. As his wife Edith wrote to Lincoln Steffens shortly after Kelly's death, her husband had helped to found a new social club in New York City during the previous winter. "You know," she wrote, "how great a field my husband thought there was for 'the Club,' and how he always maintained that Socialism was coming largely, if not altogether through the efforts of just such normal, thinking people as came together in the Liberal Club last January."

The impulse to reform society had nevertheless carried Kelly far afield from the comfortable confines of the clubhouse. After his death he was memorialized by old friends from the City Club. At another meeting in the Bowery held by the Unemployed Association, he was remembered by Ben Radman, "King of the Hoboes," as a man dedicated to those who dwelled at the bottom of society.[26]

Kelly's moral commitments, which he persistently followed, forced him to reverse the popular political wisdom of his day, and to search for a sanction for older virtues within new institutions. The collectivism which he fashioned defined society as an evolving organism which was becoming more centralized and unified in its pursuit of traditional values. The corporate economic form suggested to him that more centrally organized institutions, such as those envisioned by socialists, were the logical conclusion of his own reform efforts. The form of collectivism which he expressed thus combined the lessons of own efforts as a civic reformer with his experience as a corporation lawyer. He believed that only by translating all of the dilemmas of his day onto the grandest scale could such institutions of moral regeneration as marriage and the family be saved. The collectivist society that he desired was therefore designed to overcome a contradiction that inspired many of his efforts: How could one accept the massive new institutions of modern industrialism and still do away with the terrible side-effects of poverty and corruption? Only, he answered, by speeding the evolution of these institutions and then using the social coherence which they provided to reaffirm the Christian commonwealth.

6

King Gillette's
Social Redemption

IDEAS AS WIDESPREAD as those of collectivism invariably attracted writers who reflected the thought of their times but had little influence on it. The doors of history are generally closed to what is considered crankish thought, most often out of bewilderment. Some interesting thinkers stop short of power, influence, or even fluency, yet their lives and writings sometimes display a contour of ideas not to be found in more reasonable, dispassionate statements. In a broad, vaguely defined intellectual movement, those who carry an idea to strange or impractical conclusions sometimes test the possibilities of a set of assumptions. Occasionally, among their utopias, some of the more subtle meanings of social engineering projects such as collectivism become apparent—as much through instinct as design.

One of the most curious and persistent reform writers from the 1890's to beyond World War I was King C. Gillette, the razor man, or, as Upton Sinclair called him, the "Razor King." Gillette's utopia was an unadorned, centralized state, an immense world corporation based upon the corporate form. His literal statement of the complex collectivist ideas behind his proposals made them seem simpleminded and almost satiric. Gillette took the essential ideas of collectivism and expressed them with a maddening simplicity. His utopia was obviously unworkable and unattainable. Yet, as the founder of one of the most important corporations of his time, and always a businessman, he clearly saw the importance of the corporation as a model for social evolution, even if he did not know precisely how to articulate his discovery. His collectivist ideas made him neither radical, nor socialist, nor even a Democrat. He died in 1932, still a Republican and a 32nd-degree Mason, but also a fascinated observer of the Soviet experiment in communist collectivism. His ideas are not important for their uniqueness (though they are singular), but because of the essential similarities between his conservative business utopia and other versions of collectivism.[1]

King Camp Gillette was born in January 1855, the fifth of seven children, to George Wolcott Gillette and Fanny Camp Gillette, in Fond du Lac, Wisconsin. His father was a direct descendant of the Massachusetts Wolcotts, a successful businessman, and something of an inventor. When King was four years old, the family moved to Chicago, where King attended Skinners School. After the disastrous Chicago fire, which destroyed much of his father's property, King went to work with the hardware firm of Seeberger and Breakey. Two years later he took a similar position in New York. As he later recalled, "From the time I was twenty-one until the fall of 1904 I was a traveling man and sold goods throughout the United States and England, but traveling was not my only vocation for I took out many inventions, some of which had merit and made money for others, but seldom for myself, for I was unfortunately situated not having much time and little money with which to promote my inventions or place them on the market."

In 1890, Gillette married Alanta Ella Gaines of Willoughby, Ohio. The next year he took a position as a traveling salesman for the Baltimore Seal Company which manufactured a new mechanical bottle-stopper. The device's inventor, William Painter, encouraged Gillette to work on his own inventions. But, as Gillette writes, he needed no advice: "My impulse to think and invent was a natural one, as it was with my father and brothers—as will be found in looking over the records of the Patent Office where there are a great many inventions to our credit."[2]

Gillette's mother, Fanny Camp, must also have inspired his experimental bent. The daughter of Michigan pioneers, and educated at Albion College, Fanny Camp was also the author of one of the most famous and successful cookbooks of the nineteenth century, the *White House Cook Book*. Published first in 1887 with Hugo Ziemann, steward of the White House, as co-author, the book in its various editions eventually sold close to three million copies and was translated into five languages. While its featured sections were the grandiose menus of meals served at the White House—designed to satisfy the incredible appetites and perhaps the insatiable desire for display and luxury of late nineteenth-century politicians—less conspicuous sections of the book discussed household cures, canning, and etiquette. Mrs. Gillette was, in her own right, a scientist, a culinary engineer, and a household manager. Her second book, *The Household Gem Cyclopaedia,* published in 1901, was a compilation of advice on science, anatomy, cures, psychology, cooking, etiquette, household hints, and a dictionary of synonyms and antonyms.[3]

With a family history of tinkering and a life spent in travel from one hotel to another—and in one barber shop after another—King Gillette became interested in finding a quick and safe way to shave. Most of all, he wished to make a time-saving invention, one which would end the waste that he saw and deplored around him. As he wrote, "If the time, money, energy, and brain-power which was wasted in the barber shops of America were applied in direct effort, the Panama Canal would be dug in four hours." In 1895, Gillette began to think in earnest of a new sort of razor. A vision of his invention came to him one morning after he realized, in despair, that his old straight razor was useless: "As I stood there with the razor in my hand, my eye resting on it as lightly as a bird settling down on its nest—the Gillette razor was born."

Gillette's idea took several years and some unsuccessful and discouraging efforts to perfect. Finally, with the help of William W. Nickerson of the Massachusetts Institute of Technology, Gillette developed a useful blade and holder. In 1903 his small Gillette Company of Boston began to produce "safety razors" and blades. Almost immediately the company found an enormous market, and Gillette, overnight, became wealthy and extraordinarily successful.

After about ten years, in 1915, Gillette left active management of the razor company and moved to California where he invested heavily in real estate around Los Angeles and experimented with date-growing. He initiated an active friendship with Upton Sinclair and, with time off for several trips around the world, worked to perfect his social theories. When the crash of 1929 struck, Gillette found himself badly mortgaged and his company engaged in a battle with the Auto-Strop Corporation. Heavily overextended financially, he died in July 1932 at the age of seventy-seven, on his ranch at Calabasas, north of Los Angeles.

In one of his last letters to Upton Sinclair, Gillette wrote that he would like someday to tell the story of his life. His own autobiography, he declared, was much like Sinclair's. "My life," he said, "has been seemingly commonplace and devoted to the needs of earning a living, but after I was about forty, my life seemed to separate into two distinct entities, one devoted to earning a living and the other to the problem of how to overcome the difficulties of the industrial world, for out of its confusion there seem to flow all the troubles of humanity."[4]

This division, as Gillette identified it, actually stretched further back than he suggested, to his days as a young traveling salesman. About the same time that he began to concentrate on inventing the safety razor, he had another vision. The middle 1890's were a chaotic three or four years, with a disastrous economic crisis and, simultaneously, the emergence of gigantic corporations. During this time when American institutions were undergoing marked change, Gillette developed his plans to save society from corruption, poverty, disorder, class struggle, and exploitation, all of which were magnified by economic crisis. Gillette was obviously influenced—even transfixed—by contemporary events. One was the economic decline of 1893. A second was the appearance and growth, first, of the Bellamy Nationalist movement, and, somewhat later, the Populist movement. A further influence was the appearance of gigantic corporations such as Standard Oil, which seemed to Gillette, as well as many other observers, to be far more useful and legitimate than the crude monopolies or trusts which preceded it. To Gillette, a company such as Standard Oil was the final form of industrial evolution and the beginning of an orderly end to the chaotic and competitive world of laissez-faire capitalism. A final influence was the Chicago World's Fair of 1893, with its glittering white buildings, its planned urban character, and its suggestion that cities could be great monuments to rational, centralized living. Each of these influences became a part of Gillette's utopian thinking, a series of ideas which remained essentially unchanged by his years of failure as a social reformer and success as an entrepreneur. Gillette's industrial utopia, his corporate collectivism, was finally what it had always been—a statement of absolute faith in the ultimate consolidation of world capital.

For understandable reasons, Gillette entitled his first book on social reform, written in 1894, *Human Drift*. This short work was clearly a reaction to the author's sense of approaching catastrophe. The depression of 1893, the rising tide of crime and social violence, the general anxiety of the age required, he asserted, a drastic and immediate solution. "A year or so may be too late, and the torch applied which will set the world aflame; for there is no disease which spreads so rapidly as the intoxication of madness which is the result of injustice and unreasoning excitement." Gillette's initial reform impulse, then, was to hurry rational change in order to outdistance the terrible calamity that threatened society.

To Gillette, a perpetual sign of social and economic instability was high social mobility, for through it the impermanence of fortunes and the class struggle were expressed. It symbolized social waste and economic chaos rather than, as much popular literature had it, the means to self-fulfillment. Like Edmond Kelly, Gillette based his social theories on opposition to economic individualism. He thought society as it existed was delirious with the false premises of competition. "If I believed in a devil," he remarked, "I should be convinced that competition for wealth was his most ingenious invention for filling hell. . . ." Crime, insane asylums, social divisions were all the results of economic competition. Yet man himself was innocent and even a positively good, if repressed, being.

"The mind is naturally virtuous," he continued, "honest, ambitious, and progressive."

Amidst the deepening drift of American society, Gillette saw certain points of high ground. He was in fact optimistic about immediate change because of the singular example of order and efficiency provided by the modern industrial corporation. He and all of his traveling acquaintances agreed, he said, that the corporation was a permanent institution. Modern society was evolving toward this natural form of consolidation; it was only a question of time and tactics to reach a point of industrial peace. The Standard Oil Company, as it existed, was positive proof that competition could be eliminated. If society were modeled after this success of financial consolidation, if it could become a mirror enlargement of the industrial corporation, then the chaos would end. Private property would become public, and the sins of ruthless competition would be redeemed.

Gillette's plan was to speed up social evolution by eliminating unnecessary and, he said, artificial competition. This solution was neither religious, for there was no need to change men's hearts, nor political, for there was little hope in political candidates and parties. It was simply good business. Gillette proposed to create one gigantic United Corporation as a private corporation dedicated to revolutionary purposes. The company would ultimately offer two billion shares of its stock at one dollar each; the proceeds would be spent to enter major industries through competitive factories, and to consolidate important manufacturing sectors of the economy. Company distributing stores might also be a major activity of the corporation, Gillette suggested. Thus the United Corporation would gradually replace the private economy, until almost every business was captured by this reforming monopoly. The political flank of the movement was no cause for worry, he argued, for everything undertaken would be legal under existing laws. Of course, the United Corporation would welcome a People's party of candidates who supported economic equality and corporate reorganization. But the movement's major activity would be business. As Gillette wrote, "It is only a question of dollars to complete the evolution in a short time."

The bloodless revolution of consolidation would be accompanied, Gillette wrote, by a social and geographic consolidation of the nation, and by a kind of urban implosion. This was indeed the most striking feature of the plan. Once the company was in operation, creating a new government from the ranks of its management, the next step would be to concentrate a great proportion of the American population into one major city, possibly, as the author suggested, near Niagara Falls in upstate New York. This gigantic metropolis would be modeled after the Chicago World's Fair: "The great exposition at Chicago, especially that part devoted to manufacturing and liberal arts, is an embryo illustration of the future great manufacturing centre of North America,—a perpetual World's Fair, and educator of the people; each separate machine but an integral part of the whole vast industrial machine of the people." The city could be built by the vast army of unemployed that an efficient economy would create. The "limitless possibilities" of such a manpower pool were suggested to Gillette, as he later related, by the great organizational feats of the North during the Civil War.[5]

Gillette's utopia by Niagara would presumably tap the region's enormous potential for hydro-electric power and ultimately provide a social and economic base for thirty million residents. The city itself would be built to contain an entire society. Industry would be located in compact, efficient, centralized buildings. Inhabitants would be efficiently housed in enormous apartment buildings, twenty-four thousand of them in all, with regulation heights and room sizes. These intriguing apartment complexes, which Gillette drew in detail and reproduced in his book, might differ in exterior decoration. But all of them would be circular structures, six hundred feet in diameter. They would be located in a grid, with connections to other residences and cultural buildings and promenades between. Each apartment building would be twenty-five storeys high with a central dining room, elevator systems, and a form of air conditioning. Gillette also proposed that transportation throughout the city be on electric cars and bicycles. The surrounding countryside, indeed eventually the whole aspect of the nation, would be dramatically changed. Cities, towns, villages, farmhouses, and railroads and roads would disappear.

Gillette's utopia—apparently a traveling salesman's revenge upon the sprawling American nation—was nonetheless designed to solve social problems. The apartment-institutional living quarters would end the need for inequalities in wealth and accompanying signs of status. Money could be eliminated and a labor army created for necessary work. At the age of forty-one, men and women, if they wished, would become directors in the company (by now the whole society). There would be no politics, no corruption, and no crime. Education would be largely scientific and technical, and food preparation would be carried out under the guidance of scientists. Thus society would be redeemed, and the conscious law of right would rule. "I advocate," Gillette wrote, "a system of united and material equality, under which system, the perfection of the machinery of production and distribution would be the constant and watchful care of the individual and collective mind."[6] The result would be an efficient, vastly improved society, which would allow each man to rise to his highest intellectual level. Society would be the means for the survival of merit and the enjoyment of equality. A meritocracy would replace the precarious rule of luck in business.

At every important point in this small book, Gillette took the modern corporation as his starting point. Like the more sophisticated collectivists who followed him, he attacked competition and believed that a new stage of civilization was imminent. He disliked politics and was relatively unconcerned about the procedures of democracy. He assumed, as many later writers would, that democracy and efficiency were pretty much two different words describing the same scientific way to manage society. Many of Gillette's ideas, however, also had the ring of the Bellamyite movement. Not surprisingly, he found his most sympathetic audience in the *Twentieth Century* magazine, published in New York by the Humboldt Publishing Company, and formerly associated with the Bellamy Nationalist movement.

The magazine, which approached a circulation of ten thousand in the 1890's, was edited from 1895 to 1898 by D.

O'Loughlin, who was also the general editor of Humboldt. Gillette's relationship with the magazine was fortuitous, based entirely upon the editors' favorable reaction to his book *Human Drift*. After an enthusiastic review of the book in January 1895, *Twentieth Century* made the project of a United Corporation its primary aim and purpose. This interest in Gillette occurred at an important turning point in the life of the magazine. *Twentieth Century* had absorbed Bellamy's *New Nation* in 1894. O'Loughlin was interested, as he wrote to Bellamy in 1895, in "the practical application of the principles laid down in 'Looking Backward.' " This involved no political action, but he hoped it would help to create a national movement. "We have the best country in the world," O'Loughlin continued, "—the 'land of milk and honey.' . . . All good things can be had, justice more evenly spread and every citizen contented and happy, if we but realize that it is possible and act on that principle."

Human Drift seemed perfectly suited to this general optimism. After reviewing Gillette's book, *Twentieth Century* began to promote its sale, adding it to the extensive library of scientific and social science books and tracts which it advertised. The editors also persuaded Gillette to help with the formation of a "united company." "The human drift," the magazine editorialized, "was something that we had loved and labored for, and our hope and efforts were all directed to having the 'drift' washed up on the shores of the Cooperative Commonwealth." This reference to the Cooperative Commonwealth recalled the magazine's ties to Laurence Gronlund, author of the book by the same name. Gronlund scoffed at the direction of the *Twentieth Century* when it adopted Gillette's tract, and he accused the future razor king of copying the French reformer Fourier's style of utopia, of attempting to impose a rigid structure upon society instead of synthesizing one from its organic nature. *Twentieth Century* defended Gillette, and particularly his plan for a nonpolitical revolution which would stand capitalism on its head: "We believe," it editorialized, that "Collectivism will come in the course of evolution."[7]

It was one thing to defend Gillette's *Drift* against the sarcastic comments of former friends; it was another to work his utopia into a practical plan. Throughout 1895, O'Loughlin and the *Twentieth Century* worked to institute a huge national corporation, which they appropriately named the "People's Cooperative Trust." Gillette wrote words of encouragement to the magazine and sent explanations of his plan. Shortly before the official organization of the company in 1895, Gillette amplified the meaning of his principles, calling them an embodiment of the "power of cooperation" and an expression of economic law. His solution was not radical, he added, but healing: "I have no faith in any radical reform (and radical reform is the only reform worth the serious attention of the masses) being accomplished through political channels." Politics, he continued in his next article, was a kind of tax and espionage system which inhibited the efficiency and productive capacity of business. Society could be reformed only if reformers understood essential economics: "The system of production and distribution is not founded on theory, but upon mathematics; its gradual but sure centralization and consolidation is an economical law as positive in its application as gravity; its conclusion, final centralization in the hands of the people, is a natural sequence, which any business mind must admit."[8]

Gillette's plan was attractive to anyone who wished for profound radical change without the excesses of radicalism, and for reformers who were impelled by his utopian vision that society must someday be centrally organized into a gigantic, self-operating, perfect economic service organization. His thoughts were congenial to flush times for reform, when it was clear that economic crisis had made change inevitable. His ideas were neither Populist, nor conservative, nor socialist. They simply predicted the advance of the corporation at a geometric rate until as an institution it dominated the whole society.

In April 1895 the *Twentieth Century* announced that it had incorporated a company modeled after Gillette's plan. Gillette consented to be president of the organization, and O'Loughlin and several regular writers for the magazine named themselves its board of directors. The first order of business was the subscription of stock—even before anyone had decided what the stock might purchase or what services the company would offer. As the editors wrote, the company needed $30,000 operating capital to begin its reform activities. To prove his own commitment, O'Loughlin turned the magazine's assets over to the company. At least readers could own a share in something tangible.

The next issues of the magazine were filled with testimonial letters confessing faith in the plan and in Gillette's vision. Several had suggestions for the company's first venture. But these same issues also admitted that no real progress had yet been made. Nothing could be done until the People's Cooperative Trust had raised enough capital and decided upon a program. Some readers suggested beginning a cooperative marketing service; others wanted an insurance company; the magazine itself admitted that it was thinking about organizing a utopian agricultural community. By July the directors of the company had, by a process of progressive discouragement with alternatives, decided upon insurance as their first field of endeavor. "Through making a small beginning," the magazine reported, "we can eventually absorb one industry after the other, until the whole will be in the hands of the people." In August the editors were cheered by international developments. A British publication, *Brotherhood*, had proposed its own version of the new corporation.

The ecumenical nature of the *Twentieth Century* and the openness of the People's Cooperative Trust to a variety of proposals was reflected in the indecisive and even contradictory nature of the magazine's views of radicalism. They embraced Marx, Engels, Gillette, and the power and creativity, as O'Loughlin put it, of the middle classes. The mild socialism to which he and many of the magazine's writers subscribed was a combination of attractive elements torn from the context of their original theories and combined into a new unwieldy whole. The tentative steps to create a world corporation reflected this ambiguity. The insurance project proved difficult and complicated, and was finally abandoned. The magazine then proposed a producer-consumer exchange, accepting shipments of eggs and other food products from the Midwest for orders by Eastern consumers. This highly impractical project was also quickly scuttled. Still the magazine kept faith in Gillette. As it noted in the fall of 1895, "The evils of the competitive system, so forcibly pointed out in 'Human Drift,' have been recognized by the majority of reform journals, and, where we were at first alone in our attack upon it, we are now supported by at least one hundred: but while all recognize the evil, the Twentieth Century alone seeks to apply the remedy."[9] This sanguine report was in fact very far from the truth. In the middle of 1896 the magazine forgot its plans for the reorganization of society and began a crusade to elect Bryan President of the United States. Gillette continued to write for the *Twentieth Century,* offering infrequent glimpses of his utopian society and its cybernated city, but even he was caught up by the Bryan enthusiasm.

By supporting Bryan, Gillette was forced to contradict his own political—or anti-political—principles. To overcome his previous disparagement of politics, he simply surrounded the meaning of the election with apocryphal rhetoric. In August 1896, for example, he wrote that a "higher civilization" would be born with the election: "It is an epoch-making period in the history of man—the turning point from a government of injustice and crime to one of material equality and united intelligence." Even after Bryan's disheartening defeat, Gillette continued to write in praise of political reform movements. The ballot box, he argued in his second short book (called, appropriately, *The Ballot Box*) , was a good way to achieve reform and to employ the "magic wand of intelligence." If a truly progressive political party were to appear, he predicted, the masses of men would be drawn within the "circle of its radiance and truth."[10]

Despite this growing flirtation with politics, Gillette's paramount interest was to embellish his arguments for a corporate society. He still feared the chaos of the early 1890's, with its unemployment, class struggle, and violence, though his prediction of disaster had been wrong. Thus he returned to the theme of centralization and coordination after Bryan's defeat. The immediate need for social planning in 1897, he wrote, could be solved through a national government employment law with a guaranteed daily wage of $1.50. He proposed a program of public works to sustain the unemployed who had been dismissed from work through technological unemployment or underconsumption. This ameliorative program would force society to take a step toward "final centralization." The objections of workingmen to the consolidation of industry was a complicated question, for, as Gillette wrote, this centralization was the major cause of unemployment. A guaranteed wage would end the dangers of unemployment and convince workingmen of the need for technical and organizational innovations. Then the irresistible social law of centralization would complete its work, and the physical and material world of production would be reduced to an absolute science.[11]

In *Ballot Box*, published in 1897, and two derivative articles in the *Twentieth Century*, Gillette completed the first statement of his reform ideas. Shortly afterward he began working to perfect and manufacture his razor invention. His next book on reform did not appear until 1910, when he published a work called *World Corporation*. But a friend and fellow inventor, Melvin L. Severy of Boston, carried on Gillette's work, publishing two books, in 1907 and 1908, extolling the consolidation of industry as a system of reform. Severy was a minor novelist, a mystery writer, and an inventor, and he shared Gillette's belief that all the world's ills could be cured if men applied their intelligence to problem-solving. Severy's interest in the centralization of all business resulted in two massive manuscripts. The first, *Gillette's Social Redemption,* was a huge catalogue, almost a dictionary of the evils of modern industrial society. The second was *Gillette's Industrial Solution,* which demonstrated how those evils might be dissolved through the centralization of business and society.

Severy, like Gillette, was descended from an old Massachusetts family. He had invented and marketed his own printing devices. Like Gillette, too, he moved to Los Angeles before World War I. At about the same time Gillette sought out Upton Sinclair, Severy became interested in politics and joined the Social Democratic League, which had broken with the Socialist party. As he wrote to John Spargo in 1917, he had always leaned toward socialism, though he refused Spargo's offer to become the League's organizer in Los Angeles.

Severy's discussion of the Gillette system was an exaggeration of the already remarkable claims Gillette had made for his ideas. Yet Severy was still able to find significant parallels for his interpretations in contemporary reform writings. He blamed most of the evils of modern industrial life on trusts, monopolies, and ruthless competition. But he also saw salvation in the very corruption that had done so much to disrupt the economic fabric. The trust, he wrote, "like fire is a good *servant* but a bad *master*." Like many of his contemporaries, Severy picked a thread of economic order out of the tangled social crises of his day. He demonstrated the need to hurry the evolution of the corporation, and rejected any fundamental assault upon this form of economic organization. Quantitative change, in other words, would become qualitative change once society was completely organized into one vast corporation.[12]

The second volume of Severy's work spoke to Gillette's concrete plans for social reorganization, as well as to a number of favorite subjects of collectivism. The book examined the problem of the survival of the fittest and those sociological hypotheses derived from struggle. It described reform projects in terms of social evolution and with analogies to natural organization. Its sources were almost entirely the writings of collectivists, including Charlotte Perkins Gilman, James MacKaye, John Graham Brooks, William James Ghent, and Edmond Kelly. Severy called his system a social democracy and expressed admiration for Marx and Proudhon, but his version of reform strayed widely from European socialism. He was actually expressing the essential ideals of collectivism in Gillette's simplified, nonpolitical way.

Severy's concern, as Gillette's had been, was to liberate man through the creation of orderly, rational production. Social evils, no matter how base, were neither inevitable nor intentional. They resulted from an irrational system of individualism, unnaturally visited upon many but easy to suspend. Society needed merely to turn back to the analogies of nature, and by implication to Christianity, to derive new social laws that would work to restore the ethic of the Golden Rule. This new system would lift from humanity "those shackles which now prevent it from moving serenely with the cosmic current."

Severy's ideas were derivative, and catalogued rather than argued. He combined a labor theory of value, a denunciation of money interest, a faith in the referendum and recall, and a hatred of individualistic competition with an admiration for the corporate form, a strong attraction to Bellamy's utopian writings, a plea for Esperanto, a desire to liberate women, and, above all, a wish to implement Gillette's curious urban vision. Every social goal, he wrote, in a book curiously bursting with optimism, could be attained by manipulating the present structure of society. The most distinctive part of the Gillette plan was "that it meets the regime now existing without the slightest abruptness of gradation. It starts with affairs as they exist and, through an evolution as carefully graded as the colors of the spectrum, an ultimate result which is revolutionary in the extreme."[13] Gillette's utopia, in other words, was legal, and could be realized within existing laws. "Do you not long to be a pilgrim thither?" he asked at the end.

By 1910, King Gillette himself returned to active reform work in another attempt to found a United Corporation. Success as an entrepreneur had not changed his mind about the need to reform society, nor his belief in the salvation of incorporation. But his sense of social emergency was diminished. In his new book, *World Corporation,* he persisted in his earlier proposal of a utopian city. All social problems, he still argued, could be solved by eliminating competition and accepting the social organization that was demanded by nature and by industry. If anything, in the years since his last book he seemed to have developed an even stronger faith in the corporation. He was better acquainted with the important examples of centralized production and more impressed than ever with such corporations as United States Steel and Standard Oil. U.S. Steel, he wrote, was so advanced that it had become almost the kind of military order he greatly admired: "In everything but name it is Military, as everything should be that involves operations of numbers of people who are combined together for a specific purpose." The whole organization was also a meritocracy, with intelligent men rising to the top on the basis of their contributions to the company. The benefits of military organization (which had impressed a number of reformers) were more than the incidental results of centralization. Militarism expressed the kind of order that Gillette sought. It provided the metaphors to describe the perfectly coordinated, reformed society, just as analogies to the anthill and the beehive had suggested the proper sociological models to Gillette's friend Melvin Severy.

By 1910, Gillette had also changed the tone of his writing. His feelings of social outrage were tempered. Although he was still an avid opponent of competition, the less dramatic evils of laissez-faire capitalism now distressed him equally, especially its waste of resources and human capacity. The corporate society would eliminate such excesses by ending ownership for profit and substituting ownership with responsibility. Under this new system, the true progressive minds in industry —the specialists and scientists—would direct the economy. Industry and its divisions, labor and management, would become machinelike in their perfection: "The real machine, the Materialized Embodiment of Millions of Minds, Centralized and Working in Harmony, will be so wonderful and so beautiful in its mechanism, that only its Realization can bring it within Range of our Comprehension."[14]

Gillette had also worked out a new plan for achieving the corporate society. As before, a single business would absorb all competing industries. But this time the company would be a combination mutual fund and holding company, and not the producing corporation Gillette had suggested in the 1890's. His new world corporation would purchase dividend-bearing stocks and in this manner gradually gain control of one industry after another. He incorporated his company in Arizona in 1910, shortly before the publication of his book, and carefully reproduced for his readers the documents of incorporation. Then he offered former President Theodore Roosevelt the presidency of the corporation for four years at a salary of $1,000,000. Roosevelt declined. But Gillette still hoped to market his stock for one dollar a share, and he even made plans to begin a corporate political party and to publish a newspaper entitled *World Corporation News*.

Without the enthusiastic backing he had had in the 1890's, Gillette's Arizona company quickly melted away. By World War I he had moved to California, no longer active in the management of the razor company, and wholeheartedly involved in the real estate boom around Los Angeles. But he still held on to his dream. With the help of Upton Sinclair, he published his final statement of reform theory in 1924 in *People's Corporation.*

In his autobiography, Sinclair wrote mockingly of Gillette, who, he recalled, first came to visit him at the end of the war and announced himself by wrapping a hundred-dollar bill around his calling card. Sinclair also recalled that Gillette paid him to help revise the manuscript of *People's Corporation* during long, directionless sessions. Sinclair helped to convince Horace Liveright to publish the book, with Gillette contributing $25,000 for advertising. Sinclair also arranged a meeting between Henry Ford and Gillette to discuss the relative merits of each other's reform projects. The result, he wrote, was like the collision of two billiard balls.[15] In all, Sinclair's picture of Gillette was one of a gentle crank. While perhaps true, this story omitted two important aspects. One was Sinclair's genuine enthusiasm for the Gillette plan; the second was the long and interesting friendship that developed between the two men in the twenties and early thirties.

By 1919, Sinclair wrote to J. G. Phelps Stokes about his discovery of Gillette: "King C. Gillette, the razor man, has a plan for social reconstruction which I think is very remarkable. I have been helping him to get his manuscript into shape and have boiled it down to one hundred and ten typewritten pages. I should be deeply interested to hear your opinion of it, and I am taking the liberty of sending you a copy." Stokes was hardly enthusiastic, and wrote back dismissing the plan, recalling that Gillette had already sent him Severy's two-volume explanation of the world corporation. Still, Sinclair continued to work with Gillette on the manuscript, and according to Marie Dell, wife of the author Floyd Dell, he portrayed Gillette as a sympathetic character in his novel *100 Per Cent.*[16]

During the ten or twelve years of their friendship, Gillette and Sinclair kept up an interesting correspondence in which Gillette explained the source of his reform ideas and the reasons for his tenacious optimism. All the while he continued to talk about his new book of proposals for a world corporation. When it finally appeared, *People's Corporation,* in which Sinclair had become something of a silent partner, was fundamentally a restatement of Gillette's original plans for the corporate absorption of the world's business and the end of its social woes. They were modified only by Gillette's recognition of contemporary reform movements in industry. He was intrigued by new plans for scientific management and consequently placed greater emphasis upon managerial techniques. He also felt compelled to spell out the governmental structures of his new society more carefully than before, and added a discussion of his proposed Corporate Congress. He was more explicit about the powers to be granted to the world corporation and about the future role of ownership.

People's Corporation attracted little attention and ignited no movement. Despite its disappointing reception, Gillette often spoke of revising his plans, but he never did. One commentator who was fascinated by Gillette's book was Stuart Chase, then a young writer. Chase thought Gillette had written a compelling book, but that he had missed a significant point by ignoring the psychological aspects of social control in modern society: "His sincerity is compelling and deep; his analysis of the industrial jungle is shrewd and imaginative, but his solution is quite untouched by the realities which guard the road to Utopia."[17] Gillette's plan, Chase implied, was out of touch with the interests of social reformers who by the 1920's were suspicious of projects that avoided politics or ignored the literature on the psychology of work and politics being written by Walter Lippmann, Ordway Tead, and others. What Gillette found wrong was nonetheless appealing, and his suggestion that the solution to industrial problems lay in more industry and better organization reaffirmed the ideas of that intellectual tradition which claimed Chase among its adherents. Perhaps Gillette's most astute remark was on the function of proper management: "The manager will sweep away all forms of waste; class struggle, wars, industrial depressions, unemployment, middlemen, idle classes, living on unearned incomes, insurance, salesmanship, finance, advertising and crime."[18] Here was an oversimplified but accurate statement of the collectivist claim for the new science of management and the new social science.

After *People's Corporation,* Gillette spent the remainder of his years developing real estate holdings and working on his ranch at Calabasas, north of Los Angeles. He was never again an active reformer, but he continued to discuss his ideas with Upton Sinclair. Nothing shook his faith that some movement like his own would inevitably turn the industrial revolution into a social revolution. He continued to believe that progress and order would bring a utopia which substituted merit for class. As he wrote to Sinclair in 1919, he did not believe in a system where everyone was treated alike. A secure society "must be founded on justice and justice can only be based on ambition and individual intelligence and equality can only be attained where differences in position are automatically adjusted throughout the system." Two years later he expressed what had become a firm faith in the progress of mankind, a faith which obviously underlay his theory of the world corporation. Without the assurance that progress was automatic and history the unfolding of a higher good, belief in the evolution of society would be meaningless. "Life," Gillette wrote, "has always advanced to a higher plane—with the passage of every second of time—never has life gone backward—for that which constitutes progress is knowledge of nature and nature's laws —and this is never lost, when once gained—and the whole process is brought about through pain—through sensation. We have walking with us every moment two companions— one we seek to avoid—it is pain—the other we are seeking to grasp—it is the sensation of happiness."[19] Through a kind of dialectic of pleasure and pain, Gillette predicted that society would reach higher and higher levels of civilization and organization.

After 1925, Gillette was deeply discouraged by his personal failure in the world of reform. Perhaps as a cipher for himself, he urged Sinclair to enter politics on a platform devoted to humanity. He also softened his own dispute with American society, or clarified what he had otherwise been arguing for many years: "I now realize more than ever the need of ideals and idealists to mold public thought and opinion—but I do not believe that the overthrow of the present system, by either war or drastic confiscation, is desirable. What we need is a better understanding of those elements of our system that are fundamental and tending toward that which we seek, a system dominated and controlled by natural law." Still, Gillette's optimism was overwhelming: "I have become fully convinced that life as a whole is moving rapidly to a higher and higher plane—that knowledge is accumulating with a rapidity never before known in the world's history—and that the leavening of the great mass is gradually coming about."[20]

In this context, Gillette considered the Russian Revolution a strange but compelling example of the possibilities of a corporate society. Russia in 1930, he wrote, was on the verge of taking steps that would make it the most advanced country in the world. He regretted, he told Sinclair, that other nations had not sought and achieved the same goals by "corporation," which was "nature's means of organization and centralization." Later he proposed to publish a conversation in letters between Sinclair and himself, "from a Socialist to a Corporationist," which would discuss the tactics he had observed in Russia. Perhaps inspired by the social relevance of reform in the early 1930's, he also spoke fleetingly of reviving his plan for a world corporation.[21]

As his health failed in the last few years of his life, Gillette set aside his writing plans. He followed the Soviet experiment with great interest, interpreting it as another response to the same forces that in the United States had created the corporation. He was troubled by the immense problems which he felt the Soviets would have, but nonetheless predicted that they would complete a new society, far surpassing the United States by 1955.

In one of his last letters to Sinclair, in 1932, Gillette expressed the wish to tell his own life story, with its two distinct but simultaneous phases of business and reform. Shortly afterward he died, leaving his reform work unfinished and his understanding of the two separate parts of his life unresolved. He had scarcely begun to understand the reform principles which he had absorbed and recorded, nor had he gained much perspective on his own efforts since the middle 1890's. He had idealized the business structure in which he had worked successfully, but his understanding of corporations remained superficial. Yet there was nothing essentially unresolved about Gillette's life: though business and reform were two different activities, they both involved the same institutions and assumptions. Gillette transformed the structure of the corporation he had helped to create into the outlines of a utopia. He took the main propositions of collectivist thought and constructed from them a curious solution to the industrial crisis he sensed about him. He thought little about these propositions, and refined them only slightly from their cruder origins in the economic forms he had helped to create. He wrote literally about the new industrial model which other collectivists depicted in subtle or complex forms, as the writings of Charles Steinmetz will reveal in the next chapter. Yet Gillette anticipated the importance of the economic institutions that inspired collectivists, and which many of them argued would be the key social forms of the future.

Charles Steinmetz and the Science of Industrial Organization

INVENTOR, resident intellectual for General Electric, socialist, reformer, a shrewd, naive, wizened little man, Charles Proteus Steinmetz has for the most part been the captive of inspirational literature for boys. Better than the novels of Horatio Alger ever conceived, the life of Steinmetz seems to illustrate the marvels of social mobility. His biography is the story of a misshapen, German-speaking immigrant with a suspicious socialist background, who was hired by a major American corporation and ultimately given his own laboratory where he could smoke cigars against the rules and play practical electric jokes on his friends, while on his own time he could even become socialist head of the school board in Schenectady, New York.[1]

This smoothed-out boys' life of Steinmetz is probably true in terms of the known anecdotes about him. Yet it does not especially illustrate the benevolence of corporations, nor does it say much about Steinmetz. But the emphasis upon General Electric is apt, for if anything, Steinmetz's life dramatized—even in its eccentricities—the immense importance of the new forms of industrial organization at the turn of the century. Even his socialism in later years was a thinly veneered version of the collectivist and corporate society. General Electric depended enormously upon Steinmetz for his help in perfecting the electric motor, and granted him a corporate home in his adopted land. In return, Steinmetz accepted the corporation as the fundamental institution of a reformed society, and made it his admired social model, an extended family of social and economic relations. He called for an America that would be a hard-headed, practical man's version of Gillette's utopia.

Steinmetz was born in Breslau, Germany, on April 9, 1865, a crippled, ill-formed infant. His father was a railroad worker and his grandparents were innkeepers. Raised primarily by his grandmother, he apparently took eagerly to school. His father encouraged an interest in science and mathematics. Fortunately for his later career, the nearby University of Breslau, which Steinmetz eventually attended, was one of the few in Germany to offer courses in electricity. Although he intended at first to be an engineer, he took all theoretical courses at the university, working at home on experiments which he wrote up. He also joined the local mathematics club and began in his spare time to develop a personal system of shorthand which he later perfected and used extensively in his notes.

While at the University of Breslau, Steinmetz made friends with a number of student socialists and decided to join the German Social Democratic party. This decision was a momentous one, for it ultimately forced him to change the direction of his life. While he worked for his science degree, he also attended socialist meetings near the campus. There is no reason to agree with most of his biographers, however, that this political commitment was somehow fortuitous—or that seen through the dust of World War I it was an excusable confrontation with Bismarck's Germany. The evidence from Steinmetz's later life indicates that socialism was an intense and not a passing interest, and that whatever he meant by the term, he always sought a profound rearrangement of social relations, even while he lived in the United States. When police arrested his socialist friends in Breslau who were editing a small journal called the *People's Voice,* Steinmetz agreed to take up their precarious work on the paper. This marked him with the authorities, and soon he was warned to flee the country or face arrest. Thus, shortly after he had completed his work for a doctorate degree in 1888, Steinmetz left Germany. With the ruse of a short holiday to Switzerland, he crossed the border to Zurich.[2]

For the young Steinmetz, Zurich offered few opportunities. Within a year, with encouragement from a friend, he decided to emigrate to the United States. He arrived in 1889 with little money and almost no usable English. He was able to acquire a job with another German immigrant, named Eickemeyer, who owned a small electrical company in New York City. While working with Eickemeyer, he Americanized his name Karl to Charles, and added the middle name Proteus. He also began an active participation in the American Institute of Electrical Engineers. In 1892 he delivered to the group his famous paper on the Law of Hysteresis, and quickly became known as one of the most important electrical scientists in the country. His electrical theory solved several important questions about the use of electric motors, and brought him recognition in the scientific and business worlds as the man who had perfected the electric motor.

In 1892 and 1893 the new General Electric Company was acquiring a stable of scientists and patents by purchasing small electrical firms. To get Steinmetz, GE bought out Eickemeyer. Steinmetz was enthusiastic about the new company and first went to work at the GE plant at Lynn, Massachusetts. In 1894, when the company moved its headquarters to Schenectady, New York, Steinmetz made that upstate New York city his permanent home. As one of his biographers blithely remarks, from then on his "life story is written on a General Electric letterhead."

At General Electric, Steinmetz presided over his own laboratory, a rare situation in the days of young, parsimonious corporations. He also developed the eccentricities that have embellished the stories of his life. Most of these—for example, his habit of dumping visitors out of a canoe at his Mohawk River retreat, or literally shocking visitors to his laboratory—seem to have been pranks that allowed him to establish an equality between himself and outsiders.

Besides granting him an extraordinary degree of freedom, General Electric enveloped Steinmetz with experience in the corporation. His life was virtually defined in terms of that institution, and he inevitably made a place for this experience in his writings about socialism. While at GE, Steinmetz began a series of political and educational activities which gave practical meaning to the political writings he published before and during World War I. He experimented with forms of employee education and took time out from work to teach at Union College. He entered local politics and served as president of the Schenectady school board in the administration of socialist mayor George Lunn. His last political venture was an unsuccessful candidacy for New York State Engineer and Surveyor in 1922 for the Socialist and Farmer-Labor parties.[3] Whatever skepticism he may have had about American socialist politics, he remained a member of the party throughout World War I, and served on the advisory council of the socialist publication the *New Review*. Simultaneously, he was a member of the American Association for Labor Legislation and the American Proportional Representation League, both respectable reform groups.

Steinmetz's beliefs occasionally led beyond eccentricity to expressions of unpopular sentiments, but these did not always involve his socialism. At the beginning of World War I, he openly voiced sympathy for the Germans, though he later modified this stand and eventually offered his scientific services to the American government for ballistics work.[4] Later, in 1922, he wrote to Lenin offering to help with the electrification of the Soviet Union, and he was sufficiently interested in the Russian experiment to serve as an adviser for the Kuzbas Colony in the USSR in the same year.

One of his last and most grandiose plans was to stop Niagara Falls and harness its power to turn electrical generators. Before this idea could be very widely discussed, Steinmetz was dead. As one of his friends from General Electric later wrote, his laboratory had been like a New Atlantis: "He was peculiarly a product of the General Electric Company, and it was through him, with his magnetic personality and gift of expression, that its spirit first became widely familiar. . . . I again express the hope that a soul will be perceptible in the corporation of which I have been moved to write."[5] For some, Steinmetz evidently embodied that soul.

Beyond his practical contributions to GE, probably one of the reasons that the company tolerated Steinmetz, and even encouraged the stories of his odd habits, was the corporate image that Steinmetz helped to create. GE fed him, paid him, encouraged his work, allowed him to experiment, to play even, and to find friends. As it seemed to his friend John T. Broderick of GE and to the public that knew about him, the corporation was not an impersonal organization but an assembly of people. Using his unique relationship with the corporation, Steinmetz illustrated with his own life the possibilities of this economic institution. Like many other collectivist reformers of his day, he became convinced that business organization contained the embryo of a whole new society—reformed, efficient, and meritocratic.

Steinmetz variously called his social theories "cooperation" or socialism, but there was little of the orthodox socialist in him, even though he had once belonged to the German Social Democratic party and continued to support the American Socialist party. As early as 1893 he wrote dubiously of American socialism: "The Social Democratic Party here consists mainly of people who want to make the world over and who not only do not find it worth their while to gain knowledge of conditions here, but do not even bother to learn the language of the country." While he did join the American Socialist party and remained an active member, by 1915 and 1916, when he was busy writing on social theory, socialism had become to him a convenient, if vague, label for a theory of collectivism. He had worked too long in the corporation not to see or be impressed by the organizational possibilities of modern business. In the lives of successful inventors and engineers like himself, and in the history of industrial society, he saw the almost inevitable aggregation of socialist ideas. As he suggested in 1915, "Assuming now that society, as organized in a national or international government—a more efficient government indeed than our present—sets aside a part of all the product for use in starting further production. That is, production pays a tax which is used by society to finance further production." The result would be the end of private enterprise and the beginning of socialism. There was no impossible division between this future and the present of 1915: "How this will be brought about in the natural development of our industrial civilization, nobody can predict." But he imagined several ways: ". . . gradually by the dropping rate of interest, or by the increasing strength and ability, and the increasing entrance of the government into the industries as competitor with private capital, or by the extension of the principle of supervision and control by governmental commissions, etc."[6] Regardless of the different possibilities he saw, his most important argument was that socialism would come through the natural development of industry, that is, that socialism existed in the social relations and functions of the modern corporation.

What Steinmetz called socialism was a stage of evolution immediately beyond competitive capitalism, and a system of economic relationships which had already begun to be apparent in the world of business. Yet economics defined only a portion of the new society. Trailing behind industrial progress, he wrote, would be new social arrangements, where "self interest becomes public interest." Society would be free from anti-social actions and thus identical with "Christianity as taught by Jesus." Like a great many of his contemporaries, Steinmetz defined society first in terms of its economic relationships, even though he was deeply interested in social reform. Socialism, he argued, had nothing to do with particular forms of government, anymore than capitalism represented a system of class oppression. Capitalism was institutionalized inefficiency and competition; from its malevolent arrangement came the patterns of social behavior that produced poverty, unemployment, and crime.[7]

Steinmetz saw in his own scientific efforts, and those of his fellow engineers and inventors, a new and truly humane socializing force. Science and invention, he wrote, would be an outstanding characteristic of a socialist society; they would not die, as the upholders of laissez faire gloomily predicted. Steinmetz saw in his own work with electricity a distinct social message. As he told a church gathering in 1922 in Schenectady, ". . . Engineering is the application of science to the science of man, and so today science is the foundation not only of our prosperity, but of our very existence, and this necessarily has become the dominating power in our human society." Science could not prove or disprove the existence of God, Steinmetz confessed, but it might do something more important by creating the basis for a modern society.

As a scientist, Steinmetz felt he could understand the relationships between natural law and sociology. In a curious way he also believed in the survival of the fittest. As he wrote to a friend in Washington, "I am, and always have been, very much interested in this family of plants [cactus] for various reasons, not the least of which is their pronounced illustration of the laws of evolution and survival of the fittest." But he made it clear elsewhere that survival of the fittest meant to him the survival of intelligence and favorable social arrangements. As he warned in 1916, if America did not have a cooperative revolution, it would die economically. "Such is fate, such is the law of evolution."

The predominant importance of intelligence was best illustrated, Steinmetz wrote, in the national organizations of scientists and engineers. The scientific community, like the corporation, demonstrated the characteristics of advanced social evolution. Throughout his life Steinmetz was active in several scientific groups, and was elected president of the American Institute of Electrical Engineering in 1902.[8] The cooperative work of these scientific societies and his own disinterested research at the General Electric laboratory seemed proof to Steinmetz that men could work together in programs dedicated to human progress. In the scientific societies, in his lab, there was no need for politics or classes or organized religions; so too the reformed society might be free from these artificial divisions. Only truth and merit need count, as Steinmetz's own life testified. In the scientific world, physical handicaps were irrelevant, and nothing prevented a man such as Steinmetz from becoming one of its leading citizens.

Thus Steinmetz took the two social models he knew best, the corporation and the scientific community, and from them derived an ideal vision of the future which he described in *America and the New Epoch*. In this book he combined the notion of efficiency with an active scientific commitment to truth, identifying both traits as the best characteristics of the new society. Together with some later writings, *America and the New Epoch* contains the core of Steinmetz's social theory and offers a unique variation on collectivist thinking.

That these writings appeared between 1916 and 1918 helps to explain the edge of urgency they all exhibit. Steinmetz was of two minds about the struggle in Europe. He sympathized with Germany at first, admitting that he had always admired aspects of German social organization. But in the long run the war became further proof of the direction of social evolution, and not merely a question of good versus evil. As he told the American Institute of Electrical Engineers in 1916, "Whatever may be the military results of the war, the issue for which the war has been fought—co-operative industrial organization against industrial individualism—that issue has been decided."[9]

Steinmetz was sure that efforts to resurrect competition in the United States after the war would be ill-fated and even destructive. Competition as an evolutionary force had been replaced by organization and cooperation. The once creative chaos of individualism had become, in the twentieth century, destructive disorder: "And its place had naturally to be taken by a corporation." In an article for *Collier's* magazine in 1916, Steinmetz detailed the burdensome effects of economic competition. One was underconsumption, followed by depressing overproduction. Even the competitive model of laissez faire, he wrote, would be undercut by an inefficient price system which drove companies to commit competitive suicide in times of depression. Severe economic problems, Steinmetz concluded, could be solved only by institutions such as the corporation which eliminated competition. Steinmetz casually suggested that to achieve a new society, "All that is necessary is to extend methods of economic efficiency from the individual corporation to the national organism as a whole." Yet he was at the same time wary about the prospects of achieving this goal: "It presupposes a powerful, centralized government of competent men, remaining continuously in office, and no political government of this kind can exist in the America of to-day—nor in the America of tomorrow."[10]

Contemporary America was undergoing vast changes, but they were most apparent in the structure of corporations. The Robber Barons, who had set dramatic organizational precedents in their drive to maximize profits, were now dying out: "... Industrially, socially, politically they are a negligible factor, they are no part of our national and industrial life, and are being rapidly exterminated by race suicide." Established industries had developed complex series of relationships—productive, administrative, financial, and even social. In effect, the corporation had become a miniature society. And here, precisely, was how the corporation might use its potential as a model for a better society. If it failed to do so, Steinmetz argued, the corporation would remain incompletely developed. American corporations did not appreciate their social potential or anticipate new concepts of industrial citizenship. As Steinmetz wrote in 1922, "It is necessary to eliminate the strained relations between employer and employee which now exist to such a great extent and periodically bring about warfare and to replace them by a system of orderly cooperation." On the whole, responsibility for realizing these more perfect corporate organizations would rest with managers and engineers who, Steinmetz believed, ought to use their power and influence to end disruptive practices in industry.[11]

Steinmetz did not ignore the faults of industry, but they were far less important to him than the corporation's impressive potential for social organization. He thought that if several reforms which he proposed were realized, including better job security and unemployment compensation for workers, a new industrial patriotism would appear within the factory. All the elements of a small society would be evident within its boundaries. The reformed corporation would barely resemble older forms of industrial organization.

New principles of political science and sociology would also flow from the corporate form. Steinmetz was able to illustrate the possible interchanges between industrial organizations and political institutions because he so convincingly described corporations as political societies and not as moneymaking organizations. In most corporations, he noted, management was reelected year after year; elections had become perfunctory. "Thus the corporation government is continuous and thereby efficient." Local political government could become just as efficient if the merit tenure system of the corporation were adopted and frequent elections abandoned, thus continuing "the same men as long as they are reasonably satisfactory after picking out good and efficient men at first." Efficiency was, above all, the prime attribute of leaders who would achieve social progress.

For national government Steinmetz proposed more of the same. It might be difficult to imagine such a government in America, he admitted, but the corporation and the national scientific societies could be used as models to create a new, efficient government. Guidelines of efficiency—to eliminate duplication, for example—would represent an important step forward in reform. Another would be the nationalization of industries such as the railroads, canals, pipe lines, and telephone and telegraph companies. By controlling major corporations and directing their activities, the federal government would become, in effect, a gigantic holding company. As Steinmetz told a meeting of the National Electric Light Association in 1916, "The function of our national government thus is to codify what has been worked out as the best practice by State societies, national societies, local societies, individuals, by industries, corporations and the individual producer."[12]

This kind of national government would be organized like a corporation; its functions would reflect the priorities of efficiency, good management, and invention. The resulting state would be neutral and unbiased in dealing with its constituent parts, just as any efficient corporation had to be. For Steinmetz, this was the context for a democratic society. Like other collectivist thinkers, he avoided a political definition of democracy, nowhere citing the importance of political action or articulated systems of political organization. Instead, he defined democracy as meritocracy, and, by implication, as freedom with a just form of social and economic mobility. The government of the ideal society would include the best and most qualified men, chosen not by election but by a merit system. They would rise through the management ranks of industrial organizations to become a political elite. These experts,

Steinmetz contended, would form the membership of an industrial senate. The only political branch of government in the
new society would be confined to a Tribuniciate, which would
hold veto power over the activities of the industrial senate.
The implication was clear: positive government would come
from industrial self-management, and politics would limit this
function only in narrow ways.

Like other collectivists, Steinmetz believed in the democracy of general social mobility, and opposed the more pessimistic, tentative conception of freedom defined by laissez
faire. For him, democracy indicated the good society, and he
opposed all forms of government that restricted a "concert of
effort to secure increased leisure through a reduction of the
cost of our material wants. . . ." Thus stability, organization,
administration, and, above all, the relationships that existed
within the corporation would typify the new society. If not, he
warned, "either we enter the coming co-operative industrial
production, or we fall by the wayside. . . ." Steinmetz's clearly
drawn functional democracy was probably what attracted
such critics as Randolph Bourne, who wrote warmly of
Steinmetz's political analysis of the corporation.[13]

The practical side of Steinmetz's writing was an emphasis
on public education, through which he hoped to prepare managers and workers for their new roles in the corporation and
to speed the coming of the "new epoch." In the light of his
analysis, Steinmetz argued that the most pressing social problem of his day was the deterioration of the educational system
in the face of industrial specialization. The schools were fail-
ing to prepare citizens to face change. A small minority of men
had always ruled the country, he told the Commission on Industrial Relations in 1916, but now the masses clamored to
participate. But who was preparing them for leadership?

Steinmetz's warning about the need for comprehensive
modern education was only one statement in a larger debate
about industrial education and about the content of public
education. Before World War I, when he advanced his educational ideas and worked to accomplish reforms, there were a
number of acute educational problems in America. Rapid industrialization demanded new curricula for teaching indus-

trial functions. Management specialization and the realization that the laboring force was increasingly split between skilled and unskilled workers forced educators, business executives, and reformers to re-evaluate the public schools. To meet the demand for special administrative and business skills, a number of business schools were founded in private and state universities. Very few such schools existed before 1900, but by 1925 there were 183 institutions offering some form of advanced business training.[14]

Three groups fought to monopolize apprenticeship training: unions, corporations, and advocates of vocational education who thought that the secondary and sometimes even the primary schools ought to provide such training. If the state undertook this training, there was still a dilemma: who should control the teaching and the subject matter of special schools? Furthermore, as men like Steinmetz repeatedly asked, what would America be like if it gave industrial training to some young people and broader cultural training to others? Would this not create an educational class system? No matter what the form of one's citizenship in the corporation, as worker or manager, education for that role, Steinmetz felt, was crucial.

Businessmen did not always have confidence in the ability of educators to solve their own problems. A book written in 1903 by R. T. Crane, which drew on data compiled from a questionnaire sent to prominent educators and businessmen, reflected the prevailing dissension and confusion about education for managerial roles in modern industrial society. Many college presidents, Crane concluded, had not even begun to think about the relation of classical education to modern industrial training. This illustrated, he decided, a profound lack of business sense among educators.

The largest question facing educators as well as corporations interested in management training was, quite simply, how did one train a successful and creative executive? James Young, director of the Wharton School in Pennsylvania, writing in 1906 for a symposium in the *Annals* of the American Academy of Political and Social Science, admitted the corporation's urgent need for experts and managers. The function of university education, he noted, ought to be the teaching of broad scientific principles in business and the preparation of students for the general profession of management. The entrepreneur H. J. Hapgood agreed. The best way to create a good businessman, he argued, was through training. In 1912, however, Herman Schneider, dean of the College of Engineering at the University of Cincinnati, qualified such educational optimism. The results of his program at Cincinnati, he reported, indicated that natural business leaders could be trained—but not created. Thus Cincinnati had initiated a program to educate selected candidates chosen for their promise by local industries.[15]

Financier Frank Vanderlip, in a collection of speeches and articles published in 1907, suggested that educators had been largely ineffective in business training. He called for a central fund to administer business training in the nation, to reward good schools and eliminate ineffective ones. Educators were far too narrow in their outlook to be allowed to monopolize education. For Vanderlip, the question of good management education and proper industrial training was far more important than merely finding a quota of good managers or skillful workers. The health of the nation was at stake. Educated men, capable in commercial life, were needed to cope with a rapidly changing society: "The forces of combination—the labor union and the trusts—are united and are working in harmony to accomplish at least one thing. They are united in a tendency to make commercial or industrial automatons of a great percentage of our population." The schools could counteract this trend if only teachers would instruct students in the proper scientific approach to business and finance.[16]

Steinmetz was aware of the range of questions and proposals relating to education in modern society. His own answers would, he felt, help to achieve the potential of such institutions as the corporation. For Steinmetz there were two forms of citizenship in modern society, and therefore two varieties of education. One was civic and cultural, and carried on in the public schools; the other was industrial and mechanical, and might well take place in the corporation or in special business schools.

Steinmetz had long experience in selecting and training experts in electrical engineering. During his years at General Electric he had taught courses in electricity at nearby Union College, and had helped to recruit scientists for the company. His resulting view of the college man was profoundly skeptical: ". . . To the college training there is one great drawback—that is, that the college trained man, especially when he leaves college, often thinks that he knows all, and since nobody else agrees with him in this respect he frequently is absolutely useless until the world has knocked thoroughly out of his head the idea that he knows anything." College training in itself was insufficient to prepare men to invent new processes or run corporations.

For those workers and ordinary citizens who would not become managers, Steinmetz wanted the kind of training that would not degrade them into an ignorant proletariat. He firmly opposed vocational education in the grade schools. As he told the Commission on Industrial Relations, vocational training ought to be available after eight years of general schooling, and ought not to be a substitute for the necessary knowledge that each citizen should acquire.[17] Thus he proposed that each fraction of the new industrial society acquire a practical and a classical education.

When Steinmetz addressed the Industrial Commission, he had just served two years as president of the school board of Schenectady, under the administration of socialist Mayor George Lunn. In this capacity, Steinmetz worked out some of the practical implications of his ideas on public education, and indicated the meaning of his commitment to socialism. In 1912, when Steinmetz became head of the school board, Schenectady had a moderately sized but growing school system. During his two-year tenure, Steinmetz was instrumental in planning for a new industrial high school. This technical school offered vocational training for boys and courses in "Home Arts and Sciences" for girls—but only after an initial education in eight grades of traditional subjects. Steinmetz helped to work out the controversial problem of control of the school by bringing in the labor unions and insisting that the school's advisory board include a representative of each trade to be taught, "such as the trades of Pattern Maker, Cabinet

Maker, Carpenter, Blacksmith, Foundry Man, etc." Theoretically, then, the school would not fall under the control of businessmen. Moreover, vested control in the school board itself
meant that technical education would be administered by unbiased educators who were elected to office by all of the
citizens.

Steinmetz's sympathies with the Socialist party occasionally
showed in his activities for the school board, but his socialism
scarcely gibed with the contemporary aims of the movement.
For him, socialism was a confluence of ideas which best described the dynamics of a modern social system. His handling
of petitions from local socialist groups while he was on the
school board reveals the extent to which he felt that socialism
was simply the best science of society. When a committee of the
Socialist party asked for special exercises in the schools on
May 1 "to emphasize the Ideals of International Peace, the
Abolition of War and the supreme value of International Solidarity among the workers as a means of emancipation from
Capitalistic Masters," Steinmetz approved. As the minutes of
the school board meeting recall, "The President stated that
this request was neither religious nor political and that such
Ideals should be encouraged." Somewhat later he permitted the
Socialist party to use empty schools on Saturday and Sunday
to hold Socialist Sunday Schools, so long as no political activities took place during the meetings.[18]

If socialism represented a scientific attitude toward society
for Steinmetz, then his other activities on the board can also
be viewed as pursuing this belief. His most important project
was to create healthy children, "symmetrical" children, as he
called them. He considered physical education a prerequisite
for intellectual development, and urged more adequate programs. To an inquiry about sex education sent to the board by
the Young People's Socialist League, he replied that it might
be tried by the schools as part of its commitment to train the
whole child: ". . . It is a privilege which belongs primarily to
the parents but since the vast majority of parents neglect this
duty then it follows that the State may well interfere."

The most extensive school project under Steinmetz was the
development of a child health program. A "Committee on

School Hygiene and Sanitation" was appointed to supervise the inspection of children and schools, and to look especially for contagious diseases, mental retardation, and any "physical defects which may serve as impediments to the Symmetrical development of the child." With the completion of this program, Steinmetz's term as president of the school board ended. His theories had emphasized the development of the whole child and a well-rounded education. He had introduced measures to test the health and development of children. He had approved projects to open the schools to all elements of the community, to make them meeting places for both Boy Scouts and socialists. In the development of high school industrial education he had insisted that trades be represented in overseeing instruction, and that the schools represent all elements of the industrial community. Public education, he had illustrated, ought to prepare citizens for a modern industrial community.[19]

Steinmetz also had a hand in the education of the other half of industry, the training of management and skilled workers. He was one of the early members of the National Association of Corporation Schools, the predecessor of the American Management Association and an organization joined by many of the largest manufacturing companies in the United States. The association was established in 1913 at a convention at New York University, and was to serve as a national clearinghouse for ideas and plans of management education and personnel training. Steinmetz was elected president of the group in 1914 and remained a member through the years of World War I.

The Association of Corporation Schools was created through the efforts of Lee Galloway, a professor at NYU in charge of management training courses, and F. C. Henderschott of the New York Edison Company, who had received national publicity because of his work in company training schools. Behind the activities of these men and a number of interested corporations lay a larger history of experimentation and writing about the problems of management training and selection. This literature ranged from tests for character analysis, intelligence, and temperament, to phrenology, to the kind of training program that such firms as General Electric had carried on for a number of years.[20] Reflecting the educational crisis of the day, the organization was explicitly critical of the public schools for the poor quality of education which they passed on to students, and for their useless training methods.

The Association of Corporation Schools intended to work in the vague area between public and private institutions which Steinmetz had once called the fourth dimension of the corporation. As founder Lee Galloway remarked in his speech to the first convention: "That seems to be the highest kind of insurance that any industrial corporation can have—to insure itself by creating a strong educational system among its own industrial forces, and if our big industries are to assume the proportions of states, with great power and large incomes, they must assume some of the responsibilities of states, and one of these responsibilities is to educate the people. . . ." Galloway, Henderschott, and Steinmetz all believed that the corporation had reached the point where it resembled a political state in its power and in the control it could exert over people's lives. As Steinmetz remarked to the first convention, pioneering work had already been done by private organizations to assume new public functions. The national engineering societies and sociological societies were examples for organizing "the welfare part of the human element in modern corporations."

If, as Steinmetz believed, the corporation was a miniature version of a future society, then the problems of citizenship in that corporation society were immensely important. Two of history's most pressing demands had to be solved first within the factory system. The first of these was social mobility; the factory had to guarantee a high degree of movement from inferior to superior positions. The second, which followed, was education. The corporation had to define its various functions and create an educational system that would prepare men to be skilled workers, foremen, and managers—to achieve, in other words, the social mobility they wanted. The decisive question about modern industrial organizations, Steinmetz wrote, was "How far and how fast can we go in transforming the factory into a real school, in which opportunity shall succeed opportunity for each worker to give expression to his passion to accomplish something, where all shall learn things by doing things, and learn as many things and as important things as each is capable of doing."[21]

Steinmetz proposed these corporate ethics before the Association of Corporation Schools, hoping that the organization would get behind the training of men and women for a new industrial citizenship. His analysis of the corporation was far more utopian than Galloway's had been, less self-consciously conservative, and more flexible. Outsiders to industry, he argued, understood very little of the development of the corporation and were apt to single out those errors which reflected human ignorance. But these critics should realize that "the corporation is still imperfect and growing, just as we find human beings not completely developed." Only the lingering hulks of a previous disorganization prevented the corporation from correcting its inequities: "It is the incomplete organization of the human activities which is the cause of most of the resentment against corporations. . . ." The creation of corporation schools could help to overcome this disorganization by training individuals to achieve their highest creativity. This would result in enormous inventiveness and innovation, for human creativity, he argued, was not the product of isolation or crankish inquiry.

In his address to the third annual convention of the organization, Steinmetz developed an intellectual justification for it that most members probably either misunderstood or discounted. He called the corporation the newest, most creative economic organization in history, and of all institutions most like the probable future. As he said, "I look forward to the time when the corporation will be mankind, those times when all mankind will form a cooperative industrial organization which in its initial crude form is represented by the modern corporation." The purpose of the association, it followed, was to speed that remarkable day by developing the human and social side of industrial life.[22]

Steinmetz's last address to the organization was a defense of his belief in the corporation and a warning about its role among other institutions in society. Corporations ought to provide apprentice training, continuing schools, and management instruction, he said, but they should not encroach upon the legitimate function of public education for everyone. Neither, he warned, should the association take a stand against labor unions or management organizations. The National Association of Corporation Schools, he concluded, ought, like the corporation itself, to be an ecumenical organization.

Although Steinmetz's interest in corporation schools exceeded the bounds of personnel management, the outbreak of World War I caused new discussion among his colleagues of the problems he had raised. E. W. Rice, Jr., president of General Electric, told the Association of Corporation Schools in 1917 that industry ought to model itself after the cooperative society, "from the president and executive officers down to the humblest wage earner." As the *Bulletin* of the organization declared in 1918, the war had brought forth a new form of social cooperation and marked a significant decline of individualism. The magazine quoted the president of Bethlehem Steel approvingly to support its belief that society was becoming collectivist: "Class it socialism, social revolution, Bolshevikism, or what you will, it is a leveling process, and means that the workman without property, who labors with his hands, is going to be the man who will dominate the world."[23] Other brief effects of the war were felt in discussions of Industrial Democracy, profit-sharing schemes, and Americanization education. Fundamentally, however, the organization remained committed to more mundane tasks of training personnel for sales positions or management, or developing employee selection devices. Steinmetz had suggested a larger meaning for these programs, but few members followed his visionary lead.

The strangeness of an admitted socialist as president of an influential management organization before World War I recedes when Steinmetz's political writings and his educational activities are seen as a whole. The corporation had become, to him, the potential cooperative commonwealth, in which scientific education and organization created a new form of industrial citizenship. After all, this was the sum of his own experience, which for its special circumstances could never be reproduced or universalized. Still, Steinmetz persisted in his hopes. The corporation had the undeveloped advantages as well as many of the existing problems of a political state. Education was the instrumentality for organizing this new society so as to effect maximum social mobility and create a class system based upon merit. Good and humane social behavior existed, Steinmetz felt, in those areas of the industrial world roped off from competition by corporate centralization. Whatever the future that evolved from these advanced economic species would be called, whether socialism or cooperation or state capitalism, the key to understanding that future would always be the corporation and its superb functional organization.

This view of the business world represented the autobiography of one strange and creative man who found there a mixture of the best social and scientific relationships. Steinmetz molded collectivist assumptions, which he had gained from his participation in building the new industrial order, and proposed a utopian state ruled by benevolent corporations and expert managers. He found the modern virtues of efficiency and merit-reward to be the very essence of the new industrial and social spirit of twentieth-century America, and he wished them for a whole nation still torn by labor strife and poverty. But he had also proven by the exceptional nature of everything he did how far this dream lay from reality.

William English Walling: The Pragmatic Critique of Collectivism

To THOSE WHO celebrated progress, the gathering of reform movements in the early twentieth century promised quick success and the immediate possibility of an industrial utopia. The institutions of the good society appeared to exist all around; only men stood in the way of their final evolution. In such flush times, there were nevertheless some who suspected this optimistic appraisal, who disliked the assumptions of the collectivist intellectuals, and who mocked the gentle band of reformers that assembled behind the "somewhat red banner" of collectivism. To William English Walling, those reformers who joyfully proclaimed a new society were menacing their own best intentions. Few of them, he felt, had honestly or deeply considered the meaning of the popular attack upon individualism, or the intricate steps of social evolution. Walling regarded a socialist like Edmond Kelly as being unconsciously allied with historical forces pushing for state socialism. This highly complex and ambiguous stage of social development, Walling wrote, was filled with the kinds of dangers that Herbert Spencer had seen when he called all socialism a "coming form of slavery." Real socialism, Walling argued, was "true democracy," in which there were no social classes and divisions and all men enjoyed equal opportunity. Socialism did not mean that the industrial state, with its insatiable demands for efficiency and centralization, be allowed to swallow the political state whole.

As a leading intellectual in the American Socialist party and one who often ranged himself on the party's left wing, William English Walling occupied a kind of lone reviewing stand where the parade of reformers was thickest and their shouts strongest in the early twentieth century. He tried, from this position, to look over their heads, through the dust of their demands for reform, to the origins of social evolution and the implications of modern industrialism. And he saw a movement of awesome confusion. His doubts about collectivism appeared in three books published from 1912 to 1914, which form the core of an uneven but unjustly ignored critique of an important political persuasion. A man who read widely in contemporary socialist theory, Walling was also a confirmed individualist, anxious to preserve the social insights of such Americans as Jefferson and John Dewey. For almost three years, Walling's combined socialism of Marx, Spencer, and Kautsky, the anarchism of Max Stirner, and the poetic theories of Horace Traubel challenged the happy march of reformers toward their goal of a functional industrial pluralism. By 1915, Walling's unswerving enthusiasm for war against Germany diverted his attention from theories to conspiracies, and gradually he ceased to write about American society in a serious way. He broke with the Socialist party in 1917.[1]

Walling's career, first as a reformer and then a socialist, and the accompanying evolution of his ideas, is a fascinating and important commentary on the early development of collectivist political theory. He was a central figure in many of the major reform movements of his time, first as a social worker and resident of the University Settlement House in New York, then as a friend of Russian revolutionaries, a Socialist party member, a founder of the National Association for the Advancement of Colored People, a pro-war socialist, and, finally, an ally of Samuel Gompers. He was familiar with most of the leading reform intellectuals of his day, and sampled many of their organizations. The theories he developed to explain the appearance of collectivism were intriguing, though ultimately they were cut short by a career that was reversed in midcourse. Walling was one of the few American intellectuals to see clearly the implications of collectivism and to discuss them specifically, but he faltered in his attempt to create an alternative.

Walling was born in Louisville, Kentucky, on March 14, 1877, to a wealthy and politically prominent family. His mother was Rosalind English, daughter of William Hayden English who had been Democratic candidate for Vice-President in 1880. His father served as the American Consul in Edinburgh for four years, after which he took his family to live in Chicago. William English attended the new University of Chicago, studied economics and sociology in the graduate school there, and, giving this up, went to Harvard Law School in 1897. But he found Harvard unsatisfactory and remained there only a year.

The kind of education Walling wanted came to him only after he left the university for a career in social reform movements. In the late 1890's he returned to Chicago to settle near Hull-House. He also secured a position as a state factory inspector, in which his job was to gather statistics on the sweating system in the clothing and food industries, and to enforce newly designed state work standards. The first report of the factory inspectors, written by Florence Kelley, who later worked with the National Consumers League, described some of the outrageous working conditions that Walling surely observed. Thus, in one of his first contacts with urban poverty and industrial exploitation, Walling was exposed to some of the worst conditions in America. Some years later, looking back on his inspector's job, Walling wrote that its purpose was "to *enforce* laws." But the work was too grueling for him, and after little more than a year he quit and went west to recuperate.[2]

Walling's next project had a profound and lasting effect on the direction of his life. He went to New York City to begin residence in the University Settlement project, and there joined Walter Weyl, J. G. Phelps Stokes, Maurice Parmelee, Arthur Bullard, Ernest C. Poole, Robert Hunter, and a number of other intellectuals all destined to become important social scientists, journalists, and reformers.

The functions and purposes of the settlement house were many. To Nicholas Murray Butler, president of Columbia University and active in the University Settlement, the organization was largely an instrument for the Americanization of immigrants. Jane Addams argued more to the point of Walling's experience when she said that the key impact of the organization was often felt by the resident workers themselves. "May we not say," she said, "that their first aim is to get into such social and natural relations with their neighbors that they can reveal to themselves and to the rest of the citizens the kind of life that exists in industrial neighborhoods?—perfectly frank in regard to its limitations but also insisting that it has those fine qualities that the best human life exhibits everywhere."[3]

The University Settlement ran clubs, kindergartens, art classes, athletic programs, a "Penny Provident Bank," and a legal aid society, sponsored trade union meetings, and undertook special investigations into working and living conditions in the local community it served—the large New York Jewish ghetto which was, as the *Bulletin* of the society noted, the largest center of Jewish population in the world. For Walling this meant a unique sort of contact, and he became friends with a number of Jewish intellectuals and labor leaders. As a resident worker he served on the Child Labor Committee and wrote and lectured on the labor movement, which was considered an important aspect of the settlement's activities. As the publication of the organization explained in 1902, "The settlement workers can perhaps perform few more useful functions in this community than to assist the labor unions of the sweating trades to perfect their organization, and in this manner to improve their living conditions."[4]

The significance of this experience for Walling went far beyond his exposure to poverty or a new culture, or even his acquaintance with some of America's new labor leaders. The meaning of this work was, as J. G. Phelps Stokes suggested, a whole mixture of new ideas. Walling's friend Hutchins Hapgood revealed in his book *The Spirit of the Ghetto* the way in which contact with the Jewish community affected many American intellectuals. The spirit that Hapgood discovered was almost a purely intellectual one. Beneath the rags of a peddler he found a Talmudic scholar; in the steamy tea-rooms of the ghetto he uncovered countless men and liberated women devoted to intellectual questions and steeped in the exciting tradition of Russian literary realism and European Marxism. Although Hapgood disliked political radicalism, Walling did not, and he joined a number of other settlement house residents who made regular excursions through the ghetto's cultural and political life. Walling's friend Ernest Poole described these journeys: "With our friend Henry Moskowitz as guide, we went to countless cafes, large and small, Russian, Polish and German cafes, Socialist, Anarchist, free love, freethinker and actor and poet cafes, where, coming from the oppression of Europe into the sudden freedom here to argue and shout and write as they pleased, young Jews were burning up their lives in this great furnace of ideas." At other times, the socialist editor Abraham Cahan served as guide for these eager students of the ghetto. One common reaction to this strange exciting life was the almost mystical attitude toward Jewish immigrants that a number of settlement house workers, including Jane Addams, developed. The Jew represented to many of them the essence of what it meant to be a immigrant. Walling agreed, but felt that the Jewish immigrant was an uncommon new citizen as well. His progress after arriving in the United States was amazing. "Within one generation," Walling wrote, Jews had gone from almost medieval occupations to "lucrative and promising twentieth century pursuits in the leading center of the richest and most progressive country in the world."[5]

Beyond his reading, then, Walling's radicalism was born in his experience with ghetto radicals and in his firsthand knowledge of the painful growth of the labor movement in New York City. His contact with the Jewish community also brought him his wife, a Jewish radical and writer, Anna Strunsky. At the settlement house he met a number of exiled Russian radicals, and through them and ghetto residents he became intrigued with the events surrounding the abortive Russian Revolution of 1905. In New York he saw the events through the eyes of his friends, and even when he went to Russia in 1905 he preserved the attitudes he had learned in the

United States. One principal reason for this trip to Eastern Europe, he wrote, was to understand the Jew's position in Russia before he came to the United States, to see "conditions with our own eyes."

Like several other intellectuals of his day, Walling learned a great deal about socialism from Russian-Jewish immigrants who had come to the United States in the 1890's and begun their successful drive to unionize the workers of the ghetto. But Walling also developed a fascination with another despised group in Russia, the Dukhobors. He believed, as did many sympathizers with Russia, that the Russian peasantry—far from supporting pogroms against the Jews—lived in an almost natural equalitarian society. Through his interests, Walling was a principal element in the interchange between native American residents and Eastern European Jewish intellectuals in New York City, and he helped to initiate what became one of the most significant intellectual patterns of the twentieth century.[6]

Walling's attitude toward labor was, for his time, a radical one. From his days as a factory inspector in Chicago he had been a student of workers' organizations, and had been deeply influenced by the building strike in Chicago in 1900. As he continued to observe labor conditions in New York, and as he met AFL leaders and socialist unionists, he gradually accepted the idea that industrial unionism, not the craft organization of the AFL, would be the essential union form of the future. There were compelling reasons for industrial organization: "If the era of trusts," Walling wrote, "has required the rewriting of political economy and industrial history, the era of new unionism requires the rewriting of the economic theory of labor unions and the recasting of the history of their development." Monopolies and trusts had brought organization at the top of society, in capital and technology and in factories and workshops; but they had also created the basis for a class ideology. Walling opposed the anti-labor open-shop movement with its misleading call for "freedom of choice." He favored instead the organization of unions, because "Everything both now and in the future depends on the prosperity, health and education of our working-people."[7]

The "new unionism," as Walling defined it, was the modern response of workers to industrialism. Once organized and combined, all trade and industrial unions would enjoy a numerical majority in the industrial community: "They will then have, acting together in one organization, the majority of the consumers, voters and citizens of every industrial community in the United States."

This organizational drive necessarily implied the need for socialist political forms. There was, Walling believed, an almost inevitable relationship between industrial unionism and socialism. In a letter to his parents in 1904, he expressed the belief that company unions would mean a confusion and disarming of the forces at the bottom of society which were pressing for needed changes.

Walling's sympathy for industrial unionism led him to an ambiguous relationship with the American Federation of Labor, which was committed to the craft form of worker organization. After he attended the AFL convention in 1904, he wrote several articles explaining the different paths before labor. Given a choice "between immediate and concrete economic results and a future and intangible political program," American labor unions, he wrote, "have made a typical American and 'business' choice." At the time, Walling preferred the position of John Mitchell of the Mine Workers, which did not automatically preclude socialist politics. Yet in 1904 Walling understood the reasons why Gompers refused to enter politics. Labor, he concluded, thought it could achieve a just society without talking about socialism and without tampering with political strategies.[8]

These tactics of organized labor in America, pale as they appeared to Walling, were far more progressive than the activities of the British trade unions, though the British were committed to politics. English unions, Walling wrote, were formed for conservative purposes, that is, to preserve jobs and restrict production and the application of technology. American unions, though they were an offspring of British organizations, had outgrown their conservative parentage. They had more sympathy for the unskilled worker and were more willing to commit their resources to support strikes. British unionism and

English Fabianism were both derivatives of the same conservative attitude toward modern society, Walling thought; neither provided a model for American labor or American intellectuals. Thus quite early in his career Walling developed an antipathy toward political unionism and Fabianism, which he would later detect at the heart of collectivist theory.

Walling's labor sympathies, and, more precisely, his belief that the labor union was an instrument for social betterment, led him to help organize a trade union for women. After the AFL convention in 1903, Walling, along with Jane Addams and others, helped found the Women's Trade Union League. Mary Morton Kehew was elected president and Jane Addams vice-president, and Walling was secretary of the New York branch. At the same time he worked for the elimination of child labor and became a member of the executive committee of the Commission on Child Labor.[9]

While his interests spread out along the labor front, Walling also continued a habit he had begun in Chicago and carried over into his New York settlement house days. Rather than writing about events in theoretical detachment, Walling was accustomed to visiting scenes of social crisis, labor trouble spots, and riot areas. He earned a good deal of attention for this, but he also used this style of participatory journalism to try to influence the outcome of revolutions and social upheavals, and not merely to comment on them. Walling's trip to Russia in 1906 was a good example of this approach. It led to a series of articles in the *Independent,* and later to a book, *Russia's Message,* in 1908, which introduced American audiences to the aims and personalities of Russian revolutionary leaders. A second such trip was to Springfield, Illinois, in 1908, where Walling reported on the disastrous race war in that city and through his writings helped to spur the founding of the NAACP.

Walling became an avid spectator of Russian revolutionary movements, as he recalled, around 1904, when the Russian revolutionary Madame Bereschkovsky visited the United States. By 1905 he and a party including Arthur Bullard had decided to travel to Russia, as Walling put it, so "that the American social movement could draw inspiration and spirit from the depth and breadth and self-sacrifice of the Russian Revolutionists." Walling saw a personal tie between his own work and the efforts of young, middle-class Russians who sought to overthrow the tsar. His struggle was like theirs; change in Russia was only possible because of the activities of young agitators, all of them "brought up in some comfort and many in comparative luxury." In America there was a comparable group who were young social workers.

Walling's trip was a journey to the source of his radical inspiration—to the home of Russian revolutionaries, immigrant Jewish intellectuals, and democratic peasants. The trip itself was an exciting and even dangerous one, for Walling was arrested at one point by the tsar's police. As he interviewed one revolutionary leader after another, he felt he had gotten to the rock bottom of the revolution. In January 1906 he wrote to his parents: "I honestly believe there is no single man to whom all Russia is so open. The Revs. tell me what they tell no one else. I shall see Witte in a few days, I saw the Ministers of War & Finance—for long intimate talks last week—I dine with the leading 'black' editor and Prince A this noon." When his parents asked about his safety, he replied that he was not in danger, for he was trying to understand "the Master Minds and Forces of the Revolution," not conspiracies or violence.[10]

Walling sent back a description of Russia which emphasized the potential of peasant life, repressed in 1906 but naturally democratic. In a perceptive prediction he wrote that the peasant's struggle represented that of all humanity, and that Russia could leap from hunger and backwardness into socialism, vaulting the steps between. There was no more important world event than the Russian Revolution, for it promised to fulfill the French Revolution and conquer the "last of the rights of man" as it made its way toward socialism. The struggle, Walling acknowledged, would probably be enormously costly in terms of human life.

When Walling returned to the United States, he put his experiences together in a book published in 1908 which he called *Russia's Message*. The message was etched in terms of bleak oppressions and injustice and the overwhelming desire of the masses for political and economic freedom. Their struggle was

none other than the reaffirmation of man's need everywhere
to end all forms of tyranny, of which capitalism was the last
and most extensive. Americans, Walling argued, knew well
such institutions of oppression; they were familiar with the
"soulless corporations" which in the United States were the instruments of corruption and exploitation and in Russia were
the purveyors of the tsar's prisons.[11]

Even more interesting than Walling's identification of
America's struggles with the revolutionary battles against the
tsar were some of the other messages of his book. These said a
great deal about the development of Walling's political attitudes. He looked at Russia from the point of view of the
Jewish minority suffering there from social exclusion and frequent pogroms. In *Russia's Message* the Jew was the symbol
of all men oppressed by tsarist tyranny: "In my first chapters,"
he wrote, "I have dwelt at some length with this subject, but
I have devised the economical measure of taking the Jews as
my central theme. . . ." Far more than economy led Walling to
focus on the Jewish population. Even before his trip, Walling
had begun to view the Jewish population as symbolic of the
industrial population of twentieth-century America, laboring
to raise itself through industrial unionism to democratic citizenship.

The symbol of oppressed man in America and Russia was
the Jew, but in Russia the hope was with the peasantry.
Walling's devotion to the peasant was almost mystical, for he
regarded him as "a democrat in everything and a Socialist in
regard to the land, that he is almost without race prejudice,
and that he is liberal and even independent in his religious
views." Such men, if ever freed, would pour the intoxicant of
liberty across the borders of Europe and thereby begin a continental emancipation of mankind. Russia, if it became socialist, would replace America as the inspirational force for the
world. With the help of intellectuals and the professional
classes, the masses would transform themselves and their
nations.

Most working-class people in Russia, Walling noted, were
already socialists of one kind or another, but few were orthodox Marxists. The reason for this, according to Walling, was

that Marx's theories described more industrialized societies. The workers in Russia were only a primitive minority among the great peasant masses. Of the leaders Walling interviewed, most acknowledged the importance of the peasants in the revolution. Only one important man did not think they were decisive—Lenin, whose dismissal of the peasants as "bigoted and blindly patriotic" Walling deeply distrusted. Walling cast his lot intellectually with the Socialist Revolutionary party because of its peasant base and because of its relatively mild attacks on private property.[12]

Walling's choice of revolutionary leaders in Russia made good sense in 1908, as it might have even in 1917. His sketches of the Jewish immigrants and the Russian peasantry, however, sometimes revealed more about his own thinking than they did about reality. His strong identification with the forces which ultimately lost out in the Russian Revolution allowed him no sympathy in 1917 for what he could only understand to be a German conspiracy. His own study of Russia proved to him that Lenin's revolution was a false one which would place the fate of Europe in Germany's bloody hands. Sensitive as he was in 1906 to events in Russia, he could only explain what happened in 1917 in terms of conspiracies.

After Walling returned to the United States, he married Anna Strunsky in a wedding that was much noted in the Jewish press. Shortly afterward, he wrote what was to become his most famous article, "The Race War in the North," published in the *Independent* in 1908 and based upon observations in Springfield, Illinois. He wrote to his mother also immediately after the outbreak of violence in Springfield about his plans: "It is needless to say that we shall seek out the best known people of [every kind] for interviewing, that we shall not go near any riotous parts—if the rioting should by any chance be renewed and that I will take good care of Anna." The article exonerated the black population of Springfield and detailed the events and causes of the riots. Walling warned that the spread of race riots threatened moral degeneracy or even a profounder, deeper, "more revolutionary civil war." Somewhat later, when he wrote to Hamilton Holt, managing editor of the *Independent*, to answer criticisms of his position on the Springfield riots, he compared the exploited position of the blacks with that of the Jews in Russia.

Several months later, in an article on "Science and Human Brotherhood," Walling attacked intimations of racism which he found in socialist writings, in fashionable European philosophers such as Nietzsche, and in the "undemocratic 'culture' " of American universities. "This is not a contest between radicalism," he argued, "against conservatism, but of progress against the sinister *reaction* of Eastern Europe." He thought that two broad impulses existed in the world, one united for democracy and led by the peoples of the United States, Russia, Japan, Turkey, and Persia, and the other one racist, "supported by a bare majority of the English and Germans at the terrible expense of the lower classes of both countries and the ruin of the subjected peoples."[13]

By 1909, Walling had begun to sketch a world picture which would serve him for a number of years. It viewed such nations as Germany and England ambiguously, and identified sinister elements attempting to crush the spirit of revolt in Russia and the practice of freedom in America. Walling's socialist theories, when he came to devise them, reflected this special attitude toward Europe and a faith in forces that ultimately failed.

During his years in New York, until 1910 when he joined the Socialist party, Walling's relationship to the American socialist movement had been a strong but informal one. He had been interested in socialism for a number of years. In his school days at the University of Chicago he had helped to organize a Socialist Club. Many of his friends and fellow settlement house workers in New York had become fascinated by socialism. This group, including Phelps Stokes, Robert Hunter, Charles Edward Russell, and William James Ghent, formed an important nucleus of socialist intellectuals in New York City.

When Walling joined the party, however, he did not do so because he admired all of the programs or ideas of American socialism. He was already an established journalist and an expert on labor and immigration, and he came to the Socialist party with several fixed notions, all of which were antagonistic to what he argued was the collectivism of many of the party's members. One was the absolute need to keep the party from founding a Labor party, such as the British had done. This would be an act, Walling thought, of absolute folly, for any Labor party would by definition be a minority party. The Socialists should no doubt cooperate with the labor movement, but each had a separate function. Politics and labor agitation would coalesce naturally: "As the Socialist Party grows and obtains a foot-hold among every element of the community except the capitalists and those whose lives are guided by the ambition of becoming capitalists or of serving them, it will find every year that it is co-operating with the Labor Unions more and more on the same broad and democratic field."[14]

Walling confided his disgust for political laborism to the English socialist writer H. M. Hyndman in early 1910, remarking that he opposed it even more than capitalism. Ultimately it was more reactionary, for it would fasten the rigidity of a guild system onto society rather than allowing the natural expression of capitalist crises. "I am a democrat," he wrote, "and not in any sense a Collectivist or a State Socialist, and I consider that a Trade Union party is as great a calamity to any country as a Catholic party or an Imperialist party could possibly be." Such views clashed with the ideas of other party members, but Walling was not reluctant to name his enemies. He wrote to fellow socialist Louis Boudin in early March of that year: "I believe that he [Hillquit] and Hunter, Spargo and Berger are as dangerous and reactionary demagogues as any modern country has known and I shall also continue fighting them to the last." The proper example of a socialist movement, he continued, was the "splendid and aggressive [industrial] army of Germany," which opposed labor parties and understood the need to fight for deep and genuine reforms and not settle for the organizational evolution of corporate power. Walling thought such reforms as the initiative and referendum and other democratic procedures were far more revolutionary than the state socialism proposed by Berger and Hillquit.[15]

Walling thus made his entrance into socialist politics from the left wing and in support of political democracy. He sometimes sided with the Industrial Workers of the World and their more nonpolitical unionism, but he also had room to tolerate the anti-political AFL. Of course, Walling qualified his support for Gompers' union, just as he criticized the IWW for their "undemocratic ideals." "No matter how revolutionary they may be," he commented to Fred Warren, the editor of the Midwestern *Appeal to Reason,* "they are not democratic. Their goal is a sort of dictatorship of the proletariat in the narrow sense of the word. In spite of occasional professions to the contrary, they are hostile to farmers, to clerks, to the professional classes, etc., etc.—all proletarians in the truest sense of the word and people whom we absolutely must have in the movement. . . ."

Walling's conception of socialism blended industrial unionism with political democracy waged by a political organization. He opposed the state socialists who, he argued, were merely collectivists who wanted a labor party and more government regulation of the economy. His own socialism was far more political, and perhaps less realizable. He sought to bring the majority of the American people together into one great militant movement to isolate and destroy the power of capitalism. The working class would be only one element of the radical coalition which necessarily included professional classes and white-collar workers. This was not simply an important insight into a way of unifying the divided functional elements which industrialism had spawned, or even just the beginning of a new revolutionary theory. This definition of a radical coalition also justified Walling's role as an intellectual in the party.

Walling's sense of the different forms of unionism and radicalism enabled him to isolate different kinds of socialism within the Socialist party. Each kind, he noted, had a class basis, although "class" as he used it here had the rather special meaning of skilled worker, unskilled worker, small businessman, and large entrepreneur. He also saw a profound division between reformers and socialists on the question of state power. Reformers and nonradical socialists wanted to extend centralized control over all parts of society, including the arbitration of strikes in the interest of some vague "public." This forced arbitration would destroy independent unionism by allowing working-class organizations to grow only through the selected openings of class collaboration. Small capitalists, especially, Walling wrote, favored this arrangement to provide workers with minimal forms of unionism. These "far-sighted small capitalists," such as Theodore Roosevelt, understood the need to organize the economic system to make it safe from attacks by industrial unions. Embodied in Progressive party reforms, these moves were merely diversions from the more profound needs of the workers and their allies.

No union was yet perfect, he argued, and surely not the AFL; nor did the IWW propose a truly revolutionary analysis in its philosophy that capitalism could be overcome by strikes. But the IWW's syndicalism was important because it set socialist goals for unions. Eventually, the Socialist party and revolutionary unions might become the two arms of the socialist struggle. Thus Walling supported the left wing of the Socialist party and often the IWW because both disavowed the reformism of some elements of the party, and not because he was always sympathetic to either. Occasionally, as during the Lawrence, Massachusetts, textile strike when he defended the role of the IWW, he found himself ranged against most of the party intellectuals.[16]

A by-product of Walling's fight within the party against laborism and reformism was the elaboration of his position in a series of books. In the years from 1912 to 1916, when he was most active in the party, he published four major works which attempted to answer a number of troubling questions for American socialists: What was the distinction between reform and revolution? What sources could help to build a radical intellectual analysis of modern society? What were the class bases of political positions? What was the meaning of general social evolution and the Socialist party's role in it? What was a socialist culture? Taken together, Walling's answers represented a profound attack upon the assumptions of collectivism, and suggested a view of socialism that was independent of corporate patterns.

Socialism As It Is, written in 1912, in fact described socialism as it should not be. American society, Walling noted, was at a turning point, preparing to embrace state socialism, or state capitalism as he sometimes called it. Society was about to embark upon the collectivism proposed by H. G. Wells, Sidney Webb, Henry George, Edmond Kelly, Victor Berger, and Algie Simons. But this centralized, controlled form of private-public capitalism was profoundly different from true socialism. The gulf between them was political democracy. State capitalism, whatever its guises as municipalism or government regulation, represented an extension of power by private capital. So long as the government remained in "capitalist hands," no variety of reform at the national level would bring socialism. The evidence for this dilemma was obvious, because capitalists on their own, with no encouragement from radicals, had already begun a revolution "in the organization of labor and business by *governmental means.*"[17] Behind these reforms were groups such as the National Civic Federation, which, Walling recalled, had been formed to divert the energies of working people from socialism and revolutionary unionism into the more conservative craftism of British unions.

The class basis of true socialism was far broader than those special groups which favored state socialism. Here Walling announced his faith in majoritarian democracy. The new middle class, first described in Europe by Kautsky and other socialists, and including clerks and scientists and professional intellectuals, was a necessary part of any socialist coalition. Thus even the working class was too small a group to achieve socialism, and any direct exploitation of class hatred would be misguided because it would square one part of society off against another its equal in size. The goal of socialists, therefore, ought not to be to replace one class by another possibly smaller one, but to abolish all classes by creating a true democracy. Walling intended to isolate the capitalist forces from other members of society. Neither working-class hatred nor the piecemeal reforms of state socialism would achieve this new society. "Socialism," he declared, "can only do what capitalism, after it has reached its culmination in State capitalism, leaves undone; namely to take effective measures to establish equal opportunity and abolish class government."[18] As these ideas showed, Walling, like many of his contemporaries, was truly ambiguous about the meaning of class-consciousness, seeing it as a dangerous but perhaps necessary explosive to place under the bulwarks of conservative society. But, unlike the collectivists whom he opposed, Walling regarded political democracy as the basis of socialism.

When he discussed contemporary socialist ideas, Walling was particularly angered by the misuse of evolutionary theories which, he argued, had resulted in a babble of irrelevant and misguided notions on the left. Especially the theory that society exhibited an ever-accelerating organization, centralization, and rationalization—the explicit assumptions of most collectivist reformers and socialist intellectuals—was, Walling thought, the worst example of this thinking. Like the collectivists, he sensed the gathering of historical energies, but he was deeply suspicious of their ultimate direction. Society was obviously changing, and every reform helped to eliminate the last traces of laissez faire in favor of a form of collectivism. Perhaps state assumption of the functions of the private corporation was inevitable. State capitalism and state socialism were quite likely to be the accepted forms of political economy in the near future. But they did not equal socialism, despite the verbal trappings given them by the Fabians and by American reformers. True socialism would disintegrate society into genuinely individual units after a period of economic centralization. Socialism would be a dialectical advance beyond corporate centralism, and primarily a political and social system of true equality. "Here again," Walling wrote, "we see that Socialism, in its aversion to all artificial systems and every restriction of personal liberty, is far more akin to the individualism of Herbert Spencer than it is to the 'State Socialism' of Plato." State socialism might be an inevitable historical state, but it was not real socialism. Therefore, anyone in the Socialist party who supported reforms and economic schemes for centralization was threatening the life of the movement and agitating for what would happen anyway.

Walling's dislike of social evolutionary theories and his counter-hypothesis of development by dialectics made him more sympathetic to the traditional Marxist wing of the Socialist party. His own theory of socialism was at least analogous to Marx's in its emphasis upon evolution by negation and reaction, though he hardly agreed with Marx on the nature of the proletariat and the class struggle. His theories set him apart from other intellectuals, and from this position he felt he understood the grounds for the growing cooperation—and confusion—between socialism and reform thought in the United States. This unprincipled alliance, he argued, rested upon the fact that both parties accepted the assumptions of collectivism. Walling, unlike them, refused to denounce the era of laissez faire or its apostles such as Herbert Spencer. As an individualist he was deeply suspicious of social centralization, and worried that intellectuals spent too much time dreaming about vast new economic relationships. Whether he rightly or wrongly chose to credit Spencer with his own interpretation of individual rights was not as important as the use to which he put individualism. With his own great emphasis upon democracy, he was able to understand a fundamental determinism into which an important segment of American social and political thought had fallen.

One sign of the terrible blindness of collectivist thought, Walling argued, was its agitation for prison reform. This was no ordinary reform, he recalled, but rather an attempt by reformers to eliminate vagabondage by placing tramps on farm labor camps. These schemes were thinly disguised militarism, with their wish to put men and women into labor armies with discipline, banners, decorations, titles, and ceremonies, and where "the strain of personal initiative and responsibility would be removed." It was none other than the beginning of the Servile State which Hilaire Belloc had predicted. And the worst offenders were the state socialists, among whom Walling included Nicholas Murray Butler, Edmond Kelly, Franklin Giddings, Charlotte Perkins Gilman, and Robert W. DeForest, president of the Charity Organization Society.[19]

State socialism was not merely a quality of thought that existed in unfulfilled reforms; it also showed up in the highest places in American government. In three articles published in 1913, Walling argued that not only did collectivist thinking dominate the Socialist party and most reform proposals, it also inspired the more practical projects of President Woodrow Wilson. Wilson was a thorough state socialist, Walling decided, because he believed, like all such men, that society was an organism, and further that "government is society." Given support from labor organizations, Walling predicted, Wilson would pursue state socialist projects such as government ownership of leading industries, all in the face of big business opposition. The state socialists had defined labor as a commodity and the worker as a kind of machine, or a functional unit in production. Wilson agreed, and went on to assert the existence of another functional group, the intellectuals and experts upon whom the government would depend for advice and guidance. This latter group formed a liaison between Wilson and the important reform movements of the day.

In addition to Wilson's self-conscious reformism and his advanced state socialist attitudes, Walling found forces at the bottom of society which were also pushing toward collectivism. The alliance of top and bottom made state socialism inevitable: "Perhaps the most important law of economic evolution is the steady assumption of one industrial function after another by government." But, he noted, this centralization was often designed to accomplish conservative purposes. Thus he accused the Progressive George Perkins, and writers Lyman Abbott and Ray Stannard Baker, of attempting to divert the Socialist party from the true tasks of revolution to certain mild forms of government regulation. The intellectual ties, he concluded, that linked Progressive politicians, conservative unions, reformers, and many socialists were a visible conservatism.[20]

Walling's next major work, *The Larger Aspects of Socialism,* was his most important because it synthesized his interpretation of socialism and reformism. By all odds it was also his most interesting book, as he tried to enlist pragmatism and Marxism to do battle jointly with the prevailing ideas of collectivism. For his new vision of socialism, Walling called upon Friedrich Nietzsche, the German anarchist Max Stirner, Herbert Spencer, John Dewey, and German socialists Karl Kautsky and August Bebel for support.

Socialism, as Walling defined it, was no mere political scheme. The socialist movement throughout the world was no longer just a single radical movement for reform; it was the highest manifestation of modern thought and progress. The universal intellectual assumptions of modernity, without the chains and locks of metaphysics, were purely socialist in orientation: "Taking as my point of departure the philosophy of modern science, which I show to be wholly Socialist in its bearings, and wholly dependent upon Socialism for its practical applications, . . ." Walling began his discussion with a consideration of Dewey's pragmatism.

Walling's designation of Dewey as a major thinker in the socialist tradition involved some fascinating and strenuous logic. But it was a key element in his position, for it was part of an argument to end the reliance of socialists upon Marx, Engels, and countless revisionists who followed them. Since Dewey rightly insisted that knowledge arose from practical encounters with the social environment ("struggles," as Walling has it), then anything written in the past, held up as dogma, and then passed into party constitutions or platforms was clearly reactionary. Theory had to be based upon the reality of the socialist movement, not upon an abstract rationality or revolutionary vision. Given Walling's belief in the universal importance of the socialist movement and its potential dominance of society, the party's struggle to free men from the undemocratic structures of the capitalist state and from evolving state socialism gave rise to ideas, values, and strategies for creating a truly democratic state. Thus Walling made Dewey the philosopher of socialism and transformed pragmatism into socialism. In doing so, he violated Dewey's assumption that he had been describing the universal psychology of understanding and learning; indeed, that he was a philosopher at all. Walling did this because he believed that socialist experience was the sum of all real ideas, that useless assumptions resulted from artificial social structures, from false divisions of society, and from false consciousness. "Social truth is born in social struggles," he wrote. "This truth and this *alone* is the essence of all Socialism from Marx to modern pragmatism."[21]

All other forms of socialist thought, Walling argued, were abstractions in disguise and glorifications of an unjust society hidden in the costume of progress. Only pragmatic socialism could comprehend the yet unconscious meanings of social struggle and articulate such voiceless strivings into a program of revolutionary individualism. He wrote, as his friend and contemporary Walter Lippmann insisted that good political scientists must do, of the unspoken necessities of the soul. Politics had to encompass all kinds of social change. Pragmatism and socialism were all-inclusive because both celebrated change as social: "The genetic standpoint makes us aware that the systems of the past are neither fraudulent impostures nor absolute revelations; but are the products of political, economic, and scientific conditions whose change carries with it change in theoretical formulations." This was the basis of true socialist theory.

Walling subscribed to a philosophy of science and sociology which apparently contradicted the mock Darwinian concepts of the collectivists. He opposed their search for social laws or the accumulation of facts, and argued against establishing a "priesthood" of scientists or experts. The true philosophy of science and of socialism, he wrote, rested upon the belief that society and culture were constantly evolving away from nature in every sense. Thus socialism rejected brutal struggle as well as an organic description of society. Walling contrasted the Bergsonian definition of nature and evolution to Comte's, which, he added, was the supreme justification for state socialism. No system of metaphors that implied man's dependence upon some abstract whole or upon the state could ever be used to describe a social theory for man. The duty of socialists was to create a new environment in which all human beings would be free, socially and intellectually.

This statement of socialism depended for support upon two German philosophers of individualism, Nietzsche and Max Stirner. Walling discussed Nietzsche at length, though he was first careful to reject the philosopher's theory of aristocracy. Nietzsche, Walling wrote, was the first philosopher of true social science, for he had despised the worship of history and the canonization of laws of growth. Of all philosophers, he was closest to socialism because he understood and celebrated individualism, despite the way in which, historically, man's personality was caught and molded by society: "Nietzsche's central idea was not the 'will to power,' but that for the individual to develop his capacity it is necessary for him to use others and to be used by others. . . ." Nietzsche had understood that morality was and ought to be experimental and in the ultimate interest of the self. Supernaturalism and metaphysics in contrary philosophies were, Walling concluded, the last defenses of political elites who used ideas to confuse and divert the masses from understanding the iniquities of class rule.[22]

An even more interesting weight behind Walling's individualist convictions was his reading of Max Stirner, whose book *The Ego and Its Own* he considered a revolutionary and pragmatic primer. Stirner was a pragmatist in the most revolutionary sense: he perfectly understood the pragmatic dictum of experience, that "when a man acts in each given moment according to the dictates of his whole personality and his whole experience, he acts more effectively than he could possibly do by mastering and following the most perfect logic and philosophies the human race has ever developed." Stirner was perhaps the most radical of all individualists and also, Walling noted, the strongest opponent of state socialism. Walling was intrigued by Stirner's sense of the whole man acting from the dictates of his experience, for it was here, he had always believed, that the proof of society's need for socialism resided.

Together, Spencer, Nietzsche, and Stirner provided Walling with a phalanx of philosophic anarchism and armed his suspicions about the direction of social evolution and the effects on liberty of a modern mass society. Walling's socialism meant political and social liberation for self-fulfillment, something, he said, that could never occur in the absolutist organizational society of state socialism. Thus Walling argued from his interpretation of a radical anarchist and individualist tradition against the more predominant schools of German and French philosophy. He rejected the ideas of Hegel, Rousseau, and Comte, and what he felt was their incorporation into a modern collectivism which celebrated the state, the organic society, and materialism. Only if philosophy were experimental and educational could it be liberating. Thus the deeper meanings of socialist struggle were also the essence of a modern scientific philosophy.[23]

In a final section entitled "Socialism and Pragmatism as Seen in the Writings of Marx and Engels," Walling attempted to salvage parts of the socialist theories of these two men. He did so by citing their anticipation of pragmatism and their understanding of how social truth changed. "How does it happen," Walling asked, "that the modern Socialist philosophy did not come from the Socialist movement?" The reason was that Marx and Engels, despite their unconscious anticipation of pragmatism, were too much bent upon using Hegelian philosophy for socialist purposes. Great energy was thus spent upon the futile concept of materialist dialectics, which, Walling argued, ought to be discarded as meaningless. Walling praised Marx and Engels for their realism and for discarding abstractions and absolutes in favor of shifting and evolving assumptions. Unfortunately, however, they saw only the vague outlines of a true pragmatic socialism.

Walling was roundly attacked in the socialist press for *The Larger Aspects of Socialism,* especially in an article in the *New Review* by Robert Rives La Monte entitled "Apotheosis of Pragmatism." La Monte wondered that Walling could praise John Dewey as a socialist philosopher, and accused Walling of mixing a noxious combination of anarchism and pragmatism. Walling's friend Walter Lippmann rushed to defend him in the pages of the same journal. But the discussion did not focus upon the book's vital points, only its heresies.

Walling was obviously groping for a philosophic understanding of socialism which did not depend upon the developing outlines of mass industrial society. He had been deeply impressed by Dewey's efforts to break the dogmatic structures of nineteenth-century philosophy. Walling was one of the few radicals who did not reject Spencer, laissez faire, and the century of Victorianism out of hand. This reintroduction of complexity and ambiguity about the nineteenth century perhaps hinted at a conservative temperament. But, more important, Walling's discussion revealed possibilities for a critique of collectivism which was at once socialist, radical, and eclectic. In his antipathy to centralization, Walling anticipated much later discussions of the "new working class" when he explained the bureaucratization of certain middle-class jobs among the pro-

fessions. These new professional men were a new kind of proletarian class, he thought, with many of the same interests as
the working class.

Walling was suspicious of the evolutionary language of
much modern social science literature, which he denounced
as merely a celebration of contemporary social arrangements.
He did not define social classes, as the collectivists did, in
terms of the corporation or by work function. Finally, he
nourished the seeds of a deep hatred for German philosophy because of its statist tendencies, and he built a strong
case for the dangers of state socialism should it ever be combined with political autocracy. But of all his ideas perhaps the
most significant was his dissection of collectivist assumptions
and his discovery that they linked much of socialist thought,
reform ideas, and practical political programs. His later interpretation of collectivism and state socialism would become
confusing and directionless, but it served him well in 1913.

Walling's next book, *Progressivism—and After,* published
in 1914, was disappointing after the expectations raised by his
earlier work on socialism. It caused Walter Lippmann to comment snidely that Walling was limited by his background:
"The ideals are those of the Middle West democracy, and the
underlying prejudices are those of the Eighteenth Century,
from which the culture of the American Middle West derives."
In a certain sense Lippmann was right—there were obvious
marks of a backward movement in Walling's new book, or at
least a pause to elaborate old ideas. Lippmann was particularly upset by two of them: first, that socialism represented absolute equality in the distribution of social goods and powers,
and second, that Walling suddenly wrote as if he believed in
the inevitable progress of the Progressive movement and the
benevolent effect of all contemporary reform: "Socialists are
reduced to being people who know what is going to happen,
but that knowledge helps them not at all, because they can't
change what is going to happen."[24]

Lippmann was only partly right. But he had caught Walling
in a clumsy attempt to create a class explanation for the Progressive movement which would indicate why it happened
and why its proposed reforms could be supported by socialists.

In emphasis, this amounted to a reversal of Walling's previous attacks upon collectivism. The result was a mechanical scheme, simply formed and smoothly functioning. Walling divided society into four important groups—large capitalists, small capitalists, aristocratic labor, and nonprivileged workers. Each group had a representative political ideology which it would enforce once in power. Big business created the ideology of capitalism or laissez faire; small capitalists, led by Theodore Roosevelt and Woodrow Wilson, were creating state capitalism under the guise of the Progressive movement; other reforms leading to Industrial Democracy and the inclusion of craft unions in the councils of government would initiate state socialism. The final state of social evolution, Walling wrote, would probably be marred by increasing class-consciousness and a bitter struggle between segments of the working class. As state socialism matured, gradually the distance between classes would evaporate, and the lower classes would resist until they too were incorporated into the state. This would result in the abolition of all class privileges and the beginning of socialism. Socialism would come full circle to where American society had begun, with the abolition of hereditary privilege and a return to equal opportunity, but now in an age of industrialism.

Despite occasional heavy strokes to represent class struggle and exploitation, Walling mapped a series of placid plateaus, each with a class marker, and each representing a further step forward in the democratization of American society. Social change now meant the accumulation of the good intentions of each group that was waiting its turn to contribute to progress. First, "a certain measure of progress is to be expected through the self-interest of the governing classes." More progress would result as new elements of the middle class and wage-earners began to effect policy. Finally, with the revolt of the lower classes would come socialism: "For this is the only force that can be relied upon to put an end to class government and class exploitation of industry and to establish that social democracy which is the real or professed aim of every progressive movement."[25]

Walling felt he had created a new class interpretation of

society that was far more relevant than Marx's: "The modern Socialists do not deny the immense historic importance of Marx, they deny merely the present-day importance of his doctrine."[26] Most socialist movements, he declared, had no understanding of class; they merely projected their own middle-class values as if they were somehow radical. The British Labour movement and many German socialists made this fundamental error, and, as a result, they represented merely a left-wing version of state socialism. The proponents of collectivist thought in America, among them socialists, Progressives, and some politicians, were guilty of the same misunderstanding.

In *Progressivism—and After,* Walling had become less critical of the evolutionary version of social progress. He was now sanguine about the straight-line accretion of benefits that each class would donate to society as it committed suicide, through absorption into the state. Believing that power could absorb the energies of a class, Walling argued that by taking power, each class would extinguish the power of the previous ruling group and prepare its own doom. Government would therefore not be the arm for a class system. Walling in effect revived one of the principal collectivist arguments he had once criticized. The peaceful evolution of society became the dominant metaphor to express his socialist hopes. The vast state would gradually dissolve social passions and, in the process, obliterate itself.

Much of the anger that he had once turned against the exploitation of immigrants or Negroes was also dissipated in this book. Walling now found guilt everywhere. Many of his fellow socialists, he wrote, shared racist views. In another sense, socialism was a less effective movement because some socialists proposed programs that were already being initiated by the government. As Lippmann had remarked, the role of the socialist in such a scheme could be a highly uncomfortable one, if one did not just relax and become a political seer or prophet. How could a person act at all if socialism were only a point on the far edge of a turning wheel of progress?

The most important elements of this book, from Walling's point of view, were all directed to the tactics of the socialist movement. Walling had taken stock and catalogued the future dominance of socialism. But one task remained: to create a genuine socialist program which would not be deceived by the halfway demands of state socialism of collectivism. Socialism meant democracy, he argued, a pioneer equality operating in the context of industrialism. Walling rightfully reminded his socialist comrades that economic definitions of human freedom were incomplete, and that socialism did not simply mean efficiency and centralization and planning. He understood that socialism could never be achieved until the mass of industrial workers shared political power in their own name. But his argument became overly schematic when he turned to positive proposals. If Progressives were state capitalists of a sort, they did not, as Walling thought, represent small capitalists or the aristocratic elements of the labor movement. If there was profound agreement between large corporate owners, government, and, to some extent, the labor movement in America, this did not mean that small capitalists were now working to extend freedom and economic regulation to more underprivileged sections of society. Walling's desire to construct a class beneath every idea led him astray from the most valuable insights of his earlier books. His critique of collectivism faltered as he sought the respectability of a class analysis.

Walling's last important book on socialism was a very different attempt to discover, through American poetry, the traditions of radical individualism. His *Whitman and Traubel,* published in 1916, was a description of the socialist potential in the American character, and the last exegesis of Walling's pragmatic revolutionism. It demonstrated Walling's confirmed social and political individualism, his deep hostility to institutionalized reform, and the almost Tolstoyan anarchism in his emphasis upon spiritual individualism.

The development of American poetry in the nineteenth century from Whitman to Horace Traubel, Walling wrote, represented the flowering of American individualism. Whitman, whom he called a revolutionary because of his great desire for social equality, had an unblushing faith in the future. He was a Social Democrat in almost every respect but one: he did not understand the debilitating effects of a belief in metaphysical idealism, or how destructive were the powers of the social and

physical environment. Whitman did not realize that the frontier had also worked negatively upon the pioneers, reducing
them to "mere primitive men." Thus his emphasis upon the
westward expansion of small farming would never work as a
solution to the problems of contemporary industrial America.
Whitman might have changed, Walling added. Still, he "did
not see that the religion and metaphysics of a period are the
last stronghold of its social system. So he left these authorities
fundamentally undisturbed."[27]

Horace Traubel was Whitman's greatest interpreter. He had
refined the earlier poet's ideas, Walling argued, and had become America's first socialist writer; not a great writer whose
politics were incidentally socialistic, but one whose life and
works contained glimpses of a revolutionary future. His life
was at one with his work. As Traubel himself had explained:
"Some artists think they can't be artists if they are partizans.
Every great artist is a partizan." Walling thought Traubel's
socialism was a kind of instinctual pragmatism. Traubel rejected every form of social religion that made supplicants out
of independent citizens; he did not subscribe to older versions of science, natural law, altruism, or God, or to updated
versions of social religion or the worship of society itself.

Walling's discussion of Traubel was also an exposition of his
own view of socialist character. His enthusiastic endorsement
of the poet's social philosophy was an argument for his own
individualism. Traubel, it seemed, agreed that individualism
was at best precariously alive in any social system. But
Walling also came close to rejecting the important assumptions of the Socialist party when he seconded Traubel and
said: "A far greater danger to individual liberty, because it is
usually unexpressed, is the tendency to lay undue stress upon
institutions or institutional change."[28] Here was the fundamental reason for Walling's dislike of collectivism as well as
the source of his dissenting mood in the Socialist party.

The rest of Walling's short discussion of Whitman and
Traubel was taken up with an analysis of individualism as the
freedom of each individual to develop without the obstacles
of classes, institutions, or ideologies. This development could
take place only in a socialist society, and never in nations that

adopted state socialism or collectivism, or that worshiped social images or made spiritual integration the highest virtue. Socialism was not the idealization of the crowd but the idealization of the individual. Traubel, Tolstoy, Nietzsche, and, of course, Walling, had understood this to be the essence of liberty. Thus socialism would mean a total revolution of economics, politics, and the moral foundations of modern industrial society, and a final liberation of the self.

Walling went much further than most socialist writers in emphasizing individualism as the basic social organization of the new society, but there were elements in his theory that were also very much a part of contemporary socialist debate. The German revisionists Karl Kautsky and Eduard Bernstein had made similar distinctions between reformism and socialism. Walling, in discussing state socialism, used Bernstein's emphasis upon the cartel (or corporation) as the new element of social evolution, which performed a stabilizing and centralizing force in capitalist development. Bernstein's high praise for democracy and his description of the socialist movement as a creative social and intellectual force seconded Walling's position. As Bernstein characteristically wrote, "To me that which is generally called the ultimate aim of socialism is nothing, but the movement is everything."[29]

Of the other American socialists who, like Walling, took up the question of the corporation in modern capitalist development, perhaps the most important thinker was Walling's friend Louis Boudin. In his book *The Theoretical System of Karl Marx*, Boudin set out to "harmonize the Marxian teaching with the development of corporate methods of doing business." Boudin, following the position taken by Kautsky, understood that the function of the corporation was to end competition and destroy the system of laissez faire upon which Marx had constructed his analysis of capitalism. The old bourgeois class, as Marx had predicted, was disappearing; but a new middle strata, which was really a disguised proletariat, now appeared in its place. More important, the corporation had wrenched the whole social system out of its laissez-faire context: "The philosophy of *individualism*, ideology of private ownership of property, and particularly of individual enterprise, is doomed;

and the philosophy of *collectivism,* the ideology of the collective ownership of the means of production and the social organization of human enterprise, is fast taking its place."

This economic and ideological upheaval had created a new body of middle-class reformers: ". . . If such a makeshift may be dignified into an ideology, its ideology is State Socialism." Such reformers (and here Boudin generally referred to the Progressive movement and its allies) were tremendously insecure because their positions in society were being destroyed by the corporation. Even private property was disappearing, while the substitution of collective forms of ownership continued apace. The result was the divorce of ownership from control, until stock ownership became merely a title to revenues.[30]

Boudin agreed with Walling on several important points, particularly in his discussion of the modern role of the corporation and the source of collectivist ideology, but he made no homage to individualism. Unlike Walling, he sought to update Marx, not criticize him. He provided an important attack on collectivism, but the roots of his criticism did not lie in the individualism of such writers as Whitman, Traubel, Tolstoy, or Nietzsche. His writing was far more akin to orthodox socialism and closer to the kind of examination of modern industrialism made by Morris Hillquit. Hillquit's designation of a Progressive "transitional state" was none other than the state socialism of Boudin and Walling. Hillquit also argued that socialism could not be defended by political and economic centralism, and that collectivism could be an instrument of capitalism as well as socialism. He agreed that socialism was the final state of a long evolutionary process, without cataclysm; but neither Boudin nor Hillquit could match Walling's fervent belief in individualism, nor his willingness to discard Marx and German philosophy. Thus even in his agreement with other socialist writers, Walling stood a distance apart.[31]

The years 1914, 1915, and 1916, following his most productive intellectual days, were a time of re-evaluation for Walling. He drastically revised most of his socialist beliefs, stretching those that remained to attack the world socialist movement and to justify his support of Allied war aims. In the course of his bitter withdrawal from the radical movement, Walling ultimately condemned himself to relative obscurity, becoming the right-hand ideologist for the American Federation of Labor. His understanding of collectivism gradually collapsed as he embraced a form of Industrial Democracy. The independence of mind he had once exercised so fruitfully in the Socialist party, he now put at the services of that craft unionism he had once characterized as state socialist.

Walling's attitude toward World War I rested largely upon two immediate reactions to the outbreak of fighting. One was that Germany should be blamed for inciting the struggle, and that her behavior in Belgium and elsewhere proved that German autocracy (or state socialism, as he now sometimes called it), had to be destroyed. This was the primary issue of the war. It followed that German socialists who supported the war were guilty of upholding autocracy. Second, Walling believed that the war would destroy narrow economic nationalism and lay the groundwork for a true international system. Thus Walling was naturally attracted to Wilson's version of this idea in the Fourteen Points.

At first Walling was optimistic about the war. The struggle, he wrote in 1914, would probably lead to state socialism, perhaps even real socialism in some European nations. At a minimum, the forces it unleashed would destroy the world's most powerful autocratic governments in Russia, Austria, and Germany. While it was still unclear what the position of German Socialists would be, Walling reaffirmed his faith in their movement, feeling that the Social Democrats would oppose war appropriations and ultimately bring down the kaiser's government. As he wrote in October 1914, "Before it is finished, the present conflict will in all probability cease to be a war between nations and will become a war between autocracy and democracy." Before the German invasion of Belgium he counted on German Socialists to rise up against militarism. Soon, he argued in October, "we shall know enough of the state of mind of the German and Russian Socialists to predict with confidence the revolutionary line of action they will take"[32]

But Walling was wrong. German Socialists did not denounce the war. His first reaction was to flounder about for some interpretation of the German state that would explain why Socialists had continued to support it. His answer was, at best, confusing. Germany represented a highly nationalistic form of state socialism which all true democrats ought to reject. Yet, he argued, state socialism could be democratic; after all, he conceded, it "offers us by far the most promising bridge to the social and industrial democracy of the future." He was not sure, in other words, what it was that made Germany the militaristic, undemocratic state that it was. At the same time, he expected that the war might bring "socialism in our generation," but he rejected any socialist interpretation of the war that blamed it on capitalism. He preferred his own division of the world into nationalistic nations (bad) and internationalist ones (good). The socialist claim that war followed from imperialism, or that the struggle ought to be characterized as the internal warfare of world capitalism, was nonsense.[33]

These opinions brought him into a bitter clash that developed in the American Socialist party, which as a whole opposed the war. This opposition, Walling believed, transformed even the American party into an ally of the kaiser. It was treason to the socialist cause, made even worse because a great many capitalists, particularly in the United States, France, and England, supported what he felt was true internationalism and scoffed at pacifism or neutrality, which played into German hands. By April 1916, Walling had joined the pro-war League for the Enforcement of Peace. And in July of that same year he declared, "Prussia is at the bottom of it all."

Well into the war, Walling argued that the correct position of real socialists ought to be the creation of an armed internationalism, which would promote an international economic community of democratic nations. In January 1917, after he had proposed an international league, Walling commented: "The proposed league of nations to enforce peace must be built exclusively upon an economic foundation . . . and must set for its immediate as well as its ultimate goal the elimination of the economic causes of war." When America entered the war soon after, Walling quickly—and inevitably—endorsed Wilson's Fourteen Points.

The United States entrance into the war sharpened Walling's attacks upon his comrades in the American Socialist party, and provoked him into irrational snap judgments about the state's need to enforce wartime social order. Once an advocate of individual liberty, he wrote to former President Roosevelt in July 1917, asking him to use his influence to stop the *New York Tribune* from publishing what he considered pacifist articles. In November he claimed that pro-Germans had taken over the American Socialist party and were "capturing the masses of our cities by underground methods." He even quarreled bitterly with his wife who did not share his enthusiasm for the Allies.[34]

Walling's strident attacks on socialists led him to quit the American Socialist party in the summer of 1917, after a bitter struggle. He joined with a number of other former socialist intellectuals, including Charles Russell, Henry L. Slobodin, J. G. Phelps Stokes, James MacKaye, William James Ghent, Robert Rives La Monte, John Spargo, and Algie Simons, in the Social Democratic League, a pro-war organization.

Walling's role in the new Social Democratic League was nonetheless an uncomfortable one. His correspondence with other members of the League was often contentious and argumentative over points of organization and policy. He was particularly disturbed by the prominent role of John Spargo. Walling was not included in the first organizational sessions of the Social Democratic League, or in the later National party, a conglomerate political entity brought together by the League and consisting of leftover elements from the Progressive and Prohibition parties. As Walling wrote to Phelps Stokes, he opposed even the name National party, as well as the invocation of God in its charter: "I protest against the formation of a Socialist Party, for the purposes of a non Socialist Party."

Still, the Social Democratic League, the National party, and another organization supported by intellectuals, the American Alliance for Labor and Democracy (connected to the AFL), all provided a non-Socialist party alternative for radicals and ex-radicals who supported World War I, Woodrow Wilson, and the American Federation of Labor. Henry L. Slobodin wrote to Phelps Stokes in 1919 reminding him of this purpose: "I know that the S. D. L. was a mere makeshift for political purposes and I had no objection to you and Spargo using it as you did for the organization of the National Party."[35] Understandably, the primary activity of the League was propagandistic. For example, it sent a pro-war mission to Europe in June 1918 to try to influence the course of the Russian Revolution and to solidify European socialist support behind Allied war aims.

Walling's general agreement with these aims and his support of Wilson and Gompers made him a prominent figure in the international split in the socialist movement. In the end, he became a socialist adviser to Wilson and a strong opponent of the Russian Revolution. In the United States his attacks on the Socialist party became hysterical. In 1917, for example, he wrote that the Socialists were really the party of German agitation: "Not one of the leaders of the German agitation in this country is actually a working man (Hillquit is a corporation lawyer, Berger for many years has been a professional politician and before that was a schoolteacher). The view I represent, that the Socialist Party under its present control is directed from Berlin, is also held by A. M. Simons, Winfield Gaylord, John Spargo, Charles Edward Russell and others of the most popular of the Socialist leaders." Pacifism, he wrote, was a German trick; the Socialist party was a German front. Walling's pro-war agitation became so extreme that he grew intolerant of free speech for socialists, and even supported barring them from public office. It was too severe a position for some of the other members of the Social Democratic League, particularly Upton Sinclair, who wrote to Walling reminding him that of all socialists he (Walling) had done the most through his writings to justify a left-wing position.[36]

As Walling became an apologist for American war aims, he also relinquished his opposition to progressivism, and in fact altered his own reform aims to conform to those of the Wilson administration and the AFL. But he retained some of the style and content of his earlier theories. Thus he came to believe in two important types of reform: one Industrial Democracy and possible in the United States, and the other, state socialism, which already existed in Germany. As he wrote in 1918, "The Socialism [i.e., Industrial Democracy] at which we aim has nothing in common with the regimentation that Socialists of Prussia are forced to accept in fact and cannot get rid of in their thinking—submerged as they are in the vast sea of Prussian Kultur."

The Russian Revolution forced Walling to lop off another chunk of his socialist ideology. He had always opposed the Bolsheviks, and so he was delighted with the moderate Kerensky's victory during the first stages of the revolution. He called Kerensky the representative of all non-German socialism in Russia, and claimed further that Kerensky's socialism and internationalism were identical "point by point—with the new American internationalism voiced by Woodrow Wilson." Asked by Wilson to go with the Root Mission to Russia in the spring of 1917, Walling declined, citing his "views and my personal situation." But he agreed with one purpose of the mission, which was to keep Russia in the war. When the Bolsheviks took power in the fall, Walling was sure this was part of a larger German plot to win the war. As he wrote in 1918: "Germany did not invent Lenin but she did discover him and raise him from obscurity. Germany did not create the Bolsheviki but they have never denied that Germany backed them."[37] Walling forgot that in 1905 he had been able to find and interview Lenin in spite of his "obscurity."

Walling now wrote virulent articles attacking not only Prussianism but anyone who so much as advocated recognition of the Soviet Union. Even Woodrow Wilson could not completely pass his evangelical inspection. As he wrote his brother in 1919, "The evidence from public expressions of influential friends of Mr. Wilson is sufficient enough to make a book to prove the pro-Bolshevist tendencies of our government." The Bolsheviks, he noted, had eliminated democracy: they had "invited us to abandon institutions we have won through centuries of struggle against autocracy and to follow them." Americans, he charged, were being inundated with pro-Bolshevik propaganda; his duty was to expose it and the communist revolutionaries for what they were—German agents and barbarians.

Walling's views on the Russian Revolution were summarized and expanded in a book, *Sovietism,* published in 1920. In it he reiterated his accusation that Lenin was a tool of the Germans, arguing that most Bolsheviks were non-Slavs and spoke German as a mother tongue. Lenin's plan, he wrote, was to destroy the democratic state and experiment with new and more repressive forms of state socialism.

The worst effect of bolshevism was its perverse internationalism and its insidious growth even in the United States. The American mind was about to be suffocated by an inundation of Soviet propaganda: "A hundred thousand young American 'intellectuals,' graduates of our colleges and higher institutions of learning, are weekly being taught this anti-American, anti-democratic, pro-Soviet doctrine by certain 'high-brow' publications. . . ." Walling went on to distinguish the precise forms of pro-bolshevism, citing the *Nation,* the *Dial,* and the Progressive Raymond Robbins as active propagandists for the Russians. "More influential and dangerous than the near-Bolshevist," he concluded, "is the group that works towards political recognition of the Soviets."[38]

By 1920, Walling's inventive mind and his deep reading of socialist thought were at work constructing a world demonology peopled by Germans, Russians, and American intellectuals. His perceptive discussion of state socialism had become a tool merely to describe what he did not like about the German government and the Soviet Union. He had lent his services to powers in America which he had once labeled collectivist enemies of individualistic socialism. Undoubtedly, he would have then agreed with socialist George Herron's picture of the world, in which Satan had created the perverted messianic call of the Bolsheviks: "Indeed that is what Satan has done," Herron wrote to his friend Marion Simons in 1919, "in creating the Bolshevist peril and despotism out of an elemental and righteous yearning of a great people. Thus Bolshevism becomes the veriest Antichrist." The rewards of Walling's new position were temporary power as an adviser in the Wilson administration and recognition as an anti-Soviet expert. More lasting was the close relationship he enjoyed with Samuel Gompers and the AFL in the 1920's.[39]

The end of Walling's socialism, the interlude of war service, and his assumption of the role as the AFL's unofficial intellectual marked a distinct period in the evolution of his social thought. Cast by his own choice before World War I as an outsider writing against what he felt was the dominant American political philosophy, he now rejoined the majority. Walling's socialism had always been cantankerous and, potentially at least, disjointed. His elaborate class analyses of state capitalism and state socialism had partially blurred logical contradictions: the times had made it possible for him to say that he did not oppose Progressive measures, just "progressive men and progressive parties."[40] Walling's nightmare of a world-wide evil in the guise of kaiserism and bolshevism, and his extreme bitterness toward former comrades in the American Socialist party, made the whole notion of class revolution abhorrent to him, and the concept, if not the word, socialism extremely distasteful. The Russian Revolution had not followed the course he had predicted, nor had the peasants been allowed to create their natural democracy. Walling's almost mystical faith in the disappearance of classes into a single democratic state was a dream violently interrupted by the dictatorship of the proletariat. Thus in the twenties he began a search for a new political philosophy, and ultimately accepted the once-discarded pluralistic collectivism of the prewar period.

Walling's new political ideas, of course, contained lingering elements from his former socialist days. One of these was a violent dislike for the British Labour party and for the Fabian movement. He had long opposed a labor party, and he described the English Fabians as arrogant state socialists. He accused Ramsay MacDonald of the Labour party, for example, of leading a party under the control of Bernard Shaw and other intellectuals who felt that "Socialism means an all-powerful state, in the hands of a minority, crushing labor unionism and liberty in the interest of small property owners. . . ." At other times he characterized the Labour party as pacifist, or worse, pro-Bolshevik. Walling's anti-British stand was summarized in a letter written in the 1920's: "If it were not for the foreign elements in this country and the capitalistic elements, if it were not for the Labour Party in Great Britain and the sinister international bankers who have their headquarters in London, I would like to see an Anglo-American rapprochement."[41] These were the last vestiges of Walling's theory of state socialism, contorted by his interpretation of World War I, and finally resting as a stigma upon the mild reformism of British labor.

In America, Walling's opposition to a labor party became an integral part of his defense of Gompers' "voluntarism." Sketching a new theory of the state which emptied it of class bias and made it a place where competing economic units might resolve their interests, he wrote in 1925: "Progress by voluntary organization and progress by political democracy are not two hostile or rival movements, they are interdependent parts of a single movement—real or industrial democracy."

Walling had not only to contend with socialist attacks on his adopted union, but with business efforts to bust the unions in the twenties. In this middle position, Walling called upon the state to mediate between competing extremes of socialist and capitalist autocracy. The American government, he wrote in 1926 in *Bankers Magazine,* could not be described as a capitalist government. That term was the invention of the socialists. Actually, America was becoming less and less capitalistic; America had prevented the establishment of capitalism (by which he obviously meant laissez faire). The American system was now divided between three competing and equal groups: labor, agriculture, and business. Upon the internal organization of these functional units within the nation would depend the organization of the state: ". . . The democratic state should and probably will extend its functions only in proportion to the effective development of such organizations of producers and consumers, employers and employees, professional and technical workers."[42]

Walling's final statement of political theory and his most serious re-evaluation of socialism came in 1926 with the publication of the two-volume work *American Labor and American Democracy.* Its purpose was to justify Gompers' voluntaristic theories and to draw a theory of Industrial Democracy in the interests of American labor. The first and fundamental assumption of the book was that the American social and political system, though not perfect, required no fundamental reorganization. Needed political change would follow the recognition by society that units of economic, social, and political power had already organized themselves. Since labor was one of these functional units, it was the job of the American labor movement to force society to recognize it: "The demands of American labor in the last decade constitute an American and a democratic program looking toward a gradual reconstruction of our economic society and its transformation into an industrial and social democracy."[43] The only major threat to this democratic program was the tendency to overorganize society at the top, to create a state socialist bureaucracy sequestered in government boards and commissions and opposed to the independent organization of labor unions, consumers, farmers, and businessmen.

Walling's discussion of the pluralistic state closely resembled some of Herbert Hoover's writings on social organization. But while he often quoted Hoover and Woodrow Wilson, Walling's emphasis was more in favor of labor. More optimistic, too, he assumed that the growing power of each faction in the industrial world increased the possibilities of a viable Industrial Democracy. He thought that the corporation and the union were both endowed with larger social and political responsibilities. As both powers squared off in 1926, they were unequal, for business still by and large controlled the government. Labor, as a countervailing force, was "chief of the democratic forces preventing the full establishment of capitalism."

Labor's program therefore represented a form of social salvation, for it sought to restrain the power of the giant corporations. The best way to assure balance in industrial life might be to reproduce such tripartite commissions as the War Labor Board, which during World War I had promoted cooperation and joint control of industry by labor and management. Government in this formulation would be a "more or less separate entity which must, however, protect society from 'domination' by any one of these groups." Regulatory boards that already existed should be democratized, Walling advised, by which he meant that union representatives should be added to them.

Once done, it would be possible to reorganize government to reflect new sources of social energy and strength: "The government must be controlled, in the main, by economic organizations rather than by political parties or sectarian bodies; Congress must be organized by the great economic groups representing the entire population, or at least every economic function; the government must be divided mainly into economic bodies, representing the chief economic activities of the nation rather than the largely antiquated and often unworkable executive, legislative, and judicial departments. . . ."[44]

The end of Walling's independent and radical political activities had also marked the end of his attacks on American collectivist ideas. He reverted, instead, to labor's version of Industrial Democracy and functional pluralism; to a position which received more elaborate expression in the 1930's by the theologian Reinhold Niebuhr. The searching and independent-minded books Walling wrote before World War I had initiated a reassessment of what he felt were pervasive assumptions about the sociology of the modern industrial state. But he was never able, or perhaps never interested, in extending this thinking, and after the war he reversed his position to accept what he had once denounced. He became what in his own words was the most reprehensible of figures, a mild Fabian. Rather than an attempt to understand social movements and their philosophic justifications, most of his writings after 1920 were an ambitious defense of society as it almost was. Many of the modifications he proposed recalled collectivist ideas. Many of the causes he supported were important. But Walling had succumbed to his own fears and had subordinated his creative self to a fear of social change, a blind moralism about World War I, and an intellectual shallowness. His attempt to preserve individualism was sacrificed to a functional analysis of society as binding and narrow as the collectivist interpretation he had once fought.

9

Reinhold Niebuhr: The Theologian as Power Broker

THE NEW DEAL brought to America the Industrial Democracy that many of the early collectivists had proposed. The
consolidation of each major force within the corporation—
unions, management, and consumers—was encouraged by the
Roosevelt administration. This pluralistic arrangement of
forces strongly resembled proposals made at the end of World
War I by collectivists, and contained in the later writings of
William English Walling and other social commentators. Although the New Deal achieved what many early collectivists
had proposed, their justifications for such social changes were
antiquated by the thirties. Traditional collectivism could not
interpret new complexities, nor express the new mood of the
era. The reality of New Deal reform required a new theoretical base, close to older assumptions and expressing their mixture of Christian commonwealth, evolutionary progressivism,
and economic determinism, but fitted to a new age. The theological politics of Reinhold Niebuhr reintegrated the diverse
principles of collectivism, updated its assumptions, and sanctified the new pluralistic struggle that gave the New Deal its
dynamism.

Niebuhr's thought provided a transition between the modern theory of countervailing powers and the cruder forms of
early collectivism. Coming upon the scene at the end of a long

and contradictory intellectual development, Niebuhr was extremely critical of some of the assumptions of collectivism, especially those that influenced the Social Gospel movement. His critique of those ideas, like the writings of James Burnham, revealed some of the profound limitations as well as the expectations of collectivism. But even in his most critical moments, Niebuhr was too deeply entangled in the traditions of collectivism to discard its principles; so when he turned from criticism to rebuilding political theory, his proposals really amounted to a fresh and immensely influential restatement of collectivism. His new political theology took as a model the contours of modern corporate organization. He refined the concept of the intellectual as a member of a social vanguard, except that he defined this elite as a priesthood. The defense of his diagram of countervailing corporate powers was what it had always been for collectivists—the argument of economic inevitability. And to this program he brought the vigor of a tough-minded, pessimistic mode of expression, perfectly suited to an era of unpleasant choices and self-defensiveness.

Niebuhr's writings, always edged with paradox and irony, were also a criticism of many collectivist assumptions about the new American social order. Indeed, Niebuhr often ruthlessly denounced and ridiculed the ideas of elite rule, planned utopias, optimism, and a faith in progress. But, ironically, the critic was also an architect who, out of the rubble of wrecked assumptions, found the materials to rebuild the foundations of collectivism.

The hypotheses of the collectivist intellectuals were incomplete and sometimes altogether inadequate, but in particular their early twentieth-century utopias seemed especially jerry-built after passage through the war years. Many critics who wished to share the prewar optimism could no longer bring themselves to consider the American political and economic system a complete success after 1920. American society seemed unaffected by those benevolent evolutionary laws written during the prewar period, and the creation of a collectivist society seemed far more difficult.

In a letter to his brother Reinhold, Richard Niebuhr suggested that the two of them would make good Catholics, with

Richard as a friar and Reinhold as a pope. The papal note which Richard detected in his brother's works partly derived from Reinhold's theology and partly from his insistence upon the social relevance of religious statements. Doctrinal matters were always important to him, but in his writings the political imperatives are often more compelling than the religious ones. Each of Reinhold Niebuhr's books and articles was in a sense a position paper, and as such an addition to a growing body of Christian dogma. Niebuhr's theology and his politics joined to make an intensely personal but nonetheless universalized expression. For him, politics was the practical side of a systematic theology; such was his intellectual power and influence that he helped to create a theological revival.

As a young theological student, Reinhold Niebuhr accepted much of the intellectual content of the Social Gospel movement in American Protestantism, and was not alone among theological optimists in supporting World War I. But the devastating struggle in Europe, combined with his experience as a young minister in a working-class neighborhood of Detroit, stilled his praise of the war and made him deeply suspicious of the view that capitalism was reforming itself. Armed with a new theological pessimism, Niebuhr struck out against what he called the naive beliefs of his fellow theologians and political commentators. He clearly understood that American institutions did not automatically create justice and equality. He understood as well the weakness of the Protestant church, and worried deeply about the cohesiveness of a society which preached reason and practiced force. When he attacked what he called optimistic liberalism, he did so because he had little faith in the creative power of man's rationality; he began to doubt the benevolence of technology or the viability of the urban society which it created.

But Niebuhr's critique of these ideas—many of which were the principal tenets of collectivism—was only partial, for he struck only at their weakest points. By the end of the 1930's he had changed his mind again. After a short period of infatuation with Marxist theory, he concluded that, after all, American society was relatively successful, and that this approximately just society, whatever its shortcomings, was probably the best that civilization could hope for. Collectivism was the keystone of his writings, and his subtle arguments for a pluralistic society, based upon an equilibrium of organized power mediated by a neutral state, reproduced and updated many of the arguments made before World War I under the banner of Industrial Democracy. Unencumbered now by the troublesome ideas of human perfection and constant progress, Niebuhr used man's inevitable sinfulness to argue that America was probably the best of all possible secular worlds. In the 1940's and 1950's he ceased to argue for serious social change; still his own immensely committed life as a social reformer itself became the mirror image of the good life. In the larger sense, Niebuhr came to trust in Providence and history (intellectuals would have said "evolution" thirty years earlier) for validation of his social ideas. In the end, his new social and economic theory posited an automatically functioning society reminiscent, though on a grand scale, of laissez faire. It apotheosized an ethic of struggle. These theoretical findings he joined to the older, still intact assumptions of collectivism.

Reinhold Niebuhr was born on June 21, 1892, into a family with a longstanding ministerial tradition. "My Mother," he wrote, was the daughter of "a minister in a Church to which I belong, the Evangelical and Reformed Church. . . . She was a rather unusually active and resourceful woman, acting as a kind of assistant pastor, first to her father, then to my father, and then to me in my first parish in Detroit." His father, a German immigrant from Lippe-Detmold, settled in San Francisco, then moved his family to Missouri, and thence to Illinois. Reinhold's brother Richard was to become a noted student of the history of American Protestantism.

As a young man destined for the ministry, Niebuhr attended Yale Divinity School. Almost immediately after graduation, he took up his first pastorate, at Bethel Evangelical Church in Detroit. Here he encountered Henry Ford's working class, who sweated under the system of "welfare capitalism" to turn out the cars that filled the highways of the 1920's. Niebuhr was not beguiled by Ford's efficiency figures, nor by his bloated claims of high wages. Instead he found failure in every direction he turned: the failure of the churches to be relevant, the failure of the industrial system to provide justice, and the failure of the political system to promote change. Still a young man, he began to look for different political solutions and, at the same time, to nourish his discouragement by re-examining the optimistic premises of the Social Gospel movement that had been supported by such men as Harry F. Ward. In the early 1920's Niebuhr began to publish articles in such journals as Norman Thomas's *World Tomorrow*. Simultaneously, he began a long and important relationship with the American Socialist party, and in 1928 he joined the League for Independent Political Action. His support for the Socialists continued through the 1930's, though late in the decade he grew disillusioned with what he called their isolationism. Meanwhile, his political and theological writings earned him a position at the Union Theological Seminary in New York City, where he had a long and eminent career.[1]

As a theologian and a political observer, Niebuhr experimented with various forms of writing. He published several important books in the thirties and early forties. He also edited several magazines, the first among them being *World Tomorrow* in 1929. In 1936 he joined the Fellowship of Socialist Christians in America and became an editor of their journal, *Radical Religion*. He later founded *Christianity and Crisis*, a journal devoted to his own form of neo-orthodox Protestantism and support for America's entrance into World War II.

As for his political activities, in 1930 he ran for the New York State Senate from the 19th District in Manhattan. He supported Norman Thomas for President in 1932 and 1936, but switched to Roosevelt in 1940. After a decade of socialist politics, he helped to organize the Union for Democratic Action to gather intellectual and union support for nonsocialist political liberals. "We organized in 1941," he later explained, "in order to solidify the anti-Communist liberal forces of the country." To the union leader David Dubinsky he wrote that the Union for Democratic Action was pro-interventionist: "We are anxious to relate the fight for democracy on the foreign front with the domestic issues in a way which we believe is not being done by the interventionist organizations more broadly based than we are." He also joined the New York Liberal party as a gesture to solidify the anti-communist, pro-labor forces in that city. As he later explained: "We wanted to organize a party which would offer the workingman a chance to vote against the corruption of Tammany Hall, and secondly, against the conservatism of the Republican Party, and thirdly, against the Communism of the Labor Party."

Niebuhr widened the influence of his political ideas through membership in an amazing number of organizations, from the Delta Cooperative Farm in Hillhouse, Mississippi, to official United States missions abroad. But all of these various activities culminated in his support for the Americans for Democratic Action. This immensely important organization bore the imprint of Niebuhr's philosophy, both through his writings and through his friendship with many of its members. The ADA recognized this influence in 1957: "We look upon him as the spiritual father of the A.D.A."[2] The evolution of Niebuhr's political theology, then, took him from a reconsideration of the assumptions of prewar social thinking to the ADA—from an incomplete vision of mass industrial society to a full-blown vision of a collective though internally competitive society.

The theological context for almost all of Reinhold Niebuhr's writings (even in the forties and fifties) was the pre–World War I Social Gospel movement, just as his political writings were often pervaded by prewar political assumptions. In the prewar years the Social Gospel theologians had impressed a liberal political program upon the Protestant church, comprised of a peculiar blend of optimistic social prediction and an unswerving faith in man's rationality. Niebuhr decided, quite early on, that both this theology and its politics were wrong. He argued that the Social Gospel was the dominant ideology of the majority of liberal clergy who were bent upon ending social injustice and instituting—if not a kingdom of God on earth—at least a redeemed society. By no means, however, did this movement dominate the American pastorate, and certainly not the Protestant laity. Yet these ideas were a constant reference point in Niebuhr's writings, because the Social Gospel was a movement with which he had sympathized as a youth, and because it seemed to represent the most reform-

minded element of the church—an element whose radicalism
he intended to challenge.

Niebuhr's theological career was based upon an ever-deep-
ening dislike for the ideas of the Social Gospel and the creation of what he considered to be the only wise alternative to
it: a psychologically and politically realistic orthodoxy.
Niebuhr saw the Social Gospel and modern political and economic liberalism as two parts of the same world view, and
judged both of them guilty of the same confusions. Through
a circuitous route, he drew a new political ideology tied to a
far more pessimistic, even fatalistic, view of mankind, one
fitted to a modern world of unholy choices. Despite his withering critique of liberal assumptions, and despite his contempt
for the optimistic utopian vein of the Progressive years,
Niebuhr's new realism retained strong ties to older theories,
for the reality he so keenly stressed was the developing system
of corporate relationships. Through strenuous intellectual
effort, he forced the evolution of collectivist assumptions into
the postwar world. From American social and political institutions in the thirties and forties, he derived new laws of social
development. Although he stridently denied any such intention, his writing contained a celebration of the world as it was.
Collectivist assumptions, as tested and tempered in his writing, became more subtle than those of his predecessors and
politically more useful. By the end of the 1930's he had
developed a version of collectivism that seemed eminently realistic and altogether appropriate to the shattering events of that
decade.

The Social Gospel movement, which began in the late 1870's
and developed through the 1890's and into the twentieth century, was a theological-political movement designed by its adherents to revitalize the Protestant church. At many points it
matched the principles and general purposes of the collectivism of secular social reformers. While the movement itself
was largely led by middle-class ministers, theologians, and
laity, its goal was to deal with the enormous changes in
American society brought about by the effects of urbanization
and industrialization. The new industrial working class and
the labor violence which surrounded certain industries made

the older assumptions of ministers seem obsolete, if not reactionary. Under the new conditions of life in America, it became more and more difficult to believe in a Christianized version of Spencerism and laissez-faire economics. As one writer has put it, "Undoubtedly the realization of working class alienation caused many Protestant leaders to re-examine their social attitudes."

Instead of advising workingmen to accept their miserable callings as providential, Social Gospel ministers worked for a redeemed society for all men on earth. The movement was catholic in its tolerance and its thrust, hoping to knit some form of unity among the scattered American Protestant churches. The hope for a regenerated society reached its peak immediately before the end of World War I. Many Social Gospel ministers had invested great hope in a better world's coming into being after the war. Instead of a redeemed society and church, however, the Social Gospel movement had to face indifference in the 1920's, and even hostility from some of its former supporters—among them, Reinhold Niebuhr. The movement revived slightly in the thirties, but the most important development of that decade in American Protestantism was undoubtedly the growing importance of Niebuhr's own neo-realism. Niebuhr and his followers tried to outflank the Social Gospel from the left: "The neo-radicals were for the most part militant socialists and hoped to win the leadership of Christian socialism after Rome had announced its own social philosophy. Since Marxism was relatively weak in the United States the Protestant Christian socialists hoped to win the sympathy of American labor, and they moved decidedly 'to the left' of the platform on which the Social Gospel had stood."[3] The Social Gospel represented secularization in religion and liberalism in politics, and it was this religious and political stance which Niebuhr attacked, and against which he created his own particular formulation of the modern collective state.

Niebuhr's early falling out with the Social Gospel movement, his despair with the aftermath of World War I, and his troubling pastorate in Detroit all convinced him that modern civilization was profoundly diseased. In 1928, in one of several autobiographical articles, he wrote that he had once been an optimist: "I thought that freedom was broadening down from precedent to precedent and that virtue needed only time and the aid of electricity to win its victories. I identified civilization with the Kingdom of God. Now I saw how civilization was enlarging the areas of conflict, increasing the units of battle, and sharpening the tools of destruction." Again: "The war convinced me that religion can be effective only if it resists the embraces of civilization." Obviously, Niebuhr was upset by the moralism and piousness of ministers who had supported World War I. He was perhaps most horrified by the fact that he had been among them. But the process of disillusionment which Niebuhr describes with such apparent candor seems almost too dramatic to be accurate. The ideas he rejected, along with his expression of discouragement with "civilization," were only partly a consequence of the war. Nor could the war be said to have provided the impetus for his recurring attacks upon the premises of the Social Gospel movement and optimistic liberalism.

The war did, however, illustrate one fact about contemporary life for Niebuhr, who found in it a perfect example of the propensity for the self-deception of modern Christianity. As he wrote in 1920, the church made no profit from its support of the war; in fact, the church was not even an important force in deciding social progress. In 1923 he recorded in his diary: "Gradually the whole horrible truth about the war is being revealed. Every new book destroys some further illusion. How can we ever again believe anything when we compare the solemn pretensions of statesmen with the cynically conceived secret treaties?"[4] He next rejected the premises of social progress: "In one sense modern civilization substitutes unconscious sins of more destructive consequences for conscious sins of less destructive consequences." Although searching for the best means to reform society, Niebuhr also suspected that reforms might lead to a society worse than the present one, because of the tendency of good intentions to disguise evil motives.

Niebuhr always believed that the church ought to be at the center of reform. But, like any human institution, the church

was governed by motives other than idealism, and it was cor-
rupted by reality. "The Christian church assumes too easily,"
he wrote in 1923, "that it is the perfect instrument of its gospel.
It is too unconscious of the instincts in its corporate life that
beguile it to infidelity." If the church felt itself to be the spiritual source of reform, then its own sins of self-deception were
enormous and costly, for pride and pretense caused failure.
The mechanics of this misunderstanding and its destructive
potential fascinated Niebuhr, who began a long search for the
church's weakness in the philosophic and theological origins
of the Social Gospel and the class interests of its adherents. He
concluded, rather quickly, that the Protestant churches had
forgotten the importance of sin. Liberal Christianity, he wrote
in 1926, had become optimistic about man and social progress
because it had uncritically absorbed the assumptions of such
intellectual movements as Romanticism and reform Darwinism which worshiped reality: "Whenever God is completely
identified with the real he ceases to be a God of the ideal."
Social sin, Niebuhr decided, was far more complex and dangerous than previously assumed by theologians who mistook
sentimental good will for goodness: the church "was blind
therefore to the essentially evil attitudes into which men of
sentimental goodwill might be tempted by their environment."[5]

More injurious than self-deception, however, was the Protestant church's attachment to the American middle class.
Niebuhr condemned this tie: "The Christian church, particularly the Protestant Church, is predominantly middle class and
the middle classes are more naive in their social outlook and
less mindful of the deeper problems of social reorganizations,
not only than the disinherited, but than the more aristocratic
classes."

If the church were to redeem society and save any part of
it, in Niebuhr's view in the 1920's, it had only two options. One
was to use the institution of the church, through pastoral pressure upon the laity, to convince the middle classes to be more
sympathetic to those whom they were, in fact, oppressing.
Niebuhr wrote in 1920: "Some kind of democratization of industry and some degree of socialization of property are the ul-

timate goals toward which our whole political and social life is tending." To achieve this sanctified Industrial Democracy the church ought to appeal to the "unselfish instincts of the holding classes and will emphasize that there can be no social salvation without sacrifice. . . ." But Niebuhr soon realized that the holding classes were deaf to such solutions, and that the church, following its middle-class benefactors, was not prepared to live by such high ideals.

A far more pessimistic option was for the church to persuade society to take a realistic attitude toward reform. This meant that the churches would first have to reform themselves. No workable program was possible without a deep understanding of individual psychology and the social process. This Niebuhr set out to acquire, and it led him toward a reappraisal of some of the fundamental theological questions of the day. Protestantism historically had been aware of the nature of sin, he wrote, but while sin, self-love, and pride were obvious elements of all human actions, the modern church had forgotten these enemies of social change because it had pulled a hood of liberal optimism over its own head. Christians interested in a just society would therefore be compelled to do two things: reassert the social and psychological reality of the Christian prophecy with its emphasis upon man's moral incompleteness, and put forth a realistic description of the social forces in modern industrial society.[6]

To understand human and social reality, Niebuhr continued, it was necessary to perceive that the whole of Western civilization was obviously out of control: "The fact is that the social life of the western world is almost completely outside of ethical control." This absence of ethical restraints meant that society could no longer be described in terms of nineteenth-century social theory; it no longer conformed to the contours of classical liberalism. Therefore, even the most benevolent motivations were often twisted into blatant acts of social imperialism. The centrifugal forces of modernism and industrialism were bursting the bounds of social cohesion. Industrial civilization, as conceived by the middle classes, was on the verge of degeneration. The church, the only institution capable of regenerating cohesion, was itself the victim of the same forces. Thus the church had "lost the chance of becoming the unifying element in our American society." Using what was to become a favorite metaphoric expression, Niebuhr wrote that society was left adrift between the Scylla of chaos and the Charybdis of force.[7]

Niebuhr's rejection of the Social Gospel and political liberalism was based, then, primarily upon the theory of industrial alienation which, he felt, undercut many of the optimistic assumptions of prewar collectivism. The reality of the war's aftermath convinced him that economic and political forces were far more important than the rhetoric of self-justification. This was, in the main, his reaction to Detroit. In many of the sermons he preached there in the early 1920's, he deplored the effects of industrial civilization and the impersonality of the machine age with its destruction of man's creativity. This new civilization, he maintained, had destroyed the family and created a style of life based upon the automobile and the movie. "This sort of slavery to a machine appalls me," he wrote in a sermon. Somewhat later, in his diary, he described a trip through an automobile factory. The experience was obviously extremely distasteful: "So artificial is life that these factories are like a strange world to me, though I have lived close to them for many years. The foundry interested me particularly. The heat was terrific. The men seemed weary. Here manual labor is a drudgery and toil is slavery. The men cannot possibly find any satisfaction in their work."[8]

In the light of his Detroit experience, Niebuhr wrote two articles attacking Henry Ford and the myths that surrounded the Ford Motor Company. He argued that conditions in the plants were terrible, despite the claims put forth by Ford's press agents. In Niebuhr's view, Ford was being touted by journalists as a humane industrial leader, when he actually held a "social philosophy not advanced beyond the doctrinaire individualism of the nineteenth century." This tight-fisted, old-fashioned entrepreneur was no exceptional phenomenon, Niebuhr continued, for Henry Ford "is America."

Extending his analysis of the industrial plant, Niebuhr concluded that the whole of industrial society was essentially an alienating experience. "A big city is not a society held together by human bonds. Its people are spiritually isolated even though they are mechanically dependent upon one another. In such a situation it is difficult to create and preserve moral and cultural traditions which each individual needs to save his life from anarchy." Thus modern man stood naked before his new social creator, the machine. "What distinguishes our life from that of our fathers," Niebuhr remarked, "is the fact that our sense of the organic relationship to society and to the universe has been destroyed." The Crash of 1929 and the onset of depression strengthened Niebuhr's analysis. Progress, science, invention, and mechanization had destroyed the robust relationships of the past, until men had become the victims of their own achievements. Modern industrial life was tragic. The glib acceptance of old notions, such as the rights of property, merely made matters worse; the result was the deterioration of the human community. Only the need to change remained.[9]

By the early thirties Niebuhr had worked backward in his analysis to the very questions that had agitated the theologians of the Social Gospel and the theorists of collectivist reform. But he rejected not merely the tone of their answers but their goal of establishing a kingdom of heaven on earth. As he viewed things, the church as an institution lacked relevant answers; the middle classes saw life only through the lens of optimism; and the political ideologies of the day were all disguised justifications for evil-doing. If all this were true, what remained?

Niebuhr's pessimism provided the answer. Rather than change society, men should develop new attitudes toward social reality. Man's sinful nature, Niebuhr argued, was his fundamental nature, and this inevitably led him to assert a kind of social "imperialism" over others. (Niebuhr frequently used political terminology to describe the individual personality.) Modern society, which was far less unified than ever before, was simultaneously threatened by extreme force and anarchy—both forms of personal tyranny. Thus society magnified individual evil a hundredfold, armed it with the power of property and armies, and justified it with ideology. Contention and strife were the most elemental facts of modern industrial life. Yet here, wrote Niebuhr, also resided society's most potentially liberating forces. To be optimistic about the outcome of the struggle, given man's terrible alienation from man, was also to begin the reconstruction of social imagination. "The real battle of the day," Niebuhr wrote, "is the fight against an impersonal civilization, against the inhuman machine which has dehumanized the mechanic, against the great metropolises in which we live wherein neighborliness has been destroyed."

Discovering the basis for a realistic social imagination was the practical side of Niebuhr's search for a realistic theological psychology. He now knew, he felt, the "brutal facts of life." But he needed to place them in the context of a creative social theory. How could society, he asked, recognize industrial alienation and class struggle and still hold together? What social and religious vision could provide the social cohesion to contain the enormous wasted and conflicting energies of civilization? How could society tame the organized violence that preyed upon it?

The answers to these questions came slowly over two decades of writing and political activities. If it were true, as Niebuhr assumed, that conventional rationality, optimism, and middle-class liberalism were all feigned solutions, then perhaps struggle, violence, and social evil, the irrational effects of industrialism, provided the key to a more just society. If this were true, then how, Niebuhr asked, could prophetic Christianity reassert its supremacy over the secularized church which worshiped progress? In the grip of this dilemma, Niebuhr turned to the working class, to the disinherited who, as he warned in 1931, in their passionate hatred might make "short shrift of the whole of our civilization."[10] Here, he believed, was a vein of raw energy to tap; here, possibly, was a source for a new and "robust" social vision. Following the logic of his own paradoxes, Niebuhr was inevitably drawn to the exploited and the downtrodden, the most potentially violent of social forces.

Niebuhr was nonetheless always ambiguous about the working class and about Marxism, which he considered to be its native ideology. He never completely accepted either, for he never explicitly went on record hoping for revolution or for the rationally planned society that would follow. As a prophet, Niebuhr never wished entirely to be a participant. As a theologian, his Christian vision stood upon the shoulders of the working class. He saw in Marx both a brilliant critic of the nineteenth century and the strongest competitor for the allegiance of thinkers in the twentieth, because Marx, like himself, saw the working class as a social instrumentality. For two decades, Niebuhr worked to amalgamate Christianity and socialism, until, at the end of the 1930's, having derived the essence of his final theological position, he jettisoned the spent body of Christian Socialist theories.

During the twenties Niebuhr had become more and more interested in socialism and socialist organization. By 1930 he had visited the Soviet Union, which was becoming the final phase of the political education of many other American intellectuals. After this experience he became more sincerely a socialist. He moved closer to Marx, publishing several important books in the middle thirties, including *Reflections on the End of an Era,* and *Moral Man and Immoral Society.* He worked actively as a Christian Socialist and wrote a number of searching critiques of the New Deal. At the same time, on a contrary polarity of his mind, he made the Soviet Union a test for the theories of Marx, an experimental society whose fate would prove the truth or falsity of Marx's vision.

The Crash and the depression years, far from shaking Niebuhr's world view, tended to confirm his confidence in his own pre-thirties thinking. The tension between disorder and force more than ever became the operative dilemma in his thought. His social theories became increasingly concerned with bridging the gap between conflict and cohesion. By the end of the thirties he had decided that this cohesion was to be found nowhere in society itself, but only in the Christian prophecy. This prophecy alone could tolerate the disquieting facts of reality, the worst of which was that man's predominant social experience was conflict. Man's existence was therefore a divided and hence a tragic one. To believe otherwise was to invite self-deception.

In 1932, Niebuhr once again posed his by-now-familiar dilemma of choosing between "Catastrophe or Social Control." "We are merely a vast horde of people," he remarked, "let loose on a continent with little to unify us by way of common cultural, moral and religious traditions." But the 1930's offered several examples of previously untried social unity, and Niebuhr paid them close attention. The first of these was fascism, which, he argued, was a comprehensive attempt to revive the organic relationships that had once prevailed in Western culture. Such an effort coincided with his own long search for new sources of social cohesion. But Niebuhr was merely nostalgic about feudal relationships, and he recoiled from Germany's forced feudalization of culture. He wrote in 1935: "In spite of the fact that the superimposition of feudalistic forms, derived from an agrarian past, upon the realities of an industrial civilization leads to particularly atrocious forms of injustice and tyranny, there is a certain ironic justice in the rebirth of feudalism in our age."[11] Modernized feudalism at least confronted the central problem in modern society of the breakdown of organic and religious ties. But fascist theory and practice left nothing to emulate.

Yet the appearance of fascism made the need to reassert some form of social cohesion even more compelling than before. True social unity might come, Niebuhr concluded, from Marxism, the principal contending model of modern social organization. In 1939 he wrote that, having tried all sorts of alternatives to Christianity during the depression decade, he had found them all wanting. But Marxism was the only one which he seriously considered, and for two reasons. Marx had understood the central historical role of the working classes in a way that appealed to Niebuhr. Moreover, he provided a social vision that went far beyond the pale liberalism of his day, and that contradicted the soft-minded bourgeois sense of justice. Marx created, Niebuhr felt, a religious view which challenged Christianity, because he had understood that only a utopian vision could provide the basic impulses necessary to social action. Thus Marx was both teacher and antichrist to Niebuhr. Marx was even correct, in his view, to claim that

Christianity was the opiate of the masses. Niebuhr would have added only one qualification: that it was really the Social Gospel that was deceiving most men of religious persuasion.

What Niebuhr called "religion" in his writings was also the ideological and psychological source of social unity: "Religion is first of all a force of order and unity in the lives of individuals." Modern life would sink to incredible brutality without some object of worship, without some form of religion. "It follows," Niebuhr continued, "that the religious character of a political movement is the source of both its strength and its demonic peril." Marxism's millennial aspect provided a moral incentive to its followers. It creatively merged pessimism and optimism, reality and a vision toward altering reality.[12]

Another of Marx's ideas fascinated Niebuhr, and this was his suggestion that the very nature of social struggle was paradoxical. Marx understood that only by comprehending the reality of undisguised social competition could society even change itself. As Niebuhr paraphrased Marx in 1936: "Radicalism is more realistic than liberalism in gauging the social forces of the contemporary situation and recognizing that a new social order must emerge out of a conflict of interest and impulse as much as from a conquest of impulse by reason. . . ." Marx's great achievement, as Niebuhr saw it, was his recognition that conflict was creative. "The relation of social classes in society is conceived of wholly in terms of the conflict of power with power." The belief that Marx had discovered that society was both driven and divided by a struggle for power was the crux of Niebuhr's attraction to Marxism: "Destruction of power is regarded as a prerequisite of its attainment." Marx, the philosopher of social struggle, was a perfect match for Niebuhr's psychological theories—especially his theory that self-interest inevitably ended in antisocial behavior. Niebuhr thus extended his interpretation of Marx back into history to rewrite Marx's dialectic in terms of a continuing struggle for power.[13]

Yet Niebuhr also found himself in sharp disagreement with Marx in certain crucial areas. Marx saw a resolution to historical struggle when society finally asserted its predominance over the forces of disintegration. Niebuhr, on the other hand, saw nothing but unending competition and struggle, an infinite dialectical and possibly worsening process built into society by man's imperfections. In this disagreement lay the grounds for Niebuhr's final condemnation of Marx and his description of radicalism as a demonic force. Marx, like the liberals, was ultimately guilty of empty optimism, trapped by the false hope that the struggles of mankind would end with the achievement of a classless society. The result, Niebuhr felt, was an extraordinary piece of unconscious evil. "If we want to see the power of religion," he wrote, "functioning creatively with all the furor and all the fervor which characterize vital religion, with all of the peril of fanaticism which belongs to anything creative, we have to turn to a sect which is most vociferous in disavowing religion, the Communists." Despite all of Marx's brilliance, Niebuhr found him to have no understanding of the tragic meaning of existence.

Niebuhr's own interpretation of the concept of class revealed another disagreement with Marx. For Marx, the predominant social characteristics of a period reflected its property forms and not its power relationships. In this view, man's tyranny over man was historical, and not necessarily inborn. By shifting the focus of Marx's interpretation from the mode of production to the more generalized mode of control (that is, power), Niebuhr distorted Marx's meaning. But far more important, he revealed his own obsession with the question of power in modern society.

Niebuhr's emphasis upon power led him to the most important tenet of his social philosophy: that the goal of mankind ought to be an approximate justice based upon a temporary balance in society between eternally feuding men. "To concede that justice in political relations depends upon a balance of power," he wrote in 1936, "is to admit that even the most imaginative political policy will fail to achieve perfect justice." This statement marked a step backward from earlier positions, for Niebuhr no longer simply admitted that justice was impossible, he *asserted* it. Struggle could never be eliminated—only balanced. The root of man's social alienation was economic, and located in the division of labor: "In all optimistic utopias, pure sentimentality obscures the fact that there can never be a perfect mutuality of interest between individuals who perform different functions in society." Here was the basic premise of what was to be his version of a new pluralism.

If justice was the goal of society, then balance was the means to attain it. The place to achieve such balance was, for Niebuhr, in productive relationships and, as the collectivists had written before him, within the confines of the modern corporation. Niebuhr's interest in the working class thus appears in a different light, for it now became the force that could redress the imbalance in middle-class liberalism. If the old order died—and Niebuhr believed that this might indeed happen in the early 1930's—then the new order that would take its place must be a form of socialism which would harness the enormous creative and destructive power unleashed by the struggle of the working class to achieve justice. A better society would emerge "out of the class struggle." But it was fanciful, even evil, to imagine that the struggle would ever end or that classes might disappear. Such a belief represented the "enervation of vitality by reason." Thus did Niebuhr take the traditional liberal distrust of class struggle and make it over into the hope that struggle was itself potentially a creative force. Ironically, struggle was creative only because it could never be resolved.[14]

The content of Niebuhr's socialism was given impetus by the social discord and violence that he had seen beneath the forces that shaped world history. In 1932, when his own views were closest to those of the Socialist party, he also believed that American society was on the verge of collapse. In 1934 he gave up ten years' interest in pacifism to take up the idea of creative struggle: "As a Marxian and as a Christian I recognize the tragic character of man's social life, and the inevitability of conflict in it arising from the inability of man ever to bring his egoism completely under the dominion of conscience." He worked hard to appropriate the lessons and insights of Marxism for the Protestant church. In 1935 he noted that socialists must adopt a "catastrophic view of society." They must understand the inevitability of a new order and aid labor and the working class to achieve it. But socialists would be far wiser to ally themselves with a Christian, rather than a Marxist, movement: "I regard it as unfortunate," he wrote to Gilbert Cox in 1935, "that Christian radicalism in America should have such few resources of its own that it expresses itself in terms almost identical with those of an anti-Christian Communism." Even in his most explicitly socialist writings, Niebuhr never lost sight of his primary purpose, which was to revive the heart of Protestantism: "A Christian socialism in our day could find an adequate theology and an adequate political strategy by a return to the dialectic of prophetic religion."[15]

The position he now held was simultaneously one of involvement and noninvolvement. In his voluminous writings, Niebuhr did not spend much time saying precisely what ought to be done to reform society. The details of reform work were of secondary importance to him, a part of the world he did not inhabit but rather observed. He was more comfortable as a commentator, a prophet writing about inevitabilities, immense social struggles, and the forces of history. Psychological and social reality were the subjects of all of his books; absurdity, paradox, and tragedy were his tools of analysis. The causes he supported were innumerable, yet his own writing always came first. Niebuhr wished to create for himself the role of ultimate expert, a Christian sociologist and theologian who, because he knew the paradoxical laws of history, could write about them without contradiction. In his own person he thus reproduced the social role of expert and law-giver to reform movements that was the most essential element in collectivist thought.

The tentative conclusions which Niebuhr had reached by the middle thirties still required several more years to become clear and firm. During these years he gave up independent socialist politics and began to work for the Union for Democratic Action, for the Liberal party of New York, and finally for the Americans for Democratic Action. But his interests still remained on the ideological battlefields of the thirties. Communism, the successful and living embodiment of Marxism, became more and more important to him, because Marxism was a competing ideology and, as he saw it, a religion in its own right.

As the years passed, from the 1930's into the early 1950's,

Niebuhr wrote of the Soviet Union with ever-increasing stri-
dency. After his early trip to Russia in 1930, he reported: "The
simple fact is that a great agrarian nation in which agriculture
up to three years ago was only three per cent mechanized has
suddenly decided to make the machine its god. The real passion of Russia today is not so much socialization as industrialization." The deadly process of industrial alienation was being
consciously hastened by the proletarian revolution. What capitalism had failed to do, communism was achieving: the "ancient culture with its emphasis upon family, religion, hand-
craft and self-sufficient serenity," was capitulating before the
"unconscious imperialism in the proletarian class." The Marxist dream had been realized in mechanistic collectivism,
which, Niebuhr argued, was scarcely better than the mechanistic individualism of middle-class society.

The thirties proved to Niebuhr how much a part of the optimistic age of rationality was the belief in a proletarian revolution. Marx's faith in reason had merely sanctioned political
absolutism in Russia, with the result that organic and creative
relationships in the Soviet Union had disappeared: "Here is
one of several instances in which Communism reveals itself to
be the victim and not the nemesis of a capitalistic civilization,
destined not to correct the weaknesses of a bourgeois culture
but to develop them to the last impossible and absurd con-
sistency."[16]

The Soviet Union's experiment in applied Marxism disproved Marxist theory. "The social and political facts revealed
by the Moscow trials seriously challenge the Marxian interpretation of the state as an instrument of a classless society; they
also throw doubt upon the Marxian analysis of human nature. . . ." As he did earlier with his reaction to World War I,
Niebuhr made this communist experience in Russia the source
of innumerable lessons. Over and over he argued the same
points, each time drawing more and more pessimistic conclusions from them.

During the thirties, Niebuhr also became distressed by the
role of communists in peace and labor organizations in the
United States. His work for the Liberal party, along with his
help in founding the Union for Democratic Action, were both

inspired partly by his desire to gather anti-communist support for reform legislation. As he wrote in 1940, "I have myself worked in dozens of organizations with communists, but their present orientation is so completely under the control of Russian policy that I will not again knowingly have anything to do with any organization in which they function."[17]

Despite this attitude, Niebuhr still had hopes at the beginning of World War II of achieving a world order, with Russia acting in accord with the United States, if only because the Soviets would be too weakened to do much else. Such an order might be attained in an unspecified international framework based upon each nation's mutual self-interest. But when Russia did not behave according to plan, Niebuhr became increasingly strident in condemning Soviet society. In 1943 he compared the communists with Jesuits. By 1952 he scored them as apostates: "The rise of Communism in our world is comparable to the rise of Islam and its challenge of Christian civilization in the high Middle Ages." Communism had become a competing religion, a powerful heresy whose headquarters were in Moscow—the "hated communist conspiracy," as he called it. Niebuhr had, in effect, absolutized Marxist theory and the Russian reality; the experiment was personified as antichrist.

As Niebuhr's hatred for the communist experiment grew, and thereby further justified his pessimism about the results of rational planning, he began to view the New Deal in a more favorable light, and to theorize about its accomplishments and its compromises. Niebuhr's soured view of social alternatives, the class anarchy of bourgeois liberalism versus the rational hell of communism, made the New Deal seem immensely appealing. If life were tragic, then the vision to encompass tragedy must be invented. If balance in society approximated justice, the classes could never be eliminated without sacrificing balance and hence justice itself. If creative evolution could only occur through the struggle for power, then that struggle needed to go on. Only modern capitalism, as expressed and modified by New Deal reformism, allowed all of these forces to express themselves. Only a pluralistic collectivism, balancing management and labor in the context of the democratic

state, could make possible the hope for justice. Only a prophetic Protestantism accurately described the state of human
affairs which made such a system of government necessary. To
attempt to reform this society any further, to smooth its rough
edges, would destroy the friction that made its parts move.

Niebuhr thereupon made the surprising discovery that, inso-
far as possible, the just society had existed in the United States
all along. Historical accident had prevented the nation from
pursuing a course of complete rationalization of society. The
result was a kind of rough justice, which was all anyone could
hope for: "The virtues and the stabilities of western pluralistic
cultures and communities are thus a bequest of historical
'providence' transcending the intentions of any of the agents
of history," he wrote in 1959. The "virtues and achievements
of the pluralistic communities of the West were, in short, the
consequence of an interaction between unintended historical
contingencies and human responses to these contingencies."[18]

The Protestant version of an imperfect, sinful world, peren-
nially blighted with error and pretense, provided the strength
to accept the temporal world and, in the words of Niebuhr's
prayer, to accept the "things I cannot change."* The dangers
of communist and liberal dreams lay in their runaway rationalism and their secularism. Neither understood nor accepted
the fact that the drama of history was impossible to understand. Fortunately, through an expanding frontier, the United
States had never needed to rationalize its social structure, and
had consequently been graced by mobility and fluidity. By
historical accident, America had preserved its own internal
balance of power. The New Deal was a supreme effort to retain that balance, to preserve the "vital center."

The balance between unions and management, Niebuhr felt
during the thirties, was especially important for developing
industrial justice. The competing classes in society had devel-

---

*The complete prayer—

> O God, grant me the serenity to accept
> the things I cannot change;
> Give me the courage to change the things
> that must be changed,
> And the wisdom to distinguish the one
> from the other.

oped organizations which were capable of working together, through competition, to fulfill the purposes of the earlier prophets of Industrial Democracy. These organizations, in turn, grew out of the corporation. "The prior condition for modern large-scale social organization," Niebuhr wrote, "must be found in this large-scale economic organization." Centralization must be matched to centralization, power to power. Order and justice could be achieved from these remaining "hard shells of community" which had survived and been strengthened throughout the years of industrial development. "In the process," he concluded, "some hitherto unknown quasi-sovereignties of management and labor unions were developed which would have surprised and probably outraged both John Locke and Adam Smith."[19] In the final formulation of his theory, Niebuhr re-established some of the basic insights of collectivism.

The countervailing powers which Niebuhr discovered in labor and management, the organized arms of the corporation, required a place to thrash about in their search for conciliation and compromise. The state was such a place. There competition ended; there power balanced power. "Every human community," Niebuhr wrote, "must be organized from a given centre of power; and that centre of power must try to be impartial adjudicator of the interests of others even while it remains an interested and partial social force, individual or collective, international or intranational, among the many social forces which must be brought into an equilibrium." The state was neutral and objective so long as it did not try to end the balance between social forces.

The final development of Niebuhr's position led him back to some of the ideas of the earliest proponents of modern liberalism, Adam Smith and John Locke among them, though he lent these ideas a radically different expression. Instead of competing individuals, modern society had competing groups and corporations; instead of optimism about the future, there was the realization that perfection now or in the future was impossible. As he concluded in *The Children of Light and the Children of Darkness,* "We must be careful to preserve whatever self-regulating forces exist in the economic process. If we do not, the task of control becomes too stupendous and the organs of control achieve proportions which endanger our liberty."[20]

In the long course of his search for a realistic politics and a realistic theology, Reinhold Niebuhr had brutally attacked many of the assumptions of collectivism. But in the end he had accomplished a disarmingly complex adjustment of the collectivist style of thinking to an enormously changed American society. Much of the texture of thought from the pre–World War I period had worn thin, as Niebuhr well understood, but these same ideas persisted to give his theories simultaneously a curiously old and modern appeal. If anything, Niebuhr had made the Christian motif in collectivism even stronger than it had been before World War I. He extended its sense of universality in dealing with social reforms to encompass the whole world: every article and every book he wrote was intended as an essay on man's state. More practically, Niebuhr had preserved, even improved upon, the concept of a functional economic democracy, while bitterly casting aside historical alternatives. In his thinking, the division of labor in modern industry was reproduced as the predominant social division. Thus workers could be represented by unions, and management by management organizations. The organization, not the individual, achieved justice in society. And only in the abrasions of competitive life could liberty survive. Niebuhr also reproduced, in different form, a sense of social development which was characteristic of earlier collectivist writers. He believed he understood the laws of human development— laws which forced human evolution through change after change. He felt these, in turn, were dependent upon economics and above all upon the eternal, inherent struggle for power. Niebuhr's enormous attraction to metaphors of clash, paradox, and even violence, made his writings sound like latter-day Darwinism.

For one who spent an enormous time in the midst of argument, and whose own words were carefully considered, there was little place in Niebuhr's theory of society for creative thought. Society was guided, he argued, by unseen forces; men's lives, similarly, were ruled by accident. Planning as well as all the rationalistic visions of the past were perverse, because they did not allow for the turns of fortune, error, and conflict. Inevitably, the role of the expert and the intellectual had changed in Niebuhr's hands from the time of the earlier collectivists. Niebuhr saw two functions for the intellectual—one was adjudication; the other was prophecy. These came together in the expert who understood the laws of society, of nature, of science, and of Providence. Niebuhr's conception of his own role became actualized in his participation in such organizations as the Union for Democratic Action and the Americans for Democratic Action. Both organizations played the part of propagandist and judge, and both made the vision of a slightly more democratized America than really existed to be their best of all possible worlds.

But there remained an uncomfortable aspect to Niebuhr's politics. He remained pessimistic about man's nature and the value of social change. He was willing to accept present arrangements, and even defend them fiercely, while the older collectivists had celebrated the future. It was an imperfect world into which man was born, Niebuhr argued. He ought to make the best of it.

10

James Burnham:
Collectivism Triumphant

As COLLECTIVIST assumptions were refined and developed in the 1930's by such writers as Reinhold Niebuhr and James Burnham, their inherent difficulties became more obvious. As Burnham well understood, defining democracy in terms of functional groups, or liberty in terms of planning by experts, meant no utopia but only another form of class society. Thus Burnham's essays on modern industrial society followed collectivism to the point where it seriously compromised traditional ideas about individualism and democracy. By exposing the inner contradictions in collectivism, Burnham cleared the way for new thinking about the nature of society—but failed to follow his own lead. Instead, he chose to revive older notions of liberty which in the thirties had scarcely any hope of making a practical entry into the political, economic, and social life of the nation. Burnham chose private property to defend the integrity of the political self, and this choice placed him at one extreme of the laissez-faire-collectivist dilemma. Both extremes were unpleasant: private property had worked in an older society to enhance individualism, but it had sacrificed the community; corporate property assumed a community of interests on a grand scale, but worked against individuals. Burnham's solution was to upend the historical development of the collectivist society and call for its abolition.

Intellectual attitudes toward social planning in the thirties reveal a high degree of ambiguity toward collectivism. The enormous publicity given to the Technocracy movement in 1932 and 1933 exposed a fascinated but critical audience for the engineering paradise which Howard Scott, the leader of the movement, proposed. Seven years later, James Burnham published his widely read *Managerial Revolution,* and again a half-critical, half-believing audience appeared, this time for Burnham's biting criticism of the idea of government by experts. Scott proposed his Technocratic plans as an answer to the Great Depression and to all depressions. His government by engineers would be the ultimate "government of function," a managerial society beyond the hopes of earlier writers such as Charles Steinmetz. By the end of the decade, Scott's movement remained in a few isolated Pacific Northwest towns in Canada and the United States. Yet Burnham in his book could seriously contend that men like the Technocrats had nonetheless already revolutionized society, for they represented a well-entrenched class of industrial and political managers who owed no allegiance to traditional social classes. Scott's proposed nonviolent revolution and his engineering Technate or ruling group had assumed power even without his knowing it. Rather than celebrate this event, Burnham warned that the new society had totalitarian implications. As many other intellectuals, including Reinhold Niebuhr, argued in the late thirties, purposeful social planning was extremely dangerous.

Technocracy was not a new movement by the 1930's. Howard Scott had formulated most of his basic ideas for eliminating the price system, wages, and money—and, of course, politics—during World War I, at the height of agitation for industrial management schemes and Industrial Democracy. Before him there had been such men as Charles Ferguson in the United States, and elements of the Guild Socialist movement in England, who advised similar changes. During the 1920's, Scott had tried to interest the IWW in an energy-resource survey to prepare for the eventual syndicalist revolution. But he made little progress with his ideas until the Crash of 1929 and the ensuing depression provoked a flurry of popular interest in Technocracy. The suddenness, and probably the brevity, of interest in Technocracy came from the style of Scott's writings, which plotted an easy route to utopia—if only the nation would let the engineers run industry and eliminate capitalism. As he argued, "Technocracy, Inc., is neither radical nor reactionary, conservative nor liberal, political party nor racket. . . ."[1] It was also irrelevant.

Although the Technocracy fad died quickly, and most intellectuals decided that Scott was a crank, the basis of his popularity was symptomatic of the abiding faith that many intellectuals had in some form of social movement which would complete the economic revolution begun in the middle of the nineteenth century and create a scientifically run economic system. What they hoped for was a political economy that would embody scientific management and Industrial Democracy. Many intellectuals shared Scott's desire to eliminate politics, classes, money, and social strife, and substitute rational planning and organization. Even older collectivist prophets were occasionally resurrected in this cause, the most important being Edward Bellamy. Bellamy received attention in the early thirties as several Bellamy Clubs were organized across the country. John Dewey explained in 1934 in *Common Sense* that Bellamy had been a great American social prophet. Another reason for his revival undoubtedly was the collectivist nature of his prophecy and his picture of a post-industrial utopia.

Despite what seemed to be a sudden outbreak of planning literature, there had been much of it in the twenties, particularly in the Plumb Plan and in the discussion of Industrial Democracy and Guild Socialist ideas. The pages of such magazines as the *New Republic* were filled with pleas for a planned society. For example, George Soule, one of that magazine's most important contributors, argued typically in 1926 that the nation needed a bloodless managerial revolution to create a new social class of executives: "I believe we should rather face the fact that modern large-scale industry has developed to a point such that ownership control has lost its reality." This divorce of management from ownership created the possibility, in Soule's eyes, for a scientific, pragmatic management, and the fulfillment of Industrial Democracy. Arguments such as these were repeated uncounted times by scientific-management societies such as the Taylor Society. More concrete evidence for the preparation of a new class of managers and experts existed in the activities of engineering societies, business schools, and industrial experts.[2]

The first years of the depression brought an intensification of academic writings on social planning. Stuart Chase, Harold Ickes (later a member of the Roosevelt administration), John Dewey, Charles Beard, and others wrote books outlining the need for social planning and sketching the behavior of a reformed society. Some of this literature was a response to the Russian Five-Year Plan which had made such ideas suddenly relevant, but intellectuals were also reacting to a long tradition of interest in planning in America.[3]

Probably the most interesting and influential of these books was *The Modern Corporation and Private Property*, written by Adolf Berle and Gardiner Means. It rediscovered and reaffirmed many of the assumptions of earlier collectivist thinkers, with the evidence arranged as a kind of final tally sheet for the performance of American capitalism. Berle and Means argued that the dominance of the corporation in American life had created the basis of a collectivist society. This corporate revolution had been accomplished in the transition from individual ownership of property to corporate property, which was inherently a form of public ownership. The results had been dramatic: "New responsibilities toward the owners, the workers, the consumers, and the State thus rest upon the shoulders of those in control. In creating these new relationships, the quasi-public corporation may fairly be said to work a revolution." Ownership was now divorced from control. The direction of business had fallen into the hands of managers, who were without the inherently selfish ideology of private ownership and who wished to impose a far higher degree of social responsibility upon the massive new corporations.

Economic individualism was dead as the dominant shaping force in American society, Berle and Means argued, and indeed in all advanced industrial societies. The commissar in Russia and the corporate manager in America shared much in common because of their loyalties and the social meaning of their work. Both were fixtures within a world movement to make the corporation responsible to the public interest. Finally, Berle and Means contended, all of these developments cried out for commensurate social and political changes —a new collectivism: "It is conceivable—indeed it seems almost essential if the corporate system is to survive,—that the 'control' of the great corporations should develop into a purely neutral technocracy, balancing a variety of claims by various groups in the community and assigning to each a portion of the income stream on the basis of public policy rather than private cupidity."[4] With a slightly different emphasis, Berle and Means had reaffirmed the central insight and contention of collectivists who had written twenty or thirty years before. In a sense, too, they had advanced no further than these earlier thinkers, for their analysis was in part advice. The political and social context still was not ripe for the creation of distinctly new economic arrangements. The book was nonetheless immensely timely, however much it might owe to the past.

The theme of a managerial revolution was not new in the thirties, nor were James Burnham and Berle and Means profoundly original. But Burnham added a new interpretation to old ideas which put a finishing touch on several collectivist arguments, and he demonstrated in his own career two distinctly opposite critiques of collectivism. Burnham was one of a number of unlikely intellectuals who found themselves in the radical movement during the thirties. He was born in 1905 in Chicago into the wealthy Catholic family of George Burnham, a British-born executive vice-president of the Burlington Railroad. A scholarly young man, he took his B.A. at Princeton, where he was an editor of the *Princeton Tiger* and the *Nassau Literary Review*. After Princeton he went on to Oxford where he received a degree in philosophy in 1929. When he returned to the United States he began teaching philosophy at the Washington Square campus of New York University. At about the same time, he and the philosopher Philip Wheelwright began work on a book entitled *Introduction to Philosophic Analysis*, and founded a literary and cultural journal called *Symposium*. Burnham's development as a political radical coincided with the beginning of his teaching career. His job at New York University was particularly important because he was strongly influenced by Sidney Hook, a member of the philosophy department who was then at the height of his influence in the American radical intellectual community.

When the author and historian Matthew Josephson met Burnham in the early thirties, he had what must have been a typical reaction to the intense, detached young writer: "I found Burnham a shy young mental prodigy of that type we tend to label 'frosty intellectual.'" Perhaps Josephson sensed Burnham's philosophic training or even his tentativeness toward radicalism. Whatever the source of his observation, he was right, for there was always a cool, abstract quality to Burnham's writings, despite a constant and vivid sense of impending change. Burnham touched his articles and books with this feeling of possible catastrophe at the same time as he searched for a philosophic and political position of orthodoxy and stability. His brother Phillip, who became an editor of *Commonweal* magazine, perhaps discovered these qualities in the Catholic church. James, however, turned to Marxism.

While Burnham and Wheelwright were editing their distinguished critical magazine *Symposium,* Burnham was becoming interested in radical ideology. In 1932 and 1933 he began to publish articles on politics in the magazine. For one brief moment he was attracted to the Communist party and contributed a review to the *New Masses,* the party's chief cultural outlet. But Burnham quickly soured on the Communists and instead joined a small radical group led by A. J. Muste. In 1934 he began to contribute a regular column to *Labor Action,* the Musteite newspaper. One year later he joined Max Schachtman, who was then one of a small band of Trotskyist intellectuals in the United States, to edit the *New International,* Burnham writing under the pseudonym of John West. Within a few years Burnham had become one of the prominent members of the new Workers party (Trotskyist), writing important pamphlets, resolutions for party conventions, and articles. When the Trotskyists debated entering the Socialist party in 1936 as a left-wing caucus, Burnham was one of the leading proponents of the merger.

Although Burnham had become one of the leading spokesmen for American Trotskyism, he retained several important theoretical misgivings about Trotsky's overall position, particularly the specifics of his stand supporting the Soviet Union and his theoretical reliance upon Marxist dialectics. Together with another party member, Joseph Carter, Burnham developed a halfway position in 1937 on the question of the Soviet Union—between Trotsky's view that it was a workers' state despite a corrupt and totalitarian government, and another radical view that it was merely a state capitalist regime. Trotsky took note of Burnham's position to argue against it, and effectively silenced the American critic when he asked, Why do you propose to defend the Soviet Union in wartime, if, as you say, it is not a socialist state in any essential way? The dispute smoldered for the next two years.[5]

Burnham continued to edit the *New International* with Schachtman and began also to write for the *Partisan Review,* a literary journal which was sympathetic to Trotskyism briefly in the late thirties. By 1939, however, his own and Schachtman's disagreements with Trotsky led to a split in the party. After the Nazi-Soviet pact and Russia's invasion of Finland, neither Schachtman nor Burnham was willing to defend the Soviet Union on the supposed grounds that it was a workers' state. As the split deepened and the two factions fought for control of the American party, Trotsky himself, from exile in Mexico, directed the struggle and sent off a stream of letters and articles denouncing Burnham and Schachtman. The inevitable separation occurred, and Burnham and Schachtman founded a new party and took with them the *New International.* Within a month, Burnham had abruptly quit this party too, and by May 1940 he had completely renounced Marxism.

This same year he published his *Managerial Revolution,* a widely read book which immediately provoked a storm of protest from the left. From his position in *The Managerial Revolution,* Burnham gradually slipped to the right politically and fell into relative obscurity, though he remained close to the *Partisan Review.* By 1952, however, when it became clear that Burnham supported Senator Joseph McCarthy, whom the *Partisan Review* opposed, the last of Burnham's ties to the liberal intellectuals were cut. In 1955 he became one of the editors of the conservative *National Review*.

However interesting James Burnham's progress from radical to conservative may be, he is more important for his influence on collectivist thought, and for the curious way he developed its most extreme theoretical forms. Burnham understood that one of the most significant changes in American society had been the development of an elite of management experts. He deplored this development from much the same position taken by anti-collectivist writers of the early twentieth century. At first he expressed himself through radical politics. But as he developed his ideas, through articles and a series of reviews in which he considered the major "managerial analysis" literature of the thirties, his position became more ambiguous. In some ways, the publication of *The Managerial Revolution* was an explanation of Burnham's exodus from radicalism.

Burnham had begun as a kind of permanent, part-time intellectual in the Trotskyist movement. His commitment, while firm, was perhaps never intellectually complete. The radical movement nonetheless helped to supply him with the ideas and experiences, and the criticism of popular economic ideas, that formed his managerial thesis. He shared, but also exaggerated, certain characteristics of the intellectual life of the thirties. For one, he was often distracted by historical personalities. One of his first political articles for *Symposium* in the early thirties was a review of Trotsky's *History of the Russian Revolution*. Burnham thought Trotsky a brilliant guide for and a prophet of events that would probably occur in America one day. "We now realize clearly enough," he wrote, "that with whatever lags, in our country as well as Russia a major transition is taking place." Trotsky replied to Burnham's review in the next issue of the magazine, October 1932, disagreeing on some points but generally friendly. Burnham was enormously impressed by this attention. Later in the decade, he was embittered because Trotsky carried his attack on his (Burnham's) and Schachtman's position so far as to suggest almost a personal betrayal.[6]

Burnham also displayed—as did other intellectuals in the

thirties—a vision of inevitable catastrophe. He ended almost all of his books and articles with the same formula: only the continuation of present conditions was necessary to bring on disaster, a kind of inevitable devolution into anti-utopia. From his first article in *Symposium* in 1932 to his books and articles of the 1950's, this same tone prevailed. At first he felt that depression would be a permanent form of life for Americans; twenty years later he decided it would be eternal war against communism, and entitled his column for the *National Review,* "World War III."

During the first years of Burnham's radicalization, he was reluctant to put *Symposium* at the services of the revolution. He found a number of things about the political left distasteful. Among these was "proletarian literature," which placed ideological demands upon writers in exchange for a share of the revolution. In an article "Marxism and Esthetics," Burnham discussed his belief that while Marxism had great political value and Marxists had contributed much to contemporary cultural life, they had done little to illuminate the more important historical problems of aesthetic criticism. Shortly after this article appeared in 1933, he and Wheelwright drew up "Thirteen Propositions" to discuss the relationship of their magazine to the contemporary world crisis. They favored a revolution of property and politics but criticized the American Communist party for its weakness. Unlike the Communists, they still wished to retain the separation of art and criticism from politics.[7]

For Burnham, a separation of art and politics would force him to choose between his own strong interests in literary criticism and politics. From 1933 onward it was clear that he had chosen politics, though he never completely lost touch with literary and philosophic issues. An early sign of this political priority was his review of *The Modern Corporation and Private Property* by Berle and Means. Burnham was particularly impressed by the distinction the authors made between the functions of ownership and management in the modern corporation, a distinction upon which he later built his managerial thesis. As he wrote: "No more potentially important book than this, in its or any allied field, has been published in this country for many years." Burnham did not accept all of the book's conclusions. He disagreed, for example, that the process of specialization in the corporation had changed its members' responsibility toward the public. And he foresaw a more dramatic ending to liberal capitalism than the authors envisioned: there would either be revolution or fascism.[8]

Given this statement and others that posed the future in such sure and vivid terms, there was probably no comfortable place for Burnham in the thirties except in one or another radical political organization. After he joined the Musteites, he began to contribute a column to their paper, *Labor Action,* which he called "Their Government." In a characteristic style, he sought historical precedents for the current economic crisis, and tried to describe scientifically the causes of depression and the European political debacle. Burnham was a writer for whom the slogan "What is past is prologue" had a very curious meaning: What was past, what was present, would inevitably worsen in the future. Thus most of his articles ended with the same formula warning: unless the workers took control, America would go fascist.

When the Musteites joined the Trotskyists in late 1934, Burnham began to write for the *New International.* He quickly became that journal's expert on the New Deal and American politics. In his first article, on the Roosevelt administration, Burnham suggested that Roosevelt was trying to act above class interests, but that his response to the depression drew inspiration from the left and right politically: "To put this in another way: psychologically, and to some extent politically, the task of the administration was social democratic; whereas economically the preparation for Fascism was demanded." While this comment nowhere exactly suggests the managerial thesis, the structure of argument is remarkably similar. Burnham distinguished a developing system of government (he would call it fascism in 1935 and managerialism in 1940) sitting atop but to some extent independent of the roaring class struggle beneath it. Moreover, he suggested that the meaning of social change, such as the New Deal pursued, could be understood only beyond the historical ruse by which all major forces conspired to disguise their intents.

Burnham thought he sensed the direction of those forces, and repeatedly attacked the New Deal for being a contradictory but politically successful movement to consolidate bourgeois rule disguised as social democracy. In an uncharacteristic style for contemporary radicals, he angrily denounced the federal government's extension of control over the economy and the centralization of power in the executive branch.[9] In his discussion of the Wagner Bill (later the Wagner Act of 1935), he argued that the state could seemingly be opposed to all middle-class organizations and yet rule in their favor. This independence gave the government a life of its own: "Modern governments are gigantic bureaucracies, comprising hundreds of thousands of individuals. These too have a voice and a will, and do not want to lose their salaries. Modern government is itself the largest of giant modern industries." Burnham depicted the process of governmental growth in lurid terms. The capitalist, he noted, was fearfully watching the "monster state spread its dark wings" over all areas of society, demanding concessions of entrepreneurial freedom in exchange for social stability.

The problem of historical inevitability also troubled Burnham, and he brooded over it in an article attacking Max Eastman. No case could be made for an iron-clad inevitability, he concluded, but there were obviously laws of development. Whatever Marx had meant—and Burnham admitted the complexity of that question—his sense of inevitability could not be made historically concrete, even though it was useful. Quite so, for Burnham could hardly discard a concept which turned up frequently in his own writings. Philosophically, the notion was unprovable, but Burnham was tenacious and kept a sense of inevitability and predictability constantly in mind. Society always seemed to him at an impasse where it must make a dramatic choice.

Another element of the intellectual style which characterizes Burnham's *Managerial Revolution* was obvious in his sense of what accounted for political and social reality. Marxism and Trotskyism were, for him, tools to make incisions into reality. Nothing was ever what is seemed; historical forces conspired, movements were disguised, and meanings were hidden. Thus in 1936, when he spoke of the approaching presidential election, Burnham wrote of the secret coming of fascism to America. Wealthy Liberty Leaguers who hated Roosevelt would, of course, some day be in the ranks of a fascist movement, but never openly. FDR himself was far closer to being an effective fascist than the front-page reactionaries, because, Burnham said, he represented "veiled reaction."[10]

From hindsight it is easy to see characteristics that distinguished Burnham from his radical comrades. But these characteristics made little difference at the time. Burnham was articulate, fresh, and interesting. He had academic friends and was an adviser and contributor to the *Partisan Review*, which in 1937 had begun its rise to dominance among little magazines in the United States. Burnham's commitment to Trotskyism reflected his attitude toward full-time party work. He never fully accepted Marxism, nor would he ever devote all his activities to the party. Nonetheless, as Max Schachtman recalls, Burnham along with James Cannon and Schachtman were the three major figures in the Trotskyist movement in New York. Burnham also helped to engineer two mergers of the Trotskyists, first with the Musteites and then in 1936 with the American Socialist party. This latter alliance was especially important because it coincided with the Moscow Purge Trials of 1936 and 1937 and represented one effort of Trotsky's followers to clear the exiled revolutionary's name. Burnham helped in this struggle which ultimately resulted in the appointment of the Dewey Commission, a distinguished private panel that went to Mexico to interview Trotsky and eventually cleared him of charges that he was conspiring with the forces of fascism to overthrow the Soviet revolution.

All the while, Burnham was squabbling with Trotsky over the meaning of Marxian dialectical thought. By 1939 the dispute erupted again, this time too severe to be ignored. Other elements of the American Trotskyist movement too had begun to question Trotsky's position supporting what remained of the revolution in Russia. After the Nazi-Soviet pact and the beginning of World War II, both factions within the party began to maneuver for a larger slice of the coming split. From Mexico, Trotsky directed the fight against the Schachtman minority, and gradually Burnham was caught up in the struggle and in plans for a new party. As Schachtman wrote, this was Trotsky's last and most important factional fight before his assassination, and he turned his enormous, biting argumentative skill against the dissenters. When Burnham wrote a document called "On the Character of the War to the SWP," in which he argued that the party should not support the Soviet Union in case of war, Trotsky counterattacked. He published an article entitled "An Open Letter to James Burnham," defending his own position and attempting to smoke out the dissenter. He succeeded. Burnham was stung into reply and wrote a defense of his ideas, denying that he had slid away from Marxism and recalling his role in the party and his long admiration for Trotsky's intellectual style. The war, he noted, was the only real issue between them.[11]

As Burnham's actions would reveal, his reply was not entirely candid. By April 1940 the party had polarized and split; Schachtman and Burnham set up new headquarters, and, since they were its editors, took the *New International* with them. A month later Burnham quit the new faction and quit Marxist politics forever. In his resignation he denied that he was a Marxist and rejected many of his former ideological commitments. He would have separated himself earlier, he wrote, but for loyalty to friends in the party: "On the grounds of beliefs and interests (which are also a fact) I have for several years had no real place in a Marxist party." Within a few months he had published *The Managerial Revolution*.

Burnham's sudden rejection of his Marxist past is surprising but unimportant except as an intellectual curiosity. His new theory, however, vividly projected a mix of contradictory attitudes toward industrial organization and the collectivization of modern society. The origins of the managerial thesis obviously reflect a decade of reading and writing as well as Burnham's compulsion to explain what was wrong with Marxism. Much of what he had to say was implicit in a reading of Berle and Means. Thurmond Arnold's *Folklore of Capitalism,* which Burnham also reviewed, must have suggested some of the other major ideas in the managerial thesis. As he commented on Arnold's book in 1938: "Today we can observe the rise of a class of engineers, salesmen, minor executives, and social workers—all engaged in actually running the country's temporal affairs." Several other books strengthened Burnham's interest in the growth of a ruling elite; works by Robert Michels, by Vilfredo Pareto (*The Mind and Society* was republished in New York in 1935), and by Gaetano Mosca (*The Ruling Class* was translated in 1939), are all cited by Burnham as having influenced his thinking.[12] In sum, these books contributed the sociological background and theoretical respectability for the tentative beginnings of the managerial thesis that are everywhere apparent in Burnham's political writing in the thirties.

Burnham's fight with Trotskyism helped also to provide the texture of his thesis. Trotskyism itself, if by extension, held the beginnings of a managerial thesis. Trotsky's intellectual task in the thirties was to explain the reasons for his exile from Russia, and his theoretical objections to Stalin's political and economic policies. His resulting description of the Soviet Union vacillated between a class analysis and an attack on a ruthless personal tyrant. The Soviet Union was a degenerate workers' state ruled by a bureaucracy that was not, however, a class. Burnham simply eliminated the tension and subtlety from Trotsky's theories and came away with evidence for the historic development of an elite which could rule society with no real class interest in mind except its own.

Burnham was also influenced by the thinking of Bruno Rizzi. In a book *La Bureaucratisation de Monde,* published in Paris in 1939, Rizzi, an ex-Trotskyist, argued that Soviet Russia, Nazi Germany, and the New Deal were all forms of the same revolution. Rizzi's thesis contained all the basic elements and ideas that Burnham would later use in his managerial thesis. Some observers even found Burnham's book to be little more than a popularization of what Rizzi had written. Max Schachtman spoke of "*The Managerial Revolution,* in which Burnham adopted Rizzi's thesis virtually *in toto* and with the addition of some extravagant predictions."[13]

Whatever the precise origins of Burnham's revolutionary bureaucracy, he was plainly tempted by the idea before 1939. Moreover, *The Managerial Revolution* was a timely document of radical despair and a kind of final statement of a collectivist analysis of modern corporate society. Aggressively written, radical sounding, full of a sense of discovery, the book apparently filled a compelling need in 1939 to explain the inexorable disintegration of a familiar world. Burnham reintegrated that world with a metaphor that certainly matched the extent of the crisis. Although his final attitudes toward the new society were ambiguous, he stated his conclusions firmly. Society was quietly being revolutionized by its essential productive forces. Americans, and indeed all members of advanced industrial societies, would wake up one morning to realize that they had been ruled by a new class of managers for a long time.

The new collectivist society, so fervently predicted by intellectuals before World War I, had appeared. Capitalism, Burnham argued, which meant individualism, private initiative, natural rights, the idea of progress, and bourgeois rule, was being replaced. The new system matched the dreams of the prewar collectivists and fulfilled their assertion that the corporation would be the dominant institution in the new society. Since the corporation—in one guise or another—now ruled all industrial societies, those who dominated the corporation also led society as a whole. This new class of managers owed little allegiance to the institutions of traditional politics, as older collectivists had also predicted. Their position in the corporation was not even vaguely limited by the stock ownership of outsiders. These men ruled through a multiplicity of extrapolitical parliaments and trade associations, through government commissions, and through their dominance of political bureaucracies. They were the ideologists behind the New Deal; they proposed a system of national ownership and tight federal regulation which amounted almost to state ownership of the means of production. Here was the dark shadow of federal regulation that Burnham had so eloquently opposed in his essays for the *New International*.

Burnham made even more of his distaste for the New Deal, which, he argued, was a step toward bureaucratic miasma. He thought conservative critics of the New Deal correctly saw the drift of society toward a new form, and that they were right to note its similarities to economic and political institutions in Germany and the Soviet Union. All were becoming part of a new collectivist world: "The most conservative capitalist spokesmen have for years identified 'communism' (that is Stalinism), 'Nazism,' and 'New Dealism.'" There was no formal unity between the three systems, but, Burnham concluded, "They all have the same historical direction: away from capitalist society and toward managerial society." Russia, the "chief political enigma" of the decade, was for Burnham the least puzzling part of this historical continuity. Russia represented one form of advanced managerial society, Nazi Germany the other.

Burnham's extensive chapters on Russia and Germany carry an unconvincing argument. Burnham's model for the managerial society was not really Germany or the Soviet Union but the New Deal, which he knew best. His general observations about corporations, the functions of managers, and the nature of politics and the state were far more at home in the United States than in other countries. As he argued, "The New Deal is a phase of the transition process from capitalism to managerial society." He still felt he could see enough of the future to predict it; he was sure he had witnessed the silent revolution of the technocrats.

In some ways *The Managerial Revolution* was a troubling book because, as observers noted at the time, it was almost unconcerned about the quiet death of liberal democracy. Burnham himself seemed unsure whether to defend the last strongholds of democracy or greet the invasion force of technologists. But his pessimism prevailed. In an essay published in 1940, entitled "Is Democracy Possible?", he mused about the possibilities of preserving some form of democracy. He concluded that it could only be saved by retaining social divisiveness and by preventing social planning and political management. As Reinhold Niebuhr had done somewhat earlier, Burnham decided that capitalist society was inherently more democratic than most societies: "In spite of the incompleteness, inadequacy and hypocrisy of much of capitalist democracy, an unbiased observer can hardly deny that the capitalist social structure provided more of a basis for political democracy than any other social system so far known." Capitalism, then, and not the insidious collectivism of the day, could preserve social liberty.

By 1943, in his book *The Machiavellians,* Burnham had taken another confusing step backward. While praising such social theorists as Machiavelli, Pareto, Michels, and Mosca, he wrote that elite rule was in one sense inevitable and welcome: "Political freedom is the resultant of unresolved conflicts among various sections of the elite."[14] As he shifted his focus from democracy, which he now considered totally unreal, to individual freedom, Burnham also began a rapid drift to the political right. His hatred of the Soviet Union and his dislike for the New Deal grew together. In his next books and articles he fought imaginary wars with communism and proposed strategies for victory. By the late 1940's he had begun to sanction limits on freedom of speech and to attack such groups as the Americans for Democratic Action. In the end, by the 1950's, there was little left for Burnham but to defend a modified form of laissez-faire capitalism. He finished as did other conservative critics of collectivism, at a dead end, hoping for the revival of a system which was gone and which perhaps had never worked anyway.[15] When Burnham reaffirmed the need for economic individualism and freedom, he did so in terms of private property rights, demanding a social order that could not exist in the society he knew. His writings, which so effectively analyzed the assumptions and implications of collectivism, proposed only that society return to the beginning point of industrialism, and therefore live once more through the evolution of laissez faire into corporate capitalism.

Burnham's most important contribution to the development of collectivist assumptions is based, peculiarly, upon his attention to elites. He thought he saw a glimpse of a developing elite society in the New Deal. As a radical, he opposed its reactionary bureaucratic tendencies; later, as a conservative, he concentrated on its seeming radicalism and its supine tolerance of the Soviet Union. Taken together, his writings form a love-hate relationship with what he consistently identified as a society in which the managerial function, divorced from property, became the ruling force in society. The corporation, aggrandized through economic and political change, had become the supreme social institution. To understand American society one needed only to write about this institution. The collectivist hope for a functional democracy and society run by rational observance of natural law flickered aimlessly in Burnham's nightmarish view of the managerial society.

Burnham's political wanderings also illustrate another development of collectivism. This broad set of assumptions about modern society was obviously badly injured as it was dragged from the political left to the right. In the early thirties a number of intellectuals had spoken openly about planning and about collectivizing American society—or admitting that it was already partly collectivized. By the end of the thirties, collectivism had fallen out of the serious vocabulary of most political liberals, and was used instead as a synonym for totalitarianism. In the same way, Burnham's important and sometimes apt criticisms of the New Deal were muffled in *The Managerial Revolution* by his hatred for the Soviet Union and Nazi Germany. Thus his criticism of collectivism was lost, and when he returned to pick up the pieces in the forties and fifties, it was from the position of a crankish conservative.

Burnham also developed collectivist assumptions that the intellectual and the expert were revolutionaries. The whole collectivist argument, it could be argued, rested upon the notion that even the laws of economic history were revolutionary. In the 1930's Technocracy claimed to be the embodiment of this intellectual-revolutionary cadre. To conservatives, Roosevelt's "Brain Trust" was another. Burnham's theory of the managerial elite pointed to the specific revolutionary character of the new corporate managers. As a class, he felt, they had assumed power in the Soviet Union and Germany and were moving toward the same power in the United States. While he claimed to fear this development, he agreed with earlier collectivist writers that the major impulse of corporate capitalism, or any corporate form of society, was the tendency to create an elite corps of experts who could rule because they understood social organization and the larger movements of history. To Burnham, this meant no real reform; instead, the new managerial groups would be self-serving. Thus in Burnham's hands the collectivist notion that planning would create social progress was transformed into the idea that social progress created planning, which in turn made for totalitarianism. Instead of leading a moral crusade, experts and intellectuals had merely instituted a new form of elite rule.

Against the appalling sociological structure he described, Burnham's ultimate defense was, like Niebuhr's, based upon a clash of powers and self-interests. But Burnham found no refuge in organized group counterplay. He argued, rather effectively, that elites were nonrepresentative, that labor union leaders, for example, were part of the managerial elite and therefore to be distinguished from workers. Burnham's refuge was a private plot and the self-defense of individual property. He attacked the idea of a collectivist society with the weapons of nineteenth-century liberalism. Thus the history of collectivist thought came full circle in his hands, to fall under the assault of its old opponent, laissez faire. Yet collectivist thought reflected the enormous changes that had occurred in American society since the 1890's. Burnham had been right in his original critique of the New Deal: it did represent a great measure of collectivism. Society by the 1930's was increasingly run by elites given institutional stature through corporations, labor unions, and governmental bureaucracies. But what Burnham saw, he lost the will to change, and buried his hopes in a meaningless plea to reinstate a myth.

11

The Intellectuals and Collectivism

THE POLITICAL IDEAS I have described as collectivist have never become the universal assumptions of American political thinkers or of practical politicians. They are instead embedded in a tradition of thought which is only half-consciously recognized, lying in a limbo somewhere between academic exposition and guidelines for reform. And because they are primarily descriptive ideas, which do not demand action so much as assertion, they have appeared useful only occasionally. Yet they lie behind an important part of the discussion of modern American society, and they remain enormously helpful concepts with which to examine American history.

Collectivist ideas sprang largely from the development of massive economic units which appeared around the turn of the century. Collectivist intellectuals thought to apply their new social theories to the corporation in order to control it and complete its evolution. But at the heart of their theories was the effort to make room for themselves, and to mark off a function which would be their own specialty and justification. In a sense, they sought to lead American institutions into obeisance to larger, impersonal laws of social development, and in the process reproduce in generalized and theoretical terms their own activities in universities, corporations, government commissions, and reform institutions. The result was collectiv-

285

ism, a theory of society with elitist implications. It offered little participation for ordinary citizens outside their work roles.

Because collectivist ideas were often incomplete or ignored important precedents, they were simultaneously coherent and confused. Moreover, as a broad interpretation of modern industrial phenomena, collectivism embraced a variety of programs, including managerialism, pluralism, and theories of countervailing powers. All these were linked to the central position of the corporation, whose primacy all collectivist intellectuals were agreed upon.

The chronological development of collectivism is complicated by several factors. The tendencies, social and intellectual, that brought collectivism to life to begin with have since changed. The role of the intellectual has become more severely defined and his occupational possibilities more bureaucratized in the twentieth century. The American economy has become more centralized, and social and political institutions have reacted accordingly. The direction in which modern society is headed is therefore more obvious than it was to speculative thinkers at the turn of the century. The size and nature of major components in the industrial world have changed: labor's size and role at the beginning of the century has surely altered drastically, and so have the size, function, and social impact of corporations—to the point, indeed, where early theorists might not recognize the object of their theorizing.

Within collectivist thought itself change has been constant, particularly the shifting emphases in practical applications and reform programs. The whole nature of collectivism has been further complicated by such specific programs as scientific management or Industrial Democracy or corporatism. Thus, by the 1930's, such intellectuals as Reinhold Niebuhr and James Burnham were already writing in reaction to established collectivist ideas, though their work itself fell well within the collectivist tradition. By the thirties, too, pluralistic collectivism had become the predominant form, and therefore the writings of Niebuhr and Burnham, which specifically examined pluralism, have a special importance. They provided a significant consideration of one of the most important and constantly asked questions since the rise of Industrial Democracy—how to balance the components of industry within the political state.

Pluralism remains an important description of modern society. It has been useful to those who felt they could help guide American society toward rational reform; but the more it has been used, the less it has offered toward understanding the realities and possibilities of modern society. Clearly, by the middle of the twentieth century one could describe the United States as a collectivist society, but the values that intellectuals supposed would emerge from a collectivist society did not appear: the form existed but with little of the content. As William English Walling and James Burnham had dimly perceived, reliance upon centralization, upon administration instead of political decision-making, and upon organization and functional definitions did not do justice to the complexities of modern society and proved to be overly schematic, brittle concepts. They failed to meet the problem of achieving a humane and democratic society dominated by gigantic institutions.

Although the place of collectivist assumptions in the history of modern American reform is significant, collectivist thinking is important beyond what it reveals about the economic origins of reform thought, or even the self-interested contributions of intellectuals. Collectivist thinking reflects one of the strongest biases of American political thought—the tendency to define abstract ideals, such as freedom or the good life, in terms of economic abundance or efficient economic arrangements. In this sense the collectivists can be seen answering and updating Frederick Jackson Turner's frontier hypothesis, that popularly conceived but serious attempt to explain American social institutions in terms of mobility and character formation on the frontier. Essentially, the collectivists changed the direction, not the terms of this argument, when they confronted the important problem Turner avoided: the problem of group loyalties created by industrialization. For Turner, the frontier prevented the formation of rigid social classes by offering a continuing struggle with the environment. The collectivists, on the other hand, accepted social division as the starting point of their theories. But both Turner and the collectivists argued that economic relationships, if skillfully devised, could solve human problems. Both theories were reductive, but the collectivists particularly made social-problem solving dependent upon prosperity, and prosperity, in turn, dependent upon the oblique leadership of social engineers. The collectivists scarcely touched upon questions about the nature of men as men, and never really got beyond discussing them simply as factors of production.

Collectivism's circular assumptions define moral sanctions as if they were productive norms; hence social excellence has become synonymous with the ideal of efficiency. In collectivism, social problems were seen in isolation, appearing only during a specific breakdown of the productive apparatus, when access to information was clogged. Rarely were social problems viewed as symbolic of the whole social and economic system. Thus, as a society led by experts and even reformers, we rediscovered racism and poverty in the 1950's. Perhaps only by defining such conditions as social aberrations, only with a critical tradition devoted to problem-solving, could we ever have lost sight of them in the first place.

None of this would matter much, but for one fact: the assumptions of collectivism have become a part of the basis for modern social criticism. Collectivist assumptions lie behind much of the critical journalism that has beleaguered the last, vested interests of laissez-faire thinking in America. Collectivism is neither so rigorous as orthodox political science theory, nor as widespread as myth. But it did become the best defense of the New Deal and its method of bureaucratically centralizing social reform.

Beyond its contribution to reform, collectivism has also served the interests of technological and social progress, for implicit in it is a technique of social consolidation and manipulation. Deeply critical of nineteenth-century individualism, collectivism reflected the demands of a society whose productive forces were already highly integrated and complex, and every day becoming more so. Whether in doing so it was truly innovative, however, is quite another question. In moments of social renewal, the progress of institutions but not always of men is served. Thus collectivism, like most intellectual movements in American political thought, expressed a characteristic confusion that comes from serving two masters—a liberalism that is not liberal, and a conservatism that is not conservative. Collectivism was critical of society, at least in spheres that were socially or economically archaic, but its criticism was in terms of the most up-to-date productive relations. In their subtle restatement of the principle that whatever exists is right, collectivists gave a new expression to the most characteristic idea in the American political vocabulary.

As an important summary of our attitudes toward mature industrialism, collectivism emerged from the popular conception of modern social science. Its message was carried to audiences in those organs of opinion that catered to new educated elites and to intellectuals who were constructing institutions—the universities and institutes of research—to insure their own longevity as social engineers.

The primary influence of collectivist thought has reached beyond the relatively ineffective political science academicians, and beyond specialized journals, to those thinkers who generalized the interests of intellectuals in institutions. Their attraction to collectivism is symptomatic of the transformation of universities—and even reform organizations—into productive units. As an institution, the university epitomized this process when it developed beyond its nineteenth-century function as a gentleman's club and training center for ministers and teachers. Today the purpose of such intellectually productive units is far more complicated. In the course of its existence the university maintains and expands the class and status relationships in white-collar society, and its function inevitably reflects productive relationships. Occasionally, even, its conception of the humanities is scientized and quantifiable, as if the purposes of education could be defined by intellectual production norms.

What is true in the university is true in other areas of intellectual work, whether the intellectual finds himself in a reform organization or a corporation. He is very often a crucial link in a productive process. In their assertion of such a place for the intellectual in industrial society, the collectivists reflected a general tendency to define social relations in economic terms.

Ultimately, it is this commitment to economic determinism that betrays the weakness of collectivism, for it reduces intellectualism itself to a small factor. Too little creativity was left to men by the collectivists and far too much assigned to functional definitions, to laws, and to pseudo-science. For those who wished a different sort of world, with ideas as instruments of creativity, the corporation and the social arrangements deriving from it did not create the expected utopia. Most collectivists were right to believe that economic institutions would encompass our political possibilities. But the cost was self-denigration and a theory that transformed critics into interpreters of growth, consolidation, and change in a system that was working at the same time to make the critics themselves irrelevant.

Collectivism did not describe the only possible accommodation to modern industrial society, nor was it necessarily the best. Despite its efforts to do so, it did not comprehend work, the social implications of mass industrialism, or the role of ideas in a technological state. Instead, it chose to accept institutional compromises which already existed while it worked to smooth the abrasions that prevented quick adjustment to them. Society, it seemed, was organized for economic purposes, and it unfortunately followed that a person's loyalties and role could be defined essentially in relation to production. There was no escape from the implication that men, too, existed for the sake of production.

Notes

Introduction

1. See Richard Hofstadter, *The Age of Reform* (New York: Vintage, 1955); Robert Wiebe, *The Search for Order* (New York: Hill & Wang, 1967); Irwin Yellowitz, *Labor and the Progressive Movement in New York State, 1897–1916* (Ithaca: Cornell University Press, 1965); Roy Lubove, *The Professional Altruist: The Emergence of Social Work as a Career* (Cambridge, Mass.: Harvard University Press, 1967); Samuel P. Hays, "Politics of Reform in Municipal Government in the Progressive Era," *Pacific Northwest Quarterly*, LV (October 1964), 157–169; Arthur Mann, *Yankee Reformers in the Urban Age* (Cambridge, Mass.: Belknap Press, 1954); Howard H. Quint, *The Forging of American Socialism: Origins of the Modern Movement* (Columbia, S.C.: University of South Carolina Press, 1953); James Weinstein, *The Corporate Ideal in the Liberal State, 1900–1918* (Boston: Beacon Press, 1968); Gabriel Kolko, *The Triumph of Conservatism* (Chicago: Quadrangle, 1963); Kenneth McNaught, "American Progressives and the Great Society," *Journal of American History*, LIII (December 1966), 504–520.

2. See Wiebe, *Search for Order*, and Christopher Lasch, *The New Radicalism in America, 1889–1963: The Intellectual as a Social Type* (New York: Knopf, 1965).

CHAPTER 1: *The Collectivist Tendency*

1. H. G. Wells, *The Future in America: A Search After Realities* (New York: Harper, 1906), p. 167; Clarence S. Darrow, "The State: Its Functions and Duties," in *Echoes of the Sunset Club* (Chicago: W. W. Catlin, 1891), p. 159.

2. Van Wyck Brooks, *The World of H. G. Wells* (New York: Mitchell Kennerley, 1915), p. 182. Two books by European writers seem to have influenced American thinking on the nature of the state: Franz Oppen-

heimer, *The State: Its History and Development Viewed Sociologically* (Indianapolis: Bobbs-Merrill, 1914), and Emile Vandervelde, *Socialism Versus the State* (Chicago: Charles Kerr, 1911). However, such influence was quite narrow and very difficult to measure. Henry S. Kariel, *The Decline of American Pluralism* (Stanford: Stanford University Press, 1961), speculates on the lack of discussion about the state.

3. Laurence Gronlund, *The Cooperative Commonwealth,* ed. by Stowe Persons (Cambridge, Mass.: Harvard University Press, 1965), p. 84.

4. Franklin H. Giddings, *The Responsible State: A Reexamination of Fundamental Political Doctrines in the Light of World War and the Menace of Anarchism* (Boston: Houghton Mifflin, 1918), p. 19. William Tolman, *Social Engineering* (New York: McGraw, 1909), p. 366. One of the most interesting documents in the Stuart Chase Manuscripts at the Library of Congress in Washington, D.C., is a list of books which Chase read in 1913 and 1914. These included a great many of the authors and the books discussed in this and subsequent chapters. Chase himself was a proponent of many of the plans and programs that were popular with the collectivist intellectuals.

5. For example, Charles W. Eliot argued that centralism was the best way to defend the old values of liberty, family, and private property. Charles W. Eliot, *The Conflict Between Individualism and Collectivism in a Democracy* (New York: Scribner's, 1912).

6. It has long been assumed that elements of the Socialist party and later the Communist party were collectivist. But, as I hope to demonstrate, there was another form of collectivist thought in the United States which appeared around the turn of the century and which cannot be called revolutionary in the ordinary sense of that word. Indeed, this form of collectivism was not confined to any one political party. Some collectivist intellectuals attached their hopes to the Democratic party, some to the Republican party, and some to the Progressives and Socialists.

7. Walter Rauschenbusch, *Christianity and the Social Crisis* (New York: Harper and Row, 1964), p. 62.

8. John Dewey, *Democracy and Education* (New York: Free Press, 1966), p. 225. See also James MacKaye, *The Economy of Happiness* (Boston: Little, Brown, 1906). MacKaye was one of the most interesting writers of the period, though his style is often confusing. As a writer who was interested in "Americanizing" socialism, MacKaye, like William English Walling, attempted to find socialism in the midst of American traditions and in the works of modern American and European philosophers and sociologists.

9. Charles E. Rosenberg, "Science and American Social Thought," in David D. Van Tassel and Michael G. Hall, eds., *Science and Society in the United States* (Homewood, Ill.: Dorsey Press, 1966), pp. 135–162. See also George W. Stocking, Jr., "Lamarckianism in American Social Science," *Journal of the History of Ideas,* XXIII (April–June 1962), 239–250.

10. "Social Science and Socialism," *American Review of Reviews,* XLVI (July 1912), 87.

11. David Walter Eakins, "The Development of Corporate Liberal Policy Research in the United States, 1885–1965" (unpublished Ph.D. thesis, University of Wisconsin, 1966), pp. 25–26; Joseph Dorfman, *The Economic Mind in American Civilization,* III (New York: Viking Press, 1949), *passim.* Mark Perlman, in his book *Labor Union Theories in America* (Evanston, Ill.: Row, Peterson, 1958), demonstrates several different sources of theories about the role of trade unions in the United States.

12. Frank Parsons, "The Truth at the Heart of Capitalism and of Socialism," *Arena*, xxxvii (January 1907) , 8.

13. Nicholas Paine Gilman, *Socialism and the American Spirit* (Boston: Houghton Mifflin, 1893) , p. 119.

14. Laurence R. Veysey, *The Emergence of the American University* (Chicago: University of Chicago Press, 1965) , p. 266. E. A. Ross, *Roads to Social Peace* (Chapel Hill: University of North Carolina Press, 1924) , p. 1.

15. Lyman Abbott, *The Spirit of Democracy* (Boston: Houghton Mifflin, 1910) , p. 134.

16. Robert Hunter, *Poverty* (New York: Macmillan, 1904) . See Sidney Fine, *Laissez-Faire and the General Welfare State* (Ann Arbor: University of Michigan Press, 1956) , pp. 322–345.

17. Brooks, *The World*, pp. 11–12. See, for example, Ida Tarbell, *New Ideals in Business* (New York: Macmillan, 1916) . Among other things, the author envisions the factory as a school.

18. For example, see John Corbin, *The Return of the Middle Class* (New York: Scribner's, 1922) , pp. 10, 292. Robert Wiebe's excellent and suggestive book, *The Search for Order*, makes the point that the Progressive era was a time when middle-class intellectuals gradually developed a bureaucratic frame of mind in an effort to overcome the social fragmentation that accompanied rapid industrialization and urbanization. See also Lester Frank Ward, *Applied Sociology: A Treatise on the Conscious Improvement of Society by Society* (Boston: Ginn, 1906) .

19. John Martin, "Social Reconstruction To-Day," *Atlantic Monthly*, cii (September 1908) , 279; Brooks Adams, *The Theory of Social Revolution* (New York: Macmillan, 1914) , p. 207; William James Ghent, *Our Benevolent Feudalism* (New York: Macmillan, 1902) , p. 193. Parts of Adams' and Ghent's books appeared in the *Atlantic Monthly* and the *Independent*.

20. Dorfman, *Economic Mind*, iii, *passim;* Charles Edward Russell Papers, Library of Congress, Washington, D.C., hereafter cited as Russell MSS.

21. Robert W. Sellars, *The Next Step in Democracy* (New York: Macmillan, 1916) , p. 45.

22. See Weinstein, *Corporate Ideal*, and Samuel P. Hays, "The Politics of Reform in Municipal Government in the Progressive Era," *Pacific Northwest Quarterly*, lv (October 1964) , 157–169.

23. Charles L. Wood, "A Co-operative Trust," *Twentieth Century*, xiv (March 21, 1895) , 5; Sellers, *Next Step*, p. 219; Charles Ferguson, *The Revolution Absolute* (New York: Dodd, Mead, 1918) , most of which appeared in the *Bookman* in 1917 and 1918. See also James Myers, *Representative Government in Industry* (New York: George H. Doran, 1924) , and Parsons, "Truth," *Arena*, p. 8.

24. Harry Thurston Peck, "Special Issue on the Concentration of Wealth in the United States," *Independent*, liv (May 1, 1902) ; Herbert Croly, *The Promise of American Life*, ed. by Arthur M. Schlesinger, Jr. (Cambridge, Mass.; Harvard University Press, 1965) , p. 336; Maurice Parmelee, *Poverty and Social Progress* (New York: Macmillan, 1916) , p. 443; Edward T. Devine, *Economics* (New York: Macmillan, 1898) . Devine was general secretary of the Charity Organization Society of New York City.

25. For an excellent account of the practical work of intellectuals in

corporations, see Loren Baritz, *Servants of Power: A History of the Use of Social Science in American Industry* (Middletown, Conn.: Wesleyan University Press, 1960). John R. Commons, *Myself* (Madison: University of Wisconsin Press, 1934), p. 156.

26. Brooks Adams, "The Heritage of Henry Adams," in Henry Adams, *The Degradation of the Democratic Dogma* (New York: Macmillan, 1919); Jacob Hollander, "Testimony," *Final Report and Testimony of the Commission on Industrial Relations*, Senate Document 415, 64th Cong., 1st sess. (Washington, D.C.: U.S. Printing Office, 1916), p. 7534.

27. Two such writers were Laurence Gronlund and William English Walling.

28. John Graham Brooks, *Labor's Challenge to the Social Order: Democracy Its Own Critic and Educator* (New York: Macmillan, 1920). It is sometimes difficult to estimate how seriously intellectuals took the threat of the Wobblies. Ironically, it was taken quite seriously by, among other groups, a number of socialist intellectuals.

CHAPTER 2: *Outlines of a World View*

1. Eakins, "The Development of Corporate Liberal Policy Research"; Charles H. Page, *Class and American Sociology* (New York: Dial Press, 1940).

2. Henry C. Adams, "Relation of the State to Industrial Action," *Publications of the American Economic Association*, 1 (January 1887), 13; Simon Patten, *The New Basis of Civilization* (New York: Macmillan, 1907), p. 11; James Myers, *Representative Government in Industry* (New York: George H. Doran, 1924), p. 22.

3. Charles B. Davenport, "What Is Americanism?" *American Journal of Sociology*, xx (January 1915). S. S. McClure to Charles E. Russell, New York, December 25, 1910, Russell MSS.

4. William F. Quillian, Jr., "Evolution and Moral Theory in America," in Stowe Persons, ed., *Evolutionary Thought in America* (New York: Braziller, 1956), pp. 398–421; Malcolm Cowley, "Nationalism in American Literature," *ibid.*, pp. 390–414.

5. Washington Gladden, *et al.*, *Organized Labor and Capital* (Philadelphia: George W. Jacobs, 1904), pp. 12 ff.

6. Upton Sinclair, *The Industrial Republic: A Study of Ten Years Hence* (New York: Doubleday, Page, 1907), p. 27.

7. Arthur Morrow Lewis, *Vital Problems in Social Evolution* (Chicago: Charles H. Kerr, 1911), p. 21.

8. Franklin Giddings, *Democracy and Empire, with Studies of Their Psychological, Economic, and Moral Foundations* (New York: Macmillan, 1900), p. 344; Clarence S. Darrow and Arthur M. Lewis, *Marx Versus Tolstoy: A Debate* (Chicago: Charles H. Kerr, 1911), p. 75; Edmond Kelly, *Government or Human Evolution* (Cambridge, Mass.: John Wilson, 1901), p. 258.

9. Patten, *New Basis of Civilization*, p. 43; Page, *Class and American Sociology*, p. 139; Ordway Tead, *Instincts in Industry: A Study of Working-Class Psychology* (Boston: Houghton Mifflin, 1918), p. 219.

10. Eakins, "The Development of Corporate Liberal Research," p. 101. The Russell Sage Foundation, for example, studied social conditions in New York, covering public hygiene, employment, city planning, and a number of other topics.

11. For example, the section on public ownership in William D. P. Bliss's *New Encyclopedia of Social Reform* was in large measure based upon research done by the National Civic Federation; William D. P. Bliss, ed., *New Encyclopedia of Social Reform* (New York: Funk and Wagnalls, 1908), p. 1238; William H. Allen, "A National Fund for Efficient Democracy," *Atlantic Monthly*, CII (October 1908), 463.

12. Louis Brandeis, "Testimony," *Final Report and Testimony of the Commission on Industrial Relations,*" p. 993; George Creel, "A Way to Industrial Peace," *Century*, LXVIII (July 1915), 433–436.

13. Arthur James Todd, *Theories of Social Progress: A Critical Study of the Attempts to Formulate the Conditions of Human Advance* (New York: Macmillan, 1919), p. vii; H. G. Wells, *Wells' Social Anticipations* (New York: Vanguard, 1927), p. 105; Ward, *Applied Sociology: A Treatise on the Conscious Improvement of Society by Society*, p. 21. Sidney Reeve in his book, *The Cost of Competition* (New York: McClure, Phillips, 1906), p. 606, argues that the study of science will lead to the discovery of moral law: "I proclaim the faith that he who starts out, consistently and earnestly from careful observation, with the inductive methods of the Baconian philosophy, must inevitably end up with the moral principle of the four gospels as his scientific conclusions."

14. "Masters of Capitalism," *McClure's*, XXXVII (July 1911), 344.

15. Charles J. Bullock, "Trust Literature: A Survey and Criticism," in William Z. Ripley, ed., *Trusts, Pools and Corporations* (Boston, Ginn, 1905), pp. 428–474.

16. Arthur Swanson, "Ideals in Business," in William L. Chenery, *Ideals of America* (Chicago: A. C. McClurg, 1919), p. 177; Talcott Williams, "The Corporation," in Gladden, *Organized Labor and Capital*, p. 77. Frederic C. Howe agreed about the pervasiveness of monopoly, but opposed it: Frederic C. Howe, *Privilege and Democracy in America* (New York: Scribner's, 1912), p. 243. See also Weinstein, *Corporate Ideal*, p. 251.

17. Jeremiah Jenks, "Report of the Industrial Commission on Industrial Combinations in Europe," in *Reports of the Commission in Europe*, XVIII (Washington, D.C.: Government Printing Office, 1901), 9; Charles Edward Russell, *Why I Am a Socialist* (New York: Hodder and Stoughton, 1910), p. 301. The National Civic Federation was very optimistic about the outcome of efforts like its own before 1919; see Gordon M. Jensen, "The National Civic Federation: American Business in an Age of Social Change and Social Reform" (unpublished Ph.D. thesis, Princeton University, 1956), pp. 162–163; John R. Commons, ed., *Industrial Government* (New York: Macmillan, 1921), p. viii.

18. Charles H. Vail, *Principles of Scientific Socialism* (New York: Commonwealth, 1899), p. 27; Talcott Williams, "Corporation," in Gladden, *Organized Labor and Capital*, p. 77. Williams used the work of Jeremiah Jenks in his article. Harry Laidler argues that it was Bernard Shaw and the Fabians who first suggested the separation between the functions of manager and owner; Harry Laidler, *A History of Socialist Thought* (New York: Thomas Crowell, 1927), p. 250.

19. William Graham Sumner, "Its Justification," *Independent*, LIV (May 1, 1902), 1036; Lyman Abbott, "The Trust Problem: The Socialistic Basis," *American Journal of Sociology*, XIII (May 1908), 771; Charles R. Flint, "Concentration and Natural Law," *Independent*, LIV (May 1, 1902), 1025.

20. Samuel Gompers, "Labor and Its Attitude Toward Trusts," Address to the Chicago Conference on Trusts, Chicago, October 1907, pp. 1–4.

21. Henry D. Lloyd, "Socialist Regime," *Independent*, LIV (May 1, 1902), 1072; Arthur Jerome Eddy, *The New Competition* (Chicago: A. C. Mc-Clurg, 1913), p. 100 (much of Eddy's book was previously published in *World's Work*); Theodore E. Burton, *Corporations and the State* (New York: D. Appleton, 1911), p. 98.

22. Vida Scudder, "The Social Conscience of the Future," *Hibbert Journal*, VII (January 1909), 331; James MacKaye, *Americanized Socialism: A Yankee View of Capitalism* (New York: Boni and Liveright, 1918), pp. 80–96. Edward Bellamy, Henry D. Lloyd, Laurence Gronlund, and a number of Christian Socialists were all opposed to competition because of its extreme waste. J. J. Spengler, "Evolution in American Economics," in Stowe Persons, ed., *Evolutionary Thought*, p. 247.

23. William Sloane, "Modern Feudalism," *University Settlement Studies*, I (April 1904), 17–20; see also Ghent, *Benevolent Feudalism;* Sinclair, *Industrial Republic*, p. 259; Thorstein Veblen, *Engineers and the Price System* (New York: Huebsch, 1921), *passim.*

24. John Bates Clark, *Social Justice Without Socialism* (Boston: Houghton Mifflin, 1914), p. 48; Adams, *Social Revolution*, p. 203; Charlotte Perkins Gilman, *Human Work* (New York: McClure, Phillips, 1904), p. 299; Benjamin Radar, "Richard Ely: Lay Spokesman for the Social Gospel," *Journal of American History*, LIII (June 1966); Walter G. Cooper, *Fate of the Middle Classes* (New York: Consolidated Booksellers, 1905), p. 179. Cooper was secretary of the Atlanta Chamber of Commerce.

25. Brooks, *Labor's Challenge*, p. 377; Edwin Bjorkman, "The Unnecessary Curse of Sickness," *World's Work*, XVIII (July 1909), 11837. There were, of course, a number of important intellectuals who disliked such a description of society as an organism or even as a mechanism.

26. Abbott, "Trust Problem," p. 670.

27. Weinstein, *Corporate Ideal, passim.*

28. William James Ghent, *Mass and Class: A Survey of Social Divisions* (New York: Macmillan, 1904), pp. 9 ff., 256; Frank Parsons, *Our Country's Need* (Boston: Arena, 1894), p. 188.

29. For the importance of class struggle in the theories of American sociologists, see Page, *Class and American Sociology*, pp. 33 ff.

30. John R. Commons, "Is Class Conflict Necessary?", *American Journal of Sociology*, XIII (May 1908), 782.

31. John Elliot Ross, *Consumers and Social Reform* (New York: Devin-Adair, 1912), p. 6.

32. John Spargo, *Americanism and Social Democracy* (New York: Harper, 1918), p. 86. The *Third Triennial Report to the Commission on Social Service of the American Episcopal Church* (New York: Church Missions House, 1919), p. 104, cites a new school in American political thought which centered around a sociology of the state. Among its proponents, the report noted, were Herbert Croly and Mary Follett, and Harold Laski of England. In 1904 the Century Company published the American State Series, in which almost every book was the elaboration of one or another specific function of government. The most general and theoretical was W. W. Willoughby's *American Constitutional System* (New York: Century, 1904). This work, in its theoretical aspects, was most concerned with the question of sovereignty.

33. Hunter, *Poverty*, p. 333; Charles P. Steinmetz, *America and the New Epoch* (New York: Harper, 1916), p. 160.

34. Charles R. Van Hise, *Concentration and Control: A Solution of the Trust Problem in the United States*, rev. ed. (New York: Macmillan, 1921), p. 278; Croly, *Promise*, p. 39; Theodore Lowi writes of the rise of administrative government in America and the development of rule by experts in the United States in *End of Liberalism: Ideology, Policy, and the Crisis of Public Authority* (New York: Norton, 1969).

35. Dorfman, *Economic Mind*, III, *passim;* Jeremiah Jenks, *Governmental Action for Social Welfare* (New York: Macmillan, 1910), p. 136.

36. Randolph Bourne, *The State* (New York: Resistance Press, 1946–1947), p. 4.

37. Arthur James Todd, *The Scientific Spirit and Social Work* (New York: Macmillan, 1919), p. 45. Todd was professor of sociology and director of training for social and civic work at the University of Minnesota.

CHAPTER 3: *An Ideology Without Borders*

1. Morris Hillquit, *Loose Leaves from a Busy Life* (New York: Macmillan, 1934), *passim;* John Corbin, *The Return of the Middle Class* (New York: Scribner's, 1923).

2. MacKaye, *Economy of Happiness*, pp. 457–458.

3. Bernard Baruch to Charles Edward Russell, New York, October 13, 1920, Russell MSS.

4. Vail, *Scientific Socialism*, p. 230. George Herron is a good example of a minister who adopted the socialist movement as his new laity. Allen Davis discusses the influence of Protestantism on such movements as the settlement house movement in *Spearheads of Reform* (New York: Oxford University Press, 1967).

5. Lloyd, "Socialist Regime," *Independent*, p. 1072; Lewis, *Vital Problems*, p. 22.

6. Edwin R. A. Seligman, *Economic Interpretation of History*, 2nd ed. (New York: Columbia University Press, 1907), *passim;* Morris Hillquit, *Socialism in Theory and Practice* (New York: Macmillan, 1912). See also Samuel Chugerman, *Lester Frank Ward: The American Aristotle* (New York: Octagon, 1965), p. 75.

7. Kelly, *Government or Human Evolution*, p. 199; Gaylord Wilshire, "Herbert Spencer," *Wilshire's Editorials* (New York: Wilshire, 1906), p. 279; Steinmetz, *America and the New Epoch*, p. 166. Other writers felt that socialism was unpleasant, but possibly inevitable. See Jeremiah Strong, *The State and Government* (Chicago: A. C. McClurg, 1917), *passim.*

8. Vail, *Scientific Socialism*, p. 24; Bliss, *New Encyclopedia*, p. 1238; Charles Edward Russell, *The Heart of the Nation* (New York: John Lane, 1911); Russell, *Why I Am a Socialist*, p. 301.

9. Daniel DeLeon, "The Socialist View of the Trust," *American Fabian*, V (April 1899), 9; Jack London, *The War of the Classes* (New York: Regent Press, 1905), p. 257; John Spargo, "The Influence of Karl Marx on Contemporary Socialism," *American Journal of Sociology*, XVI (July 1910), 37.

10. Scudder, "Social Conscience," *Hibbert Journal*, p. 315; MacKaye, *Americanized Socialism*, p. 7; Walter Rauschenbusch, *Christianity and Social Crisis* (New York: Harper and Row, 1964), pp. 59–62.

11. Emile Vandervelde, *Collectivism and Industrial Evolution* (Chicago: Charles Kerr, 1901), p. 103; Louis C. Fraina, *Revolutionary Socialism: A*

Study in Socialist Reconstruction (New York: Communist Press, 1918), p. 163; Gilman, *Socialism and the American Spirit*, p. 39.

12. Howe, *Privilege and Democracy*, p. 3; Charles Edward Russell, *Uprising of the Many* (New York: Doubleday, Page, 1907), p. xi (most of this book appeared first in *Everybody's Magazine*).

13. Frederic C. Howe, *European Cities at Work* (New York: Scribner's, 1913), *passim*.

14. Charles W. Wood, *The Great Change* (New York: Boni and Liveright, p. 1918), pp. 46–47; Jenks, "Report of the Industrial Commission," p. 7.

15. MacKaye, *Americanized Socialism*, p. 4.

16. Morris L. Cooke, "Discussion: Centralization of Administrative Authority," *Bulletin of the Taylor Society*, IV (April 1919), 20.

17. Clark, *Social Justice Without Socialism;* Eddy, *New Competition;* Sinclair, *Industrial Republic,* discuss Australia and New Zealand. Despite all this, as will be shown later, English radical ideas probably had more effect on American collectivism than German ideas.

18. Giddings, *Responsible State*, p. 6; Spargo, *Americanism and Social Democracy*, p. 16.

19. Laidler, *History of Socialism, passim*.

20. The origin of this group seems to have been the Noroton Conference organized by Robert Hunter at Noroton, Connecticut; J. G. Phelps Stokes Papers, Butler Library, Columbia University, hereafter cited as Stokes MSS.

21. Jessie Wallace Hughan, *American Socialism of the Present Day* (New York: John Lane, 1912). Spargo wrote an enthusiastic introduction to the book.

CHAPTER 4: *From Fabianism to Industrial Democracy*

1. Henry George, *Social Problems* (New York, Robert Schalkenbach Foundation, 1883, 1934), p. 243.

2. Eric Goldman, *Rendezvous with Destiny* (New York: Knopf, 1952), pp. 123–124.

3. Frank Vanderlip, "Economic Analysis of American Industrial Conditions," *Bulletin of the National Association of Corporation Schools*, III (February 1916), 24. Richard Welling, *As the Twig Is Bent* (New York: Putnam's, 1942), p. 41. Edmond Kelly, "Report of the Committee on Co-operation and Affiliated Clubs," *City Club Publications* (New York: City Club of New York, 1894), p. 14; "Articles of Incorporation" (New York: City Club of New York, 1898), and City Reform Club, "Minutes" (November 5, 1892); these publications are taken from the City Club Papers at the New York Historical Association, New York City, and the City Reform Club Papers, New York Public Library, hereafter cited as CC Papers and CRC Papers, respectively.

4. Kelly, "Report of Committee on Co-operation," p. 11.

5. William F. Howes, "History of the Clubs from 1892–1922," typescript, City Club Papers, New York Public Library, hereafter cited as CC Papers (New York Public).

6. CC Papers and CRC Papers (New York Public). See Yellowitz, *Labor and the Progressive Movement*, and Alice Kessler Harris, "The Lower Class as a Factor in Reform: New York, the Jews and the 1890's" (unpublished Ph.D. thesis, Rutgers University, 1968).

7. Social Reform Club, *Annual Report* (New York, 1897), pp. 1–4; Social Reform Club, "Minutes" (New York, November 1, 1898, and October 11, 1898); Social Reform Club, *Annual Report, Constitution, List of Members* (New York, 1898), pp. 7–8. Several of these printed sources were found in the Stokes MSS.

8. Social Reform Club, "Minutes" (New York, January 15, 1897).

9. *American Fabian,* I (February 1895), 5; Quint, *Forging of American Socialism,* pp. 253 ff.; Thomas P. Jenkins, "American Fabian Movement," *Western Political Quarterly,* I (June 1943), *passim.* See also James Gilbert, "The American Fabian: An Introduction and Appraisal," *Labor History,* XI (Summer 1970), 347–350.

10. *American Fabian,* III (March 1897), 4; *ibid.,* IV (November 1898), 2.

11. The Alturian League of New York was one of the first groups to join Bliss's American Fabian Movement. *American Fabian,* I (April 1895), *passim.* A very interesting article on the relationships between American and English reformers is McNaught, "American Progressives and the Great Society," cited in the notes to the Introduction.

12. I discuss the relationship of intellectuals to the Socialist party in a later chapter on William English Walling.

13. Hillquit, *Loose Leaves,* pp. 67–70. Charles Beard to William James Ghent, New York, undated letter; William James Ghent Papers, Library of Congress, Washington, D.C., hereafter cited as Ghent MSS.

14. Collectivist Society, *Bulletin of the Collectivist Society* (New York, January 1903), p. 4; William James Ghent, "The Collectivist Society," *Commons,* IX (March 1904), 89; William James Ghent to Joan London, Washington, D.C., August 27, 1937, *passim,* Ghent MSS.

15. "Noroton Conference," Stokes MSS, and Hillquit, *Loose Leaves,* pp. 56–59.

16. Harry Laidler, "Years of Progress," in Laidler, ed., *Years of Education* (New York: League for Industrial Democracy, 1945), pp. 17–20; Upton Sinclair, *Candid Reminiscences* (London: T. Werner Laurie, 1932), p. 142. See also Philip M. Crane, *The Democrat's Dilemma* (Chicago: Regnery, 1964), *passim,* and Anne Jackson Fremantle, *This Little Band of Prophets: The Story of the Gentle Fabians* (London: Allen and Unwin, 1960), pp. 219–220.

17. Library Employees' Union of Greater New York, *Industrial Democracy, 1848–1919* (New York, 1919). This work contains a list of works on Industrial Democracy. See also Walter Lippmann, "Authority in the Modern State," *New Republic,* XIX (May 3, 1919), 149, and Franklin Giddings, "Intellectual Consequences of the War," Address to the Royal Canadian Institute, Toronto, Canada, November 30, 1918, typescript. Franklin Giddings Papers, Columbia University, New York.

18. Ida Tarbell, *New Ideals, passim.*

19. *The Mediator* (Cleveland, 1910–1915), *passim.* "Industrial Democracy" is listed as a subject in the *Reader's Guide* beginning around 1915.

20. Louis Brandeis, "Testimony," *Report of the Commission on Industrial Relations,* pp. 1005, 1008.

21. Robert Franklin Hoxie, *Scientific Management and Labor* (New York: Appleton, 1915), p. 100. See also Samuel Haber, *Efficiency and Uplift: Scientific Management in the Progressive Era, 1890–1920* (Chicago: University of Chicago Press, 1964), and Baritz, *Servants of Power, passim.*

22. Weinstein, *Corporate Ideal, passim;* Jacob M. Budish and George

Soule, *The New Unionism* (New York: Russell & Russell, 1920, 1968) , pp. 12–13; the authors contend that the agreement embodied some of the principles of Guild Socialism. See also Julius Henry Cohen, *Law and Order in Industry: Five Years' Experience* (New York: Macmillan, 1916) , pp. 44 ff., and Carle H. Mote, *Industrial Arbitration* (Indianapolis: Bobbs-Merrill, 1916) , p. 1. See Melvyn Dubofsky's excellent *When Workers Organize* (Amherst: University of Massachusetts Press, 1968) , *passim.*

23. Savel Zimand, "Guild Socialism—A Bibliography," *Library Journal,* XLV (March 15, 1920) , 258; Harry Laidler, *History of Socialism,* rev. ed. (London: Routledge and Kegan Paul, 1968) , p. 217. Peter Drucker in 1942 wrote that the "Guild Socialists" Brooks and Henry Adams in the United States and the socialists in Germany were among the first to discover the discontinuity between the modern industrial system and the political system; Peter F. Drucker, *The Future of Industrial Man* (New York: John Day, 1942) , p. 69.

24. Joint Commission of the Protestant Episcopal Church, *Third Triennial Report,* p. 104. This document traces the rise of Industrial Democracy. See also Corbin, *Return of the Middle Class,* p. 279.

25. Charles Eliot to Charles Pender, Cambridge, Mass., February 5, 1914, in "Profit-Sharing," Eliot Papers, Harvard Archives. George W. Perkins, "The America of To-Morrow," in Elisha Friedman, ed., *American Problems of Reconstruction* (New York: Dutton, 1918) , p. 51.

26. Gordon Merritt, "Factory Solidarity or Class Solidarity" (reprinted from *Iron Age,* no date) , p. 43, and Paul W. Litchfield, *The Industrial Republic: A Study in Industrial Economics* (Boston: Houghton Mifflin, 1919) , pp. 60 ff.

27. Myers, *Representative Government in Industry,* pp. 50, 193, and Leitch, *Man to Man,* p. 68. See also Robert W. Briere, "Can We Eliminate Labor Unrest?" in C. H. Crennan, "A Reconstruction Labor Policy," *Annals of the American Academy of Political and Social Science,* LXXXI (January 1919) , *passim;* Robert F. Foerster, "A Promising Venture in Industrial Partnership," in Emery R. Johnson, "The Outlook for Industrial Peace," *Annals,* XLIV (November 1912) , *passim.*

28. Goodwin to Filene, Washington, D.C., November 10, 1917, in Filene Papers, Harvard Business School, Cambridge, Mass. A. B. Wolfe, *Work Committees and Joint Industrial Councils,* U.S. Shipping Board, Emergency Fleet Corporation (Philadelphia, 1919) , pp. 34, 112–115. See also his somewhat later consideration of the problem: A. B. Wolfe, *Conservatism, Radicalism, and Scientific Method: An Essay on Social Attitudes* (New York: Macmillan, 1923) .

29. "Whitley Report," in Glenn Frank, *The Politics of Industry* (New York: Century, 1919) , p. 197; Charles G. Fenwick, *Political Systems in Transition* (New York: Century, 1920) , p. 99; Glenn Plumb and William G. Roylance, *Industrial Democracy: A Plan for Its Achievement* (New York: Huebsch, 1923) , *passim.*

30. Savel Zimand writes that a tremendous amount of literature was devoted to the Plumb Plan in American magazines. Savel Zimand, *Modern Social Movements* (New York: H. W. Wilson, 1921) , pp. 109 ff.; Laidler, *History of Socialism,* pp. 319–335; Niles Carpenter, *Guild Socialism: An Historical and Critical Analysis* (New York: Appleton, 1922) , pp. 1–92. See also Leland Olds, "Guild Socialism and Railway Brotherhoods," *Intercollegiate Socialist,* VII (April–May 1919) , p. 23; Norman Hapgood, *The*

Advancing House (New York: Boni and Liveright, 1920) , p. 169; Ordway Tead, "The Development of the Guild Idea," *Intercollegiate Socialist*, VI (April–May 1918) .

31. Some Guild Socialists wished that the state as such, and even administrators, would disappear; Laidler, *History of Socialism*, pp. 319–335.

32. See Walter Weyl's emphasis on the role of the consumer and the public; Walter Weyl, *The New Democracy* (New York: Harper, 1912, 1964) , p. 250.

33. John A. Ryan, *Distributive Justice: The Right and Wrong of Our Present Distribution of Wealth* (New York: Macmillan, 1916) ; John A. Ryan, *Social Reconstruction* (New York: Macmillan, 1920) ; John A. Ryan, *Industrial Democracy from a Catholic Viewpoint* (Washington, D.C.: Rossi-Bryn, 1925) . See also Harry F. Ward, *The New Social Order: Principles and Programs* (New York: Macmillan, 1919) , p. 362.

34. Father John Ryan was a close friend of Florence Kelley; Josephine Clara Goldmark, *Impatient Crusader* (Urbana: University of Illinois Press, 1953) , pp. 53, 150. See also Florence Kelley, "Woman's Part in Post-War Problems," (1920?) , pp. 1, 7, in National Consumers League Papers, Library of Congress, Washington, D.C. See Frank Julian Warne, *The Workers at War* (New York: Century, 1920) , p. 250. American Federation of Labor, "Reconstruction Program" (Washington, D.C.: American Federation of Labor, 1918) ; Matthew Woll, "Industrial Relations and Production," in Clyde L. King, "Labor, Management and Production," *Annals*, XCI (September 1920) , 12–13.

35. William English Walling, "Industrial Democracy or Industrial Autocracy—Which?", Stokes MSS. Author unknown, "Proposed Manifesto of the Social Democratic League," February 1917, p. 2, Stokes MSS.

36. Frank Tannenbaum, *The Labor Movement* (New York: Putnam's, 1921) , pp. 44, 197, 140.

37. Harold J. Laski, *Studies in the Problem of Sovereignty* (New Haven: Yale University Press, 1917) ; Harold J. Laski, *Authority in the Modern State* (New Haven: Yale University Press, 1919) .

CHAPTER 5: *Edmond Kelly and the Socialism of Order*

1. Shaun Kelly to Henry Nicolls, October 29, 1943, in Edmond Kelly Papers, collection of Mrs. Shaun Kelly, Boston, Massachusetts, hereafter cited as Kelly MSS. "Sketch of Edmond Kelly," in "Biography of Edmond Kelly," Kelly MSS. See also "Edmond Kelly," in *National Cyclopaedia of American Biography*, XIV (New York: J. T. White, 1917) , 222–223.

2. Eliza Palache, "James Palache," in "Family Memories," typescript (California, 1934) , p. 4, collection of Mr. Sean Kelly, Washington, D.C., hereafter cited as Sean Kelly MSS. See also E. R. Clay (Robert E. Kelly) , *The Alternative: A Study in Psychology* (London: Macmillan, 1882) , p. 16.

3. Robert E. Kelly to Edmond Kelly, May 1889 and May 1885, Kelly MSS; Edmond Kelly, *The Proposed French Corporation Law and Its Effects on American Life Insurance Companies in France* (Paris, 1885) ; and Edmond Kelly, *The French Law of Marriage* (Paris: Galignani's Library, 1885) , p. 95.

4. Edmond Kelly to ?, Paris, France, September 1, 1888, Kelly MSS; "Odds and Ends," in "Political, Historical and Social Reflections" (a journal, 1889–1896) , p. 19, Kelly MSS.

5. Kelly, "Political Reflections," pp. 16, 18–23.

6. *Ibid.*, pp. 22, 53.

7. Welling, *As the Twig Is Bent*, pp. 57, 64–65; Edmond Kelly, "Good Government Clubs," *Outlook*, L (December 29, 1894) , 1124–1125; J. Lowell to Edmond Kelly, New York, November 9, 1894. See William Howe Tolman, *Municipal Reform Movements in the United States* (New York: Fleming H. Revell, 1895) , *passim,* for a list of groups that worked for political reforms in New York City at that time.

8. Edmond Kelly, *Evolution and Effort* (New York: D. Appleton, 1895) , p. 254; Edmond Kelly, *Government or Human Evolution: Justice* (London: Longmans, Green, 1900) ; L. B. Stowe, "High Spots in the Committee's Work," in National Self Government Club Papers, New York Public Library. See also Richard Littell, typescript, in Richard Welling Papers, New York Public Library.

9. Edmond Kelly, *Government or Human Evolution: Individualism and Collectivism* (London: Longmans, Green, 1901) , p. viii.

10. Edmond Kelly to Shaun Kelly, New York, October 18, 1898, Kelly MSS; Edmond Kelly, "Report of Edmond Kelly concerning his Visit to Mrs. Piper," p. 6, undated manuscript, Kelly MSS. William James suggested that a number of his friends visit Mrs. Piper; see Gardner Murphy and Robert O. Ballou, eds., *William James on Psychical Research* (New York: Viking, 1960) , p. 104, and M. Sage, *Mrs. Piper and the Society for Psychical Research,* abridged from the French (New York: Scott-Thaw, 1904) , p. 21.

11. Kelly, *Evolution and Effort,* p. 1; Edmond Kelly, "Constitutional History and International Law," bound notes, p. 1, Sean Kelly MSS.

12. Edmond Kelly, "The Borough System in Municipal Government," *Forum,* XXVII (March 1899) , 62, 70; Edmond Kelly, "Things Municipal," *International Quarterly,* V (January 1902) , 86; Edmond Kelly, "Municipal Ownership," unpublished manuscript, p. 6, Kelly MSS.

13. Kelly, "Things Municipal," p. 92; Upton Sinclair, "Review of Twentieth Century Socialism," *Wilshire's and New Age,* 1910, from clipping file, Kelly MSS.

14. Kelly, *Justice,* p. 360.

15. Edmond Kelly, draft of a review for *Political Science Quarterly,* "La Crise Allemande de 1900–1902" (January 24, 1903) , p. 2, Kelly MSS.

16. Kelly, *Individualism and Collectivism,* pp. 4, 533; Reverend Heber Newton to Edmond Kelly, East Hampton, N.Y., 1901, Kelly MSS.

17. Kelly, *Individualism and Collectivism, passim;* John Spargo, "Twentieth Century Socialism," *Call,* May 15, 1910; Edmond Kelly, "The Class Struggle," *Call,* August 20, 1909.

18. Kelly MSS, *passim.*

19. Robert Hunter, "Edmond Kelly," 1910, in clipping file, Kelly MSS; Charles Edward Russell, *Bare Hands and Stone Walls* (New York: Scribner's, 1933) , pp. 207 ff.

20. Edmond Kelly, "Mr. Roosevelt and Looseness of Thought," p. 3, manuscript in Kelly MSS.

21. Ellison Harding (Edmond Kelly) , *The Demetrian* (New York: Brentano's, 1907) . It was immediately before this period that he composed *The Demetrian.* Upton Sinclair wrote much of his own work, the *Industrial Republic,* at the Colony; see Sinclair, *Candid Reminiscences,* pp. 159–164; Upton Sinclair, "A Home Colony," *Independent,* LX (June 14, 1906) , 1401–1409.

22. Kelly MSS, *passim;* Kelly, *The Demetrian,* p. 26.

23. Edmond Kelly, *Elimination of the Tramp* (New York: Knickerbocker, 1908), pp. 4–5; Edmond Kelly, "La Legislation Etrangère en Ce Qui Concerne le Vagabondage," *Bulletin de l'Institut Psychologique de Paris,* II (December 1902), *passim.*

24. Lebovitz to Edith Kelly, Washington, D.C., June 4, 1910, Kelly MSS.

25. Edmond Kelly, *Twentieth Century Socialism: What It Is Not; What It Is; How It May Come* (New York: Longmans, Green, 1910), pp. 8, 405–406.

26. Edith Kelly to Lincoln Steffens, Nyack, New York, November 3, 1909, Lincoln Steffens Papers, Library of Congress, Washington, D.C.; *New York Times,* November 18, 1909.

CHAPTER 6: *King Gillette's Social Redemption*

1. *New York Times,* July 11, 1932; see also Gillette Letters in the Upton Sinclair Papers, Lilly Library, Indiana University, Bloomington, Ind.; hereafter cited as Sinclair MSS.

2. "King Camp Gillette," *National Cyclopaedia of American Biography,* XIV (New York: James T. White, 1910), 504; "Look Sharp!", address by Joseph P. Spang, Jr. (New York, 1951), p. 13; King C. Gillette, "Origin of the Gillette Razor" (from an article written in 1918 with additions in 1925), pp. 1–3, from the Gillette Razor Company, Boston, Mass.; *Boston Herald,* July 11, 1932.

3. Fanny Camp Gillette, *Mrs. Gillette's Cook Book* (Akron, Ohio: Saalfield Publishers, 1908); Fanny Camp Gillette, *Household Gem Cyclopaedia* (Chicago: R. S. Peale, 1891).

4. "Look Sharp!", pp. 12–13; Gillette, "Origin of the Razor," pp. 2–3; Don Wharton, "Story of the Safety Razor," *Advertising and Selling,* XLI (March 1948), 138; Gillette to Upton Sinclair, Calabasas, Calif. no date, pp. 3–4, Sinclair MSS.

5. King C. Gillette, *The Human Drift* (Boston: New Era Publishing, 1894), *passim;* and Gillette to Sinclair, no date, p. 4, Sinclair MSS.

6. Gillette, *Drift,* p. vii.

7. D. O'Loughlin to Edward Bellamy, New York, May 18, 1895, Bellamy Papers, Harvard Library, Cambridge, Mass.; "Editorial," *Twentieth Century,* XIV (January 17, 1895), 1; Laurence Gronlund, "Now Look Out for California," *Twentieth Century,* XIV (February 7, 1895), 4–5; "Reply to Gronlund," *Twentieth Century,* XIV (February 14, 1895), 2.

8. King C. Gillette, "There Is Only One Positive Channel of Reform," *Twentieth Century,* XIV (April 11, 1895), 5.

9. *Twentieth Century,* XIV (July 4, 1895); "Editorial," *Twentieth Century,* XV (October 10, 1895).

10. King C. Gillette, "Opportunity," *Twentieth Century,* XVII (August 13, 1896), 10; King C. Gillette, *The Ballot Box* (Brookline, Mass., 1897), p. 4.

11. King C. Gillette, "Labor and Natural Law," *Twentieth Century,* XIX (September 25, 1897), pp. 9–10; King C. Gillette, "Ballot Box," *Twentieth Century,* XIX (September 4, 1897), 8–10.

12. J. G. Phelps Stokes to Melvin Severy, November 19, 1917, and Melvin L. Severy to J. G. Phelps Stokes, Los Angeles, January 28, 1918, Stokes MSS; Melvin L. Severy, *Gillette's Social Redemption* (Boston: Herbert Turner, 1907), p. 755.

13. Melvin L. Severy, *Gillette's Industrial Solution* (Boston: Ball Publishing, 1908), pp. 157, 401.

14. King C. Gillette, *World Corporation* (Boston: New England News, 1910), pp. 151, 196.

15. Upton Sinclair, *The Autobiography* (New York: Harcourt, Brace and World, 1962), pp. 236, 286.

16. Upton Sinclair to J. G. Phelps Stokes, Pasadena, Calif., May 2, 1919, and J. G. Phelps Stokes to Upton Sinclair, New York, May 8, 1919, Stokes MSS; Marie Dell to King C. Gillette, Croton-on-Hudson, New York, April 25, 1923, Sinclair MSS. From Marie Dell's remarks it appears that Gillette was friends with the Dells and had something of an intellectual salon in California. See Upton Sinclair, *100%: The Story of a Patriot* (Pasadena: Upton Sinclair, 1920); apparently Gillette is the character Lackman.

17. Stuart Chase, "A Business Man's Utopia," *Nation*, CXVIII (June 4, 1924), 651.

18. King C. Gillette, *The People's Corporation* (New York: Boni and Liveright, 1924), p. 130.

19. King C. Gillette to Upton Sinclair, November 15, 1921, p. 3, Sinclair MSS.

20. King C. Gillette to Upton Sinclair, March 5, 1925, Beverly Hills, Calif., p. 3, Sinclair MSS.

21. King C. Gillette to Upton Sinclair, Calabasas, September 16, 1930, p. 2, and October 17, 1930, p. 2, Sinclair MSS.

CHAPTER 7: *Charles Steinmetz and the Science of Industrial Organization*

1. See, for example, J. W. Hammond, *Charles Proteus Steinmetz* (New York: Century, 1924); Jonathan Norton Leonard, *Loki: The Life of Charles Proteus Steinmetz* (Garden City, N.Y.: Doubleday, 1929); Sigmund A. Levine, *Steinmetz, Maker of Lightning* (New York: Dodd, Mead, 1955); John Anderson Miller, *Modern Jupiter* (New York: American Society of Mechanical Engineers, 1958).

2. Hammond, *Steinmetz*, pp. 1–82; Levine, *Steinmetz*, p. 9; Leonard, *Loki*, pp. 11–49; Miller, *Modern Jupiter*, p. 30.

3. Levine, *Steinmetz*, p. 188; Leonard, *Loki*, p. 124; Miller, *Modern Jupiter*, p. 56.

4. Charles Steinmetz to William English Walling, Schenectady, N.Y., February 17, 1915, Charles Steinmetz Papers, Schenectady County Historical Society, hereafter cited as Steinmetz MSS, Historical Society; Elmer Rice, Jr., to Charles Steinmetz, New York, July 10, 1918, Steinmetz MSS, Historical Society.

5. John T. Broderick, *Steinmetz and His Discoverer* (Schenectady: Robson and Adee, 1924), pp. 8, 40–41; Hammond, *Steinmetz*, pp. 320–359.

6. Charles Steinmetz to Mr. and Mrs. Hinz, Lynn, Massachusetts, October 25, 1893, quoted in Justin G. Turner, "Steinmetz," *Manuscripts* (Manuscript Society, Fall 1963), p. 34, from the Charles Steinmetz Papers, Union College, Schenectady, N.Y., hereafter cited as Steinmetz MSS, Union College. Charles Steinmetz to Charles Henry Davis, March 5, 1915, pp. 2–3, Steinmetz MSS, Union College.

7. Charles Steinmetz, "What Is Socialism?", manuscript copy, July 18, 1921, pp. 1, 4, Steinmetz MSS, Union College.

8. Broderick, *Steinmetz*, p. 19; Charles Steinmetz, "The Place of Religion in Modern Scientific Law," copy of a sermon delivered to Unitarian Church of Schenectady, November 5, 1922, pp. 1, 11, Steinmetz MSS, Union College; Miller, *Modern Jupiter*, p. 89; Steinmetz, *America and the New Epoch*, p. 228; Charles Steinmetz, "Presidential Address," Nineteenth convention of the American Institute of Electrical Engineering, manuscript copy, June 2, 1902, Steinmetz MSS, Union College.

9. Charles Steinmetz, "Effect of the European War on American Industries," Speech to the American Institute of Electrical Engineers, shorthand report, October 25, 1916, Chicago, p. 25, Steinmetz MSS, Union College.

10. Charles Steinmetz, "Competition and Cooperation," *Collier's*, LVIII (September 23, 1916), 22; Charles Steinmetz, "Industrial Efficiency and Political Waste," *Harper's*, CXXXIII (November 1916), 926; Steinmetz, *America and the New Epoch*, pp. 50, 160.

11. John T. Broderick, *Pulling Together*, with introduction by Charles Steinmetz (Schenectady, New York: Robson and Adee, 1922), p. i; Charles Steinmetz, *Industrial Co-Operation* (New York: Industrial Extension Institute, 1919), p. 8, Steinmetz MSS, Union College.

12. Steinmetz, *America and the New Epoch*, pp. 139, 140–159; Charles Steinmetz, Address to the International Association of Engineers and National Electric Light Association, August 22, 1916, p. 4, Steinmetz MSS, Union College.

13. Steinmetz, *America and the New Epoch*, pp. 182, 228; Randolph Bourne, "Review of *America and the New Epoch*," *Intercollegiate Socialist*, V (February–March, 1917), 22–23.

14. Frances Ruml, "The Formative Period of Higher Commercial Education in American Universities," in L. C. Marshall, *The Collegiate School of Business* (Chicago: University of Chicago Press, 1928), pp. 45–74.

15. R. T. Crane, "The Utility of an Academic or Classical Education for Young Men Who Have to Earn Their Own Living and Who Expect to Pursue a Commercial Life" (Chicago, 1903), pp. 12, 33, 107, Charles Eliot Papers, Harvard Archives, Cambridge, Mass., hereafter cited as Eliot MSS; James T. Young, "Business and Science," and H. J. Hapgood, "College Men in Business," in "Business Professions," *Annals*, XXVIII (July 1906), 28–37, 58–69; Herman Schneider, "Education and Industrial Peace," *Annals*, XLIV (November 1912), 119–129.

16. Frank A. Vanderlip, *Business and Education* (New York: Duffield, 1907), pp. 3, *passim*. These writings are collected speeches and articles.

17. Charles Steinmetz, "The Future of Electricity," Address to students at the New York Electrical School, New York, 1910?; "Testimony of Dr. Steinmetz," *Final Report and Testimony of the Commission on Industrial Relations*, U.S. Senate, II (Washington, D.C.: Government Printing Office, 1916), 1829–1830.

18. "Minutes of the Board of Education, Schenectady, New York," November 12, 1912, April 30, 1912, and November 12, 1912, from Records of the Schenectady Public Schools, hereafter cited as Schenectady School MSS; "Testimony," *Final Report of Commission on Industrial Relations*, pp. 1833, 1835.

19. "Minutes of the Board of Education," June 7, 1913, and September 13, 1913, Schenectady School MSS; Charles Steinmetz, "The World Belongs to the Dissatisfied," *American Magazine*, LXXXV (May 1918), pp. 39–40, 79–80.

20. W. J. Donald, "The Work and Program of the American Management Association," *Annals*, CXXIII (May 1925), 1–2; "Establishing the Science of Personnel Management," *Industrial Management*, LX (December 15, 1920), 10; F. C. Henderschott, "Methods of Selecting Men in Business," *Monthly Bulletin of the National Association of Corporation Schools*, I (March 1914), 37.

21. Charles Steinmetz, "Address," *Proceedings of the National Association of Corporation Schools* (New York, 1914) pp. 351, 425; Charles Steinmetz, "Engineering Schools of Electrical Manufacturing Companies," *Bulletin of the National Association of Corporation Schools*, I (March 1914), 25–28; Charles Steinmetz, "Incentive and Initiative," in Ernest Caldecott and Philip L. Alger, eds., *Steinmetz the Philosopher* (Schenectady, N.Y.: Mohawk Development, 1965), p. 159.

22. Charles Steinmetz, "Address" and "Response and Annual Address," *Proceedings of the National Association of Corporation Schools* (New York, 1914), pp. 54, 58–59; Charles Steinmetz, "Address," *Proceedings of the National Association of Corporation Schools* (New York, 1915), p. 840.

23. "Ex-President Steinmetz Sounds a Note of Warning," *Bulletin of the National Association of Corporation Schools*, III (July 1916), 5–8; "A Statement," *Bulletin of the National Association of Corporation Schools*, V (March 1918), 101.

CHAPTER 8: *William English Walling: The Pragmatic Critique of Collectivism*

1. William English Walling, *Socialism As It Is: A Survey of the World-Wide Revolutionary Movement* (New York: Macmillan, 1912), pp. 124–128; William English Walling, "State Socialism and the Individual," *New Review*, I (May 1913), 506–510.

2. Louis Arrington, "Seventh Annual Report of the Factory Inspectors of Illinois" (Springfield, Ill.: Phillips Brothers, 1900), p. 234; Jack Meyer Stuart, "William English Walling: A Study in Politics and Ideas" (unpublished Ph.D. thesis, Columbia University, 1968), p. 7; William English Walling Papers, State Historical Society, Madison, Wisc., hereafter cited as Walling MSS. See also William English Walling, "What Are Factory Inspectors For?", *Charities*, XIII (January 14, 1905), 375; Florence Kelley, *et al.*, "First Annual Report of the Factory Inspectors of Illinois" (Springfield, Ill.: H. W. Rokker, 1894), pp. 7–14.

3. Jane Addams, "Address of Miss Addams," in "Sixteenth Annual Report of the University Settlement Society" (New York, 1902), p. 51; and Nicholas Murray Butler, "Address of Dr. Nicholas Murray Butler," in "University Settlement Society Report for 1903" (New York, 1903), p. 42.

4. "A Day at the University Settlement," in "Sixteenth Report of Settlement Society," pp. 12, 32.

5. Ernest Poole, "William English Walling," in Anna Strunsky Walling, *et al.*, *William English Walling: A Symposium* (New York: Stackpole, 1938), p. 25; Ernest Poole, *The Bridge: My Own Story* (New York: Macmillan, 1940), p. 73; Howard Brubaker, "William English Walling," in *Walling Symposium, passim.* See also William English Walling, "What the People of the East Side Do," *University Settlement Studies*, I (July 1905), 85.

6. William English Walling to his mother, July 23, 1905, Walling MSS; Moses Rischin, *The Promised City: New York's Jews, 1870–1914* (Cambridge, Mass.: Harvard University Press, 1962) , pp. 2, 162–163. Howells and a number of other American writers and intellectuals had worked in the organization called the American Friends of Russian Freedom. See also Melech Epstein, *Jewish Labor in the U.S.A.: An Industrial, Political and Cultural History of the Jewish Labor Movement, 1882–1914*, 2 vols. (New York: Trade Union Sponsoring Committee, 1950) , I, 119.

7. William English Walling to his father, May 18, 1904, Walling MSS; William English Walling, "The New Unionism—The Problem of the Unskilled Worker," *Annals*, XXIV (September 1904) , 296–315; Commons, *Myself*, p. 79; William English Walling, "Can Labor Unions Be Destroyed?", *World's Work*, VIII (May 1904) , 4755.

8. Walling, "New Unionism," *Annals*, p. 315; William English Walling, "Open Shop Means the Destruction of the Unions," *Independent*, LVI (May 12, 1904) , 1069; William English Walling to his parents, Budapest, October 16, 1904, Walling MSS; William English Walling, "The Convention of the American Federation of Labor," *World To-Day*, VIII (January 1905) , 91; William English Walling, "The Defeats of Labor," *Independent*, LVIII (February 23, 1905) , 419; William English Walling, "Why American Labor Unions Keep Out of Politics," *Outlook*, LXXX (May 20, 1905) , 184.

9. William English Walling, "British and American Trade Unionism," *Annals*, XXVI (November 1905) , 109–126; William English Walling, "A Children's Strike on the East Side," *Charities*, XIII (December 24, 1904) , 305; William English Walling, "Child Labor in the North," *Ethical Record*, IV (December 1902–January 1903) , *passim*.

10. William English Walling, "The Call to the Young Russians," *Charities*, XVII (December 1, 1906) , 373, 376; William English Walling to his parents, January 29, 1906, and to his mother, no date or place, Walling MSS.

11. William English Walling, "The Peasant's Revolution," *Independent*, LXII (September 26, 1907) , 910; William English Walling, "Civil War in Russia," *Independent*, LXII (April 4, 1907) , 779; William English Walling, *Russia's Message* (New York: Knopf, 1917; Doubleday, 1908) , p. 220.

12. Walling, *Russia's Message*, pp. 6, 188.

13. William English Walling to his mother, Chicago, 1908, and William English Walling to Hamilton Holt, New York, February 1, 1909, Walling MSS; William English Walling, "The Race War in the North," *Independent*, LXIV (September 3, 1908) , 534; William English Walling, "Science and Human Brotherhood," *Independent*, LXVI (June 17, 1909) , 1327.

14. Anna Walling, "Walling," in *Walling Symposium*, p. 8; J. G. Phelps Stokes to William English Walling, December 12, 1908, Walling MSS (this letter refers to efforts to save the socialist paper, the *Call*) . See also William English Walling, "Laborism Versus Socialism," *International Socialist Review*, IX (March 1909) , 688.

15. William English Walling to H. M. Hyndman, New York, February 19, 1910, Walling MSS; and William English Walling to Louis Boudin, March 12, 1910, pp. 2–3, in Louis Boudin Papers, Columbia University Library, New York.

16. William English Walling to Fred Warren, February 26, 1910, New York, Walling MSS; William English Walling, "Labor-Union Socialism and Socialist Labor-Unionism" (Chicago: Charles Kerr, 1912) , *passim;* Wil-

liam English Walling, "Industrial or Revolutionary Unionism," *New Review*, I (January 18, 1913), 90–91.

17. Walling, *Socialism As It Is*, p. 228.

18. *Ibid.*, p. 276.

19. William English Walling and Harry Laidler, *State Socialism: Pro and Con* (New York: Henry Holt, 1917); Walling, "State Socialism," *New Review*, XLIV, *passim*.

20. William English Walling, "Woodrow Wilson and State Socialism," "Woodrow Wilson and Business," and "Woodrow Wilson and Class Struggle," *New Review*, I (March 15, 22, and 29, 1913), 329–335; 364–369; 399–405; William English Walling, "Industrialism or Revolutionary Unionism," *New Review*, I (January 18, 1913), *passim*; William English Walling, "Government Ownership Contrasted with Collective Ownership Under Socialism," *Intercollegiate Socialist* (February–March 1913), 9.

21. William English Walling, *The Larger Aspects of Socialism* (New York: Macmillan, 1913), p. xv.

22. *Ibid.*, pp. 190–256.

23. *Ibid.*, p. 143. See also Max Stirner, *The Ego and His Own* (New York: Benjamin Tucker, 1907).

24. Robert Rives La Monte, "The Apotheosis of Pragmatism," *New Review*, I (July 1913), 661–664; Walter Lippmann, "Walling's *Progressivism—and After*," *New Review*, II (June 1914), 346–348.

25. William English Walling, *Progressivism—and After* (New York: Macmillan, 1914), p. 321.

26. *Ibid.*, p. 327.

27. William English Walling, *Whitman and Traubel* (New York: Albert and Charles Boni, 1916), p. 140.

28. *Ibid.*, p. 69.

29. Karl Kautsky, *The Social Revolution*, trans. by A. M. and May Simons (Chicago: Charles Kerr, 1902), *passim*.

30. Louis B. Boudin, *The Theoretical System of Karl Marx* (Chicago: Charles Kerr, 1912), pp. 210–214.

31. Morris Hillquit, *Socialism Summed Up* (New York: H. K. Fly, 1912); Morris Hillquit, *Socialism in Theory and Practice* (New York: Macmillan, 1912).

32. William English Walling, "The Socialists and the Great War," *Independent*, LXXIX (August 24, 1914), 268–269; William English Walling, "The Socialist View: The Real Causes of the War," *Harper's*, LIX (October 10, 1914), 346–347; William English Walling, "Socialists and the War," *Harper's*, LIX (October 3, 1914), 319.

33. William English Walling, "Nationalism and State Socialism," *American Sociological Society*, X (1915), 92; William English Walling, "The Remedy: Anti-Nationalism," *New Review*, III (February 1915), 77–85; William English Walling, "Review of Socialism and the War," *Intercollegiate Socialist*, IV (April–May 1916), 28–29; William English Walling, "The Great Illusions," *New Review*, III (June 1, 1915), 49–50.

34. "Economic Internationalism Condition Precedent to World Peace, Says William English Walling," *Public Forum Weekly*, I (June 5, 1915); Walling, "Review of Socialism and War," *Intercollegiate Socialist*, p. 28; William English Walling to his mother, Nantucket, Mass., July 12, 1916, Walling MSS; William English Walling, "An Economic League to Enforce Peace," *Monthly Bulletin of the Society to Eliminate Economic*

Causes of War, January 1917, p. 1; William English Walling to Theodore Roosevelt, Indianapolis, Ind., July 12, 1917, Walling MSS; Stuart, "William English Walling," p. 138.

35. William English Walling to J. G. Phelps Stokes, December 27, 1917, Stokes MSS; Henry L. Slobodin to J. G. Phelps Stokes, March 22, 1918, Stokes MSS.

36. William English Walling to the *Globe,* May 3, 1917, Walling MSS; Upton Sinclair to William English Walling, February 17, 1920, Stokes MSS.

37. William English Walling, "A Program of Social Reconstruction after the War" (Social Democratic League of America, 1918), p. 5 (Walling claims that he wrote most of this pamphlet); William English Walling, "The Wilson-Kerensky Peace Policy," *Proceedings of the Academy of Political Science,* June 1917, p. 320; William English Walling, "The Pro-Bolshevik Propaganda in America," typescript, circa 1918, p. 6, Walling MSS.

38. William English Walling to Willoughby Walling, May 19, 1919, Walling MSS; William English Walling, "The German Socialists: Do They Stand for a Democratic Peace? Will They Revolt?", copies of articles (1918), Walling MSS; William English Walling, *Sovietism: The ABC of Russian Bolshevism—According to the Bolshevists* (New York: Dutton, 1920), p. 121.

39. George Herron to Marion Simons, April 26, 1919, Geneva, Switzerland, in Algie Simons Papers, State Historical Society, Madison, Wisconsin. See also Ronald Radosh, *American Labor and United States Foreign Policy* (New York: Random House, 1969), *passim,* for the long and complicated story of Walling's State Department relationships and his efforts in behalf of Wilson.

40. William English Walling, "Why a Socialist Party," *New Review,* II (July 1914), 403.

41. William English Walling to ?, circa 1920's, Walling MSS; William English Walling, "Premier MacDonald and the International Bankers," December 15, 1929, International Labor New Service, Walling MSS; William English Walling, "Program of the British Labor Party," *Current History,* XIX (February 1924), 749.

42. William English Walling, "Is Labor Divided as to Political Principle?", *American Federationist,* XXXII (May 1925), 350; William English Walling, "Capitalism—Or What?", *Bankers' Magazine,* CXIII (September 1926), 309–311; and William English Walling, "Labor's Attitude Toward a Third Party," *Current History,* XXI (October 1924), 32–40.

43. William English Walling, *American Labor and American Democracy* (New York: Harper, 1926), p. 170.

44. *Ibid.,* pp. 163–164.

CHAPTER 9: *Reinhold Niebuhr: The Theologian as Power Broker*

1. Reinhold Niebuhr to Verne Kaub, June 7, 1951, pp. 1–2, Reinhold Niebuhr Papers, Library of Congress, Washington, D.C., hereafter cited as Niebuhr MSS; Donald B. Meyer, *The Protestant Search for Political Realism, 1919–1941* (Berkeley: University of California Press, 1960), p. 231.

2. Reinhold Niebuhr to David Dubinsky, New York, October 7, 1941; Reinhold Niebuhr to William Foster, New York, November 1, 1949, and

Robert A. Latham, New York, March 28, 1961; ADA Resolution, March 1957, Niebuhr MSS.

3. Herbert Wallace Schneider, *Religion in Twentieth Century America* (Cambridge, Mass.: Harvard, 1952), p. 136.

4. Reinhold Niebuhr, "Religion's Limitations," *World Tomorrow*, III (March 1920), 77–78; Reinhold Niebuhr, *Leaves from the Notebook of a Tamed Cynic* (New York: Richard Smith, 1929), p. 42.

5. Reinhold Niebuhr, "Does Religion Quiet or Disquiet?", *World Tomorrow*, IX (November 1926), 221; Reinhold Niebuhr, "The Paradox of Institutions," *World Tomorrow*, VI (August 1923), 233.

6. Reinhold Niebuhr, "Sermon," undated in box of unpublished sermons, Niebuhr MSS; Reinhold Niebuhr, "The Church and the Industrial Crisis," *Biblical World*, LIV (November 1920), 590, 592; Reinhold Niebuhr, "Would Jesus Be a Churchman Today?", *World Tomorrow*, XI (December 1928), 493; Niebuhr, *Leaves*, p. 94; Reinhold Niebuhr, "Mechanical Man in a Mechanical Age," *World Tomorrow*, XIII (December 1930), 493.

7. Reinhold Niebuhr, "Our Secularized Civilization," *Christian Century*, XLIII (April 22, 1926), 508; Niebuhr, *Leaves*, p. 78.

8. Reinhold Niebuhr, unpublished sermon, Box 15, Niebuhr MSS; Niebuhr, *Leaves*, p. 78.

9. Reinhold Niebuhr, "Ford's Five-Day Week Shrinks," *Christian Century*, XLIV (June 9, 1927), 714; Reinhold Niebuhr, "How Philanthropic Is Henry Ford?", *Christian Century*, XLIII (December 9, 1926), 1516; Niebuhr, *Leaves*, p. 116; Niebuhr, "Mechanical Men," p. 492; Reinhold Niebuhr, "Property and the Ethical Life," *World Tomorrow*, XIV (January 1931), 20.

10. Reinhold Niebuhr, "Religious Imagination and the Scientific Method," *Proceedings of the National Conference of Social Work* (Chicago: University of Chicago Press, 1928), p. 51; Niebuhr, "Property and Ethical Life," p. 20.

11. Reinhold Niebuhr, *Reflections on the End of an Era* (New York: Scribner's, 1936); Reinhold Niebuhr, *Moral Man and Immoral Society* (New York: Scribner's, 1932); Reinhold Niebuhr, "Catastrophe or Social Control?: The Alternatives for America," *Harper's*, CLXV (June 1932), 118; Reinhold Niebuhr, "The Revival of Feudalism," *Harper's* CLXX (March 1935), 483.

12. Reinhold Niebuhr, "Ten Years That Shook My World," *Christian Century*, LVI (April 26, 1939), 546; Reinhold Niebuhr, "Marxism and Religion," *World Tomorrow*, XVI (March 15, 1933), 255; Reinhold Niebuhr, *The Contribution of Religion to Social Work* (New York: Columbia University, 1932), p. 34; Reinhold Niebuhr, "The Problem of Communist Religion," *World Tomorrow*, XVII (July 1934), 379; Reinhold Niebuhr, "The Religion of Communism," *Atlantic Monthly*, CXLVII (April 1931), 463.

13. Niebuhr, *Reflections*, p. 210; and Niebuhr, *Moral Man*, pp. 10–14, 146, 163.

14. Niebuhr, *Contribution of Religion*, p. 59; Niebuhr, *Reflections*, p. 243; Niebuhr, *Moral Man*, p. 195.

15. Reinhold Niebuhr, *The Nature and Destiny of Man*, I (New York: Scribner's, 1942), pp. 50–51; Reinhold Niebuhr, "Why I Leave the F. O. R.," *Christian Century*, LI (January 3, 1934), 18; Reinhold Niebuhr, "The Revolutionary Movement," *American Socialist Quarterly*, IV (June 1935), 11–13; Reinhold Niebuhr to Gilbert Cox, February 27, 1935, Niebuhr MSS; Reinhold Niebuhr, "Marx, Barth and Israel's Prophets," *Christian Century*, LII (January 30, 1935), 140.

16. Reinhold Niebuhr, "Russia Makes the Machine Its God," *Christian Century*, XLVII (September 10, 1930), 1080; Niebuhr, *Reflections*, pp. 102, 173.

17. Reinhold Niebuhr, "Russia and Karl Marx," *Nation*, CXLVI (May 7, 1938), 530; and Reinhold Niebuhr to Charles Schweise, New York, May 20, 1940, Niebuhr MSS.

18. Reinhold Niebuhr, *The Irony of American History* (New York: Scribner's, 1952), p. 128; Reinhold Niebuhr, "Democracy and Party Spirit," in D. B. Robertson, *Love and Justice: Selections from the Shorter Writings of Reinhold Niebuhr* (Philadelphia: Westminster Press, 1957), p. 69; Niebuhr, *Nature and Destiny*, I, 51; Reinhold Niebuhr, *Nations and Empires: Recurring Patterns in the Political Order* (London: Faber and Faber, 1959), p. 294.

19. Niebuhr, *Irony of American History*, p. 103; Niebuhr, in *Love and Justice*, p. 68; Reinhold Niebuhr, "Commentary," in Kenneth E. Boulding, *The Organizational Revolution: A Study in the Ethics of Economic Organization* (New York: Harper, 1953), p. 230; Niebuhr, *Nations and Empires*, p. 61.

20. Reinhold Niebuhr, *The Nature and Destiny of Man* (London: Nisbet, 1943), II, 93; Reinhold Niebuhr, *The Children of Light and the Children of Darkness* (New York: Scribner's, 1944), p. 76.

CHAPTER 10: *James Burnham: Collectivism Triumphant*

1. Frederick L. Ackerman, *The Facts Behind Technocracy* (New York: Continental Committee on Technocracy, 1933), p. 4; see news of Howard Scott's trips to Technocracy locals in *Technocracy*, July 1937; *Technocracy*, May 1935, p. 3; George Frederick, *For and Against Technocracy: A Symposium* (New York: Business Bourse, 1933), pp. 222–229.

2. John Dewey, "A Great American Prophet," *Common Sense*, III (April 1934), 6–7; George Soule, "On Changing Control," in Harry Laidler and Norman Thomas, eds., *New Tactics in Social Conflict* (New York: Vanguard, 1926), pp. 9, 11.

3. See, for example, Rexford G. Tugwell, *The Industrial Discipline and the Governmental Arts* (New York: Columbia University Press, 1933); John Dewey, *Liberalism and Social Action* (New York: Putnam's, 1935); Charles A. Beard, *America Faces the Future* (Boston: Houghton Mifflin, 1932); Stuart Chase, *A New Deal* (New York: Macmillan, 1932); George Soule, *A Planned Society* (Gloucester, Mass.: Peter Smith, 1932).

4. Adolf A. Berle, Jr., and Gardiner C. Means, *The Modern Corporation and Private Property* (New York: Macmillan, 1933), p. 356.

5. "James Burnham," *Current Biography* (New York: H. W. Wilson, 1941), p. 121; Matthew Josephson, *Infidel in the Temple* (New York: Knopf, 1967), p. 108; personal interview with Max Schachtman, August 16, 1970, Floral Park, N.Y.

6. James Burnham, "The History of the Russian Revolution," *Symposium*, III (July 1932), 380.

7. James Burnham, "Marxism and Aesthetics," *Symposium, passim;* and James Burnham and Philip Wheelwright, "Thirteen Propositions," *Symposium*, IV (April 1933), 127–134.

8. James Burnham, "Comment," *Symposium*, IV (July 1933), 259–279.

9. John West (James Burnham), "Roosevelt and the New Congress," *New International*, II (January 1935), 1; and John West (James Burnham),

"The Roosevelt 'Security' Program," *New International*, II (March 1935), 42.

10. John West (James Burnham), "The Wagner Bill and the Working Class," *New International*, II (October 1935), 186; John West (James Burnham), "Max Eastman's Straw Man," *New International*, II (December 1935), 222–225; John West (James Burnham), "Will Roosevelt Be Re-elected?", *New International*, II (April 1936), 36.

11. Schachtman interview; Leon Trotsky, *In Defense of Marxism*, ed. by Joseph Hansen and William F. Warde (New York: Merit, 1965), pp. IX, 188–210, especially James Burnham, "Science and Style: A Reply to Comrade Trotsky," Appendix.

12. James Burnham, "Letters of Resignation," in Trotsky, *Defense*, pp. 207–210 (Appendix); James Burnham, *The Machiavellians: Defenders of Freedom* (New York: John Day, 1943), pp. 87, 166; Ernest S. Bates, "The Pareto Craze," *Modern Monthly*, IX (January 1936), 469–473.

13. Max Schachtman, "1939: Whither Russia? Trotsky and His Critics," *Survey*, XLI (April 1962), 103; Isaac Deutscher, *The Prophet Outcast* (London: Oxford University Press, 1963), p. 463.

14. James Burnham, *The Managerial Revolution* (New York: John Day, 1941; Indiana University Press, 1960), p. 196; James Burnham, "Is Democracy Possible?", in *Whose Revolution?: A Study of the Future Course of Liberalism in the United States*, ed. Irving DeWitt Talmadge (New York: Howell, Soskin, 1941), p. 196; Burnham, *The Machiavellians*, p. 254.

15. James Burnham and André Malraux, *The Case for DeGaulle* (New York: Random House, 1948), p. 55; James Burnham, *Suicide of the West: An Essay on the Meaning and Destiny of Liberalism* (New York: John Day, 1964), *passim*.

A Note on Sources

MANUSCRIPT SOURCES

City Club Collection, New York State Historical Association
City Club Papers, New York Public Library
City Reform Club Papers, New York Public Library
Richard Welling Papers, New York Public Library
National Self Government Papers, New York Public Library
J. G. Phelps Stokes Papers, Butler Library, Columbia University
Louis Boudin Papers, Butler Library, Columbia University
Franklin Giddings Papers, Butler Library, Columbia University
Florence Kelley Papers, Butler Library, Columbia University
Charles Steinmetz Papers, Union College, Schenectady, New York
Charles Steinmetz Papers, Schenectady County Historical Society, Schenectady, New York
Schenectady School Board Minutes
Charles Eliot Papers, Harvard Archives
Edward Bellamy Papers, Houghton Library, Harvard University
National Consumers League Papers, Library of Congress
Reinhold Niebuhr Papers, Library of Congress
Stuart Chase Papers, Library of Congress
William James Ghent Papers, Library of Congress
Charles Edward Russell Papers, Library of Congress
Upton Sinclair Papers, Lilly Library, Indiana University
Edmond Kelly Manuscripts, Mrs. Shaun Kelly, Boston, Massachusetts
Kelly Family Manuscripts, Sean Kelly, Washington, D.C.
William English Walling Papers, Wisconsin Historical Society, Madison, Wisconsin

Algie Simons Papers, Wisconsin Historical Society, Madison, Wisconsin

Americans for Democratic Action Papers, Wisconsin Historical Society, Madison, Wisconsin

SECONDARY WORKS

The aim of this book has been to explain the ideas that justified the centralization of the American political economy, a movement which forced intellectuals to think about a mass rather than an individualistic society. There were, of course, many levels of such thought, but the most profound division, it seems to me, lay between those men and women who made actual decisions—corporate leaders, important experts, and politicians—and those who counted themselves reformers but made little real impact on the course of events. This latter group, which is in some ways the most quixotic, has been the most interesting to me because their task was to explain to themselves, and to as many others who would listen, what was happening to American society. Unbothered by the demands for political relevance (in fact, often embittered by the dishonesty which they sensed to be at the core of the political process), these intellectuals speculated about the larger meanings of the new industrial society.

Most important as sources for explaining the activities of these intellectuals is the descriptive literature of the "Progressive era," so named by historians. This is a vast and fascinating literature, so much so that I can discuss only a few of the books that I have consulted. However one may appraise it, the "progressivism" of the early twentieth century is today still felt by historians to have a vague familiarity, but beyond it, in the nineteenth century, there is a distant world of gentility and strangers. As historians have rightly understood, the political and ideological dramas of the present were born in progressivism. That era contained the vague and tentative questions and answers about modern society that starkly confront us today.

Historical literature about progressivism is interesting for its methodological variety, and for the several arguments developed to explain social and intellectual behavior. Some recent works have made the need to discuss the ideas of intellectuals in this period a far more interesting and complicated task. One of the books most helpful to me has been James Weinstein's *The Corporate Ideal in the Liberal State* (Boston, 1968). Weinstein's thesis attempts to explain the manner in which Progressive reform projects drew support and inspiration from the most sophisticated elements of corporate management and labor. His discussion of reform legislation in the context of class struggle is a fascinating one. The book, of course, did not seek to explain the behavior of intellectuals, but I feel that the very ingenuity of Weinstein's arguments demands that historians ask a number of questions about reformers whose role in Progressive reforms now seems more ambiguous and uncertain. Gabriel Kolko's *The Triumph of Conservatism* (New York, 1963) is another extremely important book on progressivism. Kolko's description of reform legislation as an attempt by larger businesses to bring order and stability to industry is a particularly apt one. Far more than Weinstein's work, Kolko suggests a conspiracy of sorts and thus makes the task of explaining the nature of reform thought even more important.

Richard Hofstadter's *The Age of Reform* (New York, 1955) is well known to American historians. His thesis of changing status, mobility, and immobility in the early years of the twentieth century has been a kind of first consideration for anyone wishing to explore progressivism. Yet Hofstadter's work also places ideas in suspicious categories by making them functions of social adjustments or part of a broad sociological analysis. Robert Wiebe's *The Search for Order* (New York, 1967) attempts a synthesis of several contradictory works on progressivism, and succeeds in pointing out the bureaucratic biases of many intellectuals, reformers, and politicians. As one book in a series, Wiebe's suffers from the breadth of subjects he discusses. His sense of a general social disorder and, in opposition to it, a search for order, is enormously suggestive, but I think still unproven. Moreover, Wiebe does not consider at much length the nature of the bureaucratic order which intellectuals pursued.

Two books that do not deal explicitly with progressivism have nonetheless been very helpful for their discussions of intellectuals and reform. The first of these is George M. Fredrickson's *The Inner Civil War: Northern Intellectuals and the Crisis of Union* (New York, 1965). Fredrickson's discussion of intellectuals and their relation to the Civil War, and the impact of that struggle upon their formulation of political and literary realism, perhaps attempts too much by way of explanation. But his method is an important example of assessing the relationship between experience and reform sentiments. Perhaps the most interesting of all of the recent books which seek to relate intellectuals to major reform movements is Christopher Lasch's *The New Radicalism in America* (New York, 1965). Lasch's short introduction is a marvelous essay on the relationships between social structure (and especially family life) and the reactions and pursuits of intellectuals in the twentieth century. Many of his subsequent essays on individual "radical" intellectuals are successful examples of how one can relate intellectual production to an identifiable social type. The overall success of this method, however, is in its flashes of insight rather than any developing argument; the book is more important for its parts than its thesis.

Several other books have attempted to deal specifically with the nature of intellectual life in the Progressive era, though they are less important for their method than for the kinds of interpretations they propose. David Noble's *The Paradox of Progressive Thought* (Minneapolis, 1958), suggests that Progressive intellectuals believed in progress yet advanced the cause of an ethically neutral science. It is an abstract way of recounting positions held at the time, but it remains a useful study. Arthur Mann's *Yankee Reformers in the Urban Age* (Cambridge, Mass., 1954) is an effort to understand the more moderate reformers of the late nineteenth century, typified by such figures as Frank Parsons. Eric Goldman's *Rendezvous with Destiny* (New York, 1952) is, as the title suggests, an attempt to trace elements of reform movements until they became part of the Democratic party. Sidney Fine's *Laissez-Faire and the General Welfare State* (Ann Arbor, 1956) makes the case that the "general welfare state" of modern America was a compromise between the extremes of laissez faire and socialism. Morton White's *Social Thought in America: The Revolt Against Formalism* (New York, 1949) deals with the philosophic base of social modernism. Theodore Lowi's *The End of Liberalism* (New York, 1969) is an interesting analysis of the modern administrative state and its pluralistic ideology.

I have found a number of more specialized books and articles useful in determining the intellectual and social context of collectivist thought. Joseph Dorfman's *The Economic Mind in American Civilization* (New York, 1949) is a good general survey of economic thinking. Robert Wiebe's *Businessmen and Reform* (Cambridge, Mass., 1962) depicts the factionalism among businessmen during the Progressive era. Mark Perlman's *Labor Union Theories in America* (Evanston, Ill., 1958) explores various theories about the rise of labor unions. *Labor and the Progressive Movement in New York State* by Irwin Yellowitz (Ithaca, 1956) surveys the development of unions in New York.

The nature of reform work in the late nineteenth and early twentieth centuries is the subject of two interesting and helpful books by Roy Lubove, *The Professional Altruist* (Cambridge, Mass., 1965), and *Progressives and the Slums* (Pittsburgh, 1962). A particularly useful study of intellectuals and the efficiency movement is Samuel Haber's *Efficiency and Uplift: Scientific Management in the Progressive Era* (Chicago, 1964). *Servants of Power: A History of the Use of Social Science in American Industry,* by Loren Baritz (Middletown, Conn., 1960), is interesting for its discussion of intellectuals and their contribution of social and psychological tools for business management. Unfortunately, Baritz's work has not led to the further studies it suggested. "The Development of Corporate Liberal Policy Research in the United States," a doctoral dissertation by David Eakins (University of Wisconsin, Madison, 1966), is a helpful examination of research organizations. Two works on the settlement house movement have been particularly useful to me: Allen F. Davis, *Spearheads for*

Reform: The Social Settlements and the Progressive Movement (New York, 1967), and a master's thesis by Harrison Graham Lowry, "The Social Settlement and the Search for Community" (University of Wisconsin, Madison, 1968). Finally, Gordon Jensen's doctoral dissertation, "The National Civic Federation: American Business in an Age of Social Change and Social Reform" (Princeton University, 1956) is an intriguing history of the Federation which attracted businessmen, labor leaders, and intellectuals.

Historians have done a great deal of work on particular intellectuals or groups, and a number of the participants in reform movements have left memoirs or autobiographies. The problem of assessing the meaning of reform experience, however, has been a slightly different problem than merely recounting the adventures of changing society. Charles Forcey's *Crossroads of Liberalism: Croly, Weyl, Lippmann, and the Progressive Era* (New York, 1961) discusses, with a good deal of insight, the forces that brought the New Republic into existence. A good many articles have enriched the study of reform movements around the turn of the century and beyond. These include Kenneth McNaught, "American Progressives and the Good Society," *Journal of American History* (December 1966); Benjamin G. Rader, "Richard T. Ely: Lay Spokesman for the Social Gospel," *Journal of American History* (June 1966); Sidney Kaplan, "Social Engineers as Saviors: Effects of World War I on Some American Liberals," *Journal of the History of Ideas* (June 1956); and John P. Diggins, "Flirtation with Fascism: American Pragmatic Liberals and Mussolini's Italy," *American Historical Review* (January 1966).

Several other specialized books and articles have been helpful. Howard H. Quint's *The Forging of American Socialism: Origins of the Modern Movement* (Columbia, S.C., 1953) is still the best discussion of socialism in the formative period, though I think the ideas of socialists still have not received the kind of treatment they deserve. I have found Samuel P. Hays's "The Politics of Reform in Municipal Government in the Progressive Era," *Pacific Northwest Quarterly* (October 1964), to be the best short examination of the Progressive impulse. Daniel Bell's *Work and Its Discontents: The Cult of Efficiency in America* (Boston, 1956) is an important study.

One of the most intriguing problems in American intellectual history since 1890 is the relationship of Anglo-Saxon Americans to immigrants, particularly Jewish immigrants. Alice Kessler Harris' doctoral dissertation, "The Lower Class as a Factor in Reform: New York, the Jews and the 1890's" (Rutgers University, 1968) contains some useful information on this important interchange. Several books, primarily on American Jewish history, have also been useful, and include Moses Rischin's *Inventory of American Jewish History* (Cambridge, Mass., 1954), and, more specifically, his *The Promised City: New York's Jews, 1870–1914* (Cambridge, Mass., 1962). Melech Epstein's two-volume work, *Jewish Labor in the U.S.A.: An Industrial, Political and Cultural History of the Jewish Labor Movement, 1882–1914* (New York, 1950) is a helpful general survey.

Biographical material on Edmond Kelly, Charles Steinmetz, William English Walling, Reinhold Niebuhr, and King Camp Gillette, is, for the most part, scanty. Jack M. Stuart's dissertation "William English Walling: A Study in Politics and Ideas" (Columbia University, 1968) is an adequate, general work. There are several biographies of Steinmetz, but none of particular merit. King Camp Gillette and Edmond Kelly are discussed only obliquely in the memoirs of Upton Sinclair and Richard Welling. There are, of course, a great number of books on Reinhold Niebuhr, the most useful of which is Donald Meyer's *The Protestant Search for Political Realism* (Berkeley, 1960).

Index

A NOTE ON THE AUTHOR

James Gilbert was born in Chicago in 1939 and
grew up near that city. He studied at Carleton
College and the University of Wisconsin, and is now
Associate Professor of History at the University of
Maryland. Mr. Gilbert's articles and reviews have
appeared in the *New Republic*, the *Nation, Partisan Review, Radical America, Studies on the Left*
(where he was an associate editor), and other journals and magazines here and abroad, and he has
written *Writers and Partisans*, a study of the *Partisan Review*.